# CLINICAL GUIDE TO COMMONLY USED CHINESE HERBAL FORMULAS

John Scott, DOM
Lorena Monda, DOM
John Heuertz, DOM

5th Edition
Herbal Medicine Press


Herbal Medicine Press
PO Box 781
Placitas, New Mexico 87043

**The information in this book is strictly educational and should not be used to treat medical conditions except by knowledgeable health practitioners.**

# *TABLE OF CONTENTS*

# *PINYIN TABLE OF CONTENTS*

# *THE FORMULAS*

# AMBER STONE-TRANSFORMING FORMULA

**Amber Stone-Transforming Formula** *(Hu Po Hua Shi Pian)* was created by Jake Paul Fratkin, OMD, based on current research in China regarding the dissolution of kidney and bladder stones. The synergistic combination of lysimachia *(guang jin qian cao)* and lygodium (*hai jin sha)* dissolves the stone. In acute blockage, it can actually dissolve the stone enough to allow passage, especially when combined with acupuncture. Besides intervention during acute attacks, the formula can be given as a preventative for patients with a history of kidney stones.

## Ingredients

Lysimachiae Herba (Lysimachia / **Jin Qian Cao**) 15%
Lygodii Spora (Lygodium Spores / **Hai Jin Sha**) 15%
Imperatae Rhizoma (Imperata Rhizome / **Bai Mao Gen**) 12%
Pyrrosiae Folium (Pyrrosia Leaf / **Shi Wei**) 12%
Lonicerae Flos (Japanese Honeysuckle Flower / **Jin Yin Hua**) 9%
Spatholobi Caulis (Spatholobus / **Ji Xue Teng**) 8%
Notoginseng Radix (Tienqi Ginseng, Pseudoginseng Root / **San Qi, Tian Qi**) 8%
Dianthi Herba (Chinese Pink, Dianthus / **Qu Mai**) 7%
Succinum Resina (Amber / **Hu Po**) 7%
Orthosiphon Herba (Orthosiphon / **Hua Shi Cao**) 7%

## Chinese Medical Actions

Expels stones, drains damp-heat, moves qi, clears heat and resolves toxin, invigorates blood, stops bleeding, relieves pain.

## Indications

Bladder stones, acute or chronic
Blood in urine from kidney or bladder stones
Kidney stones, acute or chronic
Pain and pressure in lower back and abdomen from stones
Urinary tract infection
Urination, pain with

**Tongue:** Red and scalloped, red on the edge or tip, yellow or white coating. **Pulse:** Big, rapid, rolling.

## Contraindications

DO NOT USE DURING PREGNANCY.

**Dosage:** For acute obstruction: take 2-5 tablets every 3-5 hours until pain is gone. If pain has not significantly decreased in 12 hours, patient should consult heath practitioner. For prevention: take one dose 2 times a day for a 3-4 day course, once monthly.

**Note:** This formula is most effective when combined with acupuncture.

# ANDROGRAPHIS FORMULA

**Andrographis Formula** *(Chuan Xin Lian Kang Yan Pian)* is used to clear acute heat-toxin in the blood, lymph, or at the organ level. The chief herb, andrographis *(chuan xin lian)*, is noted for its strong anti-viral, anti-bacterial, anti-pyretic, and anti-inflammatory actions. Isatis *(ban lan gen)* clears heat-toxin, cools the blood and benefits the throat. It has anti-bacterial and anti-viral actions. Dandelion *(pu gong ying)* clears both interior and exterior heat, resolves toxin, eliminates damp-heat, and has anti-bacterial actions. With its broad therapeutic scope, **Andrographis Formula** can be used to clear heat-toxin anywhere in the body. It is especially effective for treating viruses affecting the throat, lymph, or liver.

## Ingredients

Andrographitis Herba (Andrographis / **Chuan Xin Lian**) 50%
Isatidis seu Baphicacanthis Radix (Isatis Root / **Ban Lan Gen**) 25 %
Taraxaci Herba (Dandelion / **Pu Gong Ying**) 25 %

## Chinese Medical Actions

Clears heat, resolves toxin, cools blood, disperses swelling. Clears heat and reduces inflammation in the three burners.

## Indications

Bronchitis
Carbuncle
Chicken pox
Common cold, from wind-heat
Dysentery, bacterial
Ear infections
Fever
Gastroenteritis, acute
Gum infections
Hepatitis
Herpes simplex
Herpes zoster
Influenza
Kidney infection
Laryngitis
Lymph nodes, enlarged
Measles
Mouth sores
Mumps
Pelvic Inflammatory Disease
Respiratory infections
Sinus inflammation or infection
Skin infections such as boils
Strep throat
Throat, sore
Tonsillitis
Urinary tract infections

**Tongue:** Red or red spots.
**Pulse:** Rapid.

## Contraindications

The herbs used in this formula are cold in nature. Prolonged use may injure stomach fire and lead to digestive hypofunction or epigastric discomfort.

# ASTRAGALUS FORMULA

**Astragalus Formula** *(Huang Qi Jian Zhong Tang)* is also known as "Astragalus Decoction to Construct the Middle" because it builds the qi of the spleen and stomach or "middle qi." It is a major pediatric tonic formula used for children with delicate constitutions or who have chronic ear infections.

## Ingredients

Maltosum (Barley Malt Sugar / **Yi Tang**) 32.3%
Paeoniae Radix, alba (Chinese White Peony / **Bai Shao**) 19.4%
Cinnamomi Ramulus (Cassia, Cinnamon Twig / **Gui Zhi**) 9.7%
Zingiberis Rhizoma Recens (Fresh Ginger / **Sheng Jiang**) 9.7%
Jujubae Fructus (Jujube Fruit, Chinese Red Date / **Hong Zao, Da Zao**) 9.7%
Astragali Radix (Astragalus / **Huang Qi**) 6.4%
Glycyrrhizae Radix Preparata (Chinese Licorice Root, honey-fried / **Zhi Gan Cao**) 6.4%
Atractylodis Macrocephalae Rhizoma (White Atractylodes Rhizome / **Bai Zhu**) 6.4%

## Chinese Medical Actions

Warms and supplements the middle burner, dispels cold, supplements qi.

## Indications

Abdominal pain
Allergies, chronic
Appetite, poor
Back spasms
Body weakness and heaviness
Children, poor health in
Cold limbs
Complexion, pale or lusterless
Constitution, delicate
Digestion, weak
Ear infections, chronic
Fatigue
Fever, low grade or occasional
Fright, in children
Hemorrhoids
Immune system weak
Post-operative pain
Shortness of breath
Sweating, nocturnal or spontaneous
Ulcer, peptic
Weakness, general or after illness

**Tongue:** White coating.
**Pulse:** Thin and weak.

## Contraindications

Do not use with signs of heat, with heat from yin deficiency, or in cases with abdominal distension.

# ASTRAGALUS & LIGUSTRUM FORMULA

**Astragalus & Ligustrum Formula** *(Huang Qi Dong Qing Pian)*. This formula evolved from *fu zheng* therapy research done in modern China. "Fu zheng" means "support the normal or righteous" qi, which helps protect the body from adverse influences. *Fu zheng* therapy originally used tonic or adaptogenic herbs to protect the immune systems of cancer patients from the toxic effects of radiation or chemotherapy. Currently this therapy is used in the treatment of patients who are HIV+ or have AIDS Related Complex (ARC), AIDS, Chronic Epstein-Barr Virus (CEBV), and patients with other immune deficiency syndromes. The focus of **Astragalus & Ligustrum Formula** is on supplementing the qi by supporting the spleen and kidneys. In addition to the tonic herbs, this formula has poria *(fu ling)* to drain dampness, and tangerine peel *(chen pi)* to move the qi. *Chen pi* also helps prevent the bloating and stagnation, which can occur when taking tonic herbs.

## Ingredients

Astragali Radix (Astragalus / **Huang Qi**) 18.9%
Ligustri Lucidi Fructus (Ligustrum, Privet Fruit / **Nu Zhen Zi**) 9.4%
Codonopsis Pilosae Radix (Codonopsis / **Dang Shen**) 7.6%
Paeoniae Radix, alba (Chinese White Peony / **Bai Shao**) 7.6%
Atractylodis Macrocephalae Rhizoma (White Atractylodes Rhizome / **Bai Zhu**) 7.6%
Poria (Poria, Hoelen, Tuckahoe / **Fu Ling**) 7.6%
Scrophulariae Radix (Scrophularia, Figwort Root / **Xuan Shen**) 7.6%
Acanthopanacis Senticosi Radix et Caulis (Eleuthero Root / **Wu Jia Shen**) 7.6%
Schisandrae Fructus (Schisandra Fruit / **Wu Wei Zi**) 6.3%
Citri Reticulatae Pericarpium (Tangerine Peel / **Chen Pi**) 5.6%
Glycyrrhizae Radix (Chinese Licorice Root / **Gan Cao**) 5.6%
Ganoderma (Reishi, Ganoderma Mushroom / **Ling Zhi**) 3.7%
Epimedii Herba (Epimedium / **Yin Yang Huo**) 3.7%
Cinnamomi Cortex (Cassia Bark, Cinnamon Bark / **Rou Gui**) 1.2%

## Chinese Medical Actions

Builds qi, nourishes blood and kidneys, supports the *wei* qi, spleen, and stomach.

## Indications

Chemotherapy, side effects of
Fatigue, chronic
Immune deficiency syndromes
Immune system impaired
Post-partum fatigue
Post-operative fatigue
Weakness, general

## Contraindications

During pregnancy, consult a health practitioner before taking. This formula can be combined with an appropriate anti-toxin formula, like **Viola Clear Fire Formula,** in cases with microbial activity or heat-toxin. It can also be combined with tonic formulas to build qi, blood, and yin.

# BLOOD PALACE FORMULA

**Blood Palace Formula** *(Xue Fu Zhu Yu Tang),* also known as "Drive Out Stasis in the Mansion of the Blood Decoction" or "Persica and Carthamus Formula," is used for blood stasis in the upper part of the body, which results in headaches, pain in the chest and hypochondriac region, and many types of emotional symptoms.

## Ingredients

Persicae Semen (Peach Kernel, Persica Seed / **Tao Ren**) 14.8%
Carthami Flos (Safflower, Carthamus Flower / **Hong Hua**) 11.1%
Angelicae Sinensis Radix (Dong Quai, Tang Kuei / **Dang Gui**) 11.1%
Cyathulae Radix (Cyathula Root / **Chuan Niu Xi**) 11.1%
Rehmanniae Radix (Rehmannia Root, unprocessed / **Sheng Di Huang**) 11.1%
Paeoniae Radix, rubra (Chinese Red Peony / **Chi Shao**) 7.4%
Aurantii Fructus (Bitter Orange / **Zhi Ke**) 7.4%
Curcumae Radix (Turmeric, Curcuma Tuber / **Yu Jin**) 7.4%
Chuanxiong Rhizoma (Ligusticum Wallichii Rhizome / **Chuan Xiong**) 5.6%
Platycodi Radix (Platycodon Root, Balloon Flower Root / **Jie Geng**) 5.6%
Bupleuri Radix (Bupleurum Root / **Chai Hu**) 3.7%
Glycyrrhizae Radix (Chinese Licorice Root / **Gan Cao**) 3.7%

## Chinese Medical Actions

Moves blood, dispels blood stasis, spreads liver qi, unblocks the channels, alleviates pain.

## Indications

Afternoon fever
Angina
Breast lumps
Chest, pain or stifling sensation in
Coronary artery disease
Depression w/ sensation of warmth in chest
Dry heaves
Emotional outbursts or instability
Fibromyalgia w/ blood stasis
Headache w/ fixed, piercing pain
Hiccough, chronic
Hypertension
Hypochondriac pain
Insomnia and restless sleep
Intercostal neuralgia
Irritability
Palpitation
Post-concussion syndrome

**Tongue:** Purple or dark red, with dark or purple spots on sides. **Pulse:** Tight, choppy, or wiry.

## Contraindications

DO NOT USE DURING PREGNANCY. Do not use in cases with heavy menstrual bleeding or any active hemorrhagic disorder.

# BONE & SINEW FORMULA

**Bone & Sinew Formula** *(Zheng Gu Xu Jin Fang)* is a combination of Du Huo and Loranthus Formula *(Du Huo Ji Sheng Tang)* and Decoction for Removing Blood Stasis in the Channels *(Shu Jing Huo Xue Tang)* with herbs added to supplement the kidneys and knit bones and sinews. It is intended to treat the second and third stages of trauma where initial swelling and inflammation have dissipated and what remains is blood stasis and invasion of wind and dampness. The herbs in this formula center on moving and supplementing blood to dispel blood stasis, supplementing the kidney to heal bones and sinews, and dispelling wind and dampness to drive out *bi* and prevent its return. It is ideal for speeding the healing of torn ligaments or tendons, broken bones, or damaged cartilage.

## Ingredients

Taxilli Herba (Loranthus, Chinese Mistletoe / **Sang Ji Sheng**) 10%
Angelicae Sinensis Radix (Dong Quai, Tang Kuei / **Dang Gui**) 8%
Lycopodii Herba (Clubmoss, Lycopodium / **Shen Jin Cao**) 8%
Acanthopanacis Giraldii Cortex (Acanthopanax Stem Bark / **Hong Mao Wu Jia**) 8%
Spatholobi Caulis (Spatholobus / **Ji Xue Teng**) 8%
Eucommiae Cortex (Eucommia Bark / **Du Zhong**) 8%
Angelicae Pubescentis Radix (Pubescent Angelica Root / **Du Huo**) 8%
Drynariae Rhizoma (Drynaria Rhizome / **Gu Sui Bu**) 7%
Psoraleae Fructus (Psoralea Fruit / **Bu Gu Zhi**) 7%
Dipsaci Radix (Japanese Teasel Root, Dipsacus / **Xu Duan**) 7%
Olibanum (Frankincense / **Ru Xiang**) 6%
Myrrha (Myrrh / **Mo Yao**) 6%
Notopterygii Rhizoma seu Radix (Notopterygium / **Qiang Huo**) 5%
Jujubae Fructus (Jujube Fruit, Chinese Red Date / **Hong Zao, Da Zao**) 3%
Pyritum (Pyrite / **Zi Ran Tong**) 1%

## Chinese Medical Actions

Dispels wind and dampness, knits bones and sinews, supplements and moves blood, relieves pain.

## Indications

Fractures or broken bones
Bone weakness or degeneration
Cartilage damage
Ligaments or tendons, torn
Sprains

## Contraindications

DO NOT USE DURING PREGNANCY.

**Note:** If used for an extended period, it is best to combine this formula with one that addresses the patient's constitutional imbalance. For example, if yin deficiency is prominent, combine **Bone & Sinew Formula** with **Rehmannia Six Formula**, or if liver qi stagnation is an underlying issue, combine this formula with **Bupleurum & Tang Kuei Formula** or **Free & Easy Wanderer Plus**.

# BUPLEURUM & CINNAMON FORMULA

**Bupleurum & Cinnamon Formula** (*Chai Hu Gui Zhi Tang)* is a traditional formula from the *Shang Han Lun*, and is a combination of Cinnamon Twig Formula *(Gui Zhi Tang)* and Minor Bupleurum Formula *(Xiao Chai Hu Tang)*. This formula treats simultaneous tai yang and shao yang disorders. It is used to harmonize the interior and exterior, and in shao yang disorders, when the exterior has not been completely released. It is commonly used for digestive disorders resulting from disharmony of liver and spleen. This formula can be used for psychological boundary issues seen in socially uncomfortable patients who have hostile outbursts or are passive-aggressive.

## Ingredients

Bupleuri Radix (Bupleurum Root / **Chai Hu**) 23.6%
Codonopsis Pilosae Radix (Codonopsis / **Dang Shen**) 17.6%
Pinelliae Rhizoma Preparatum (Pinellia, ginger-cured / **Zhi Ban Xia**) 11.8%
Cinnamomi Ramulus (Cassia, Cinnamon Twig / **Gui Zhi**) 8.8%
Scutellariae Radix (Chinese Scullcap, Scutellaria, Scute / **Huang Qin**) 8.8%
Paeoniae Radix, alba (Chinese White Peony / **Bai Shao**) 8.8%
Zingiberis Rhizoma Recens (Fresh Ginger / **Sheng Jiang**) 8.8%
Jujubae Fructus (Jujube Fruit, Chinese Red Date / **Hong Zao, Da Zao**) 5.9%
Glycyrrhizae Radix (Chinese Licorice Root / **Gan Cao**) 5.9%

## Chinese Medical Actions

Releases muscle layer, expels wind, releases shao yang-stage disorders, harmonizes interior and exterior, harmonizes nutritive *(ying)* and protective *(wei)* qi.

## Indications

| | |
|---|---|
| Abdominal distension | Joint pain w/ crackling sensation |
| Chills | Muscular tension |
| Common cold w/ chest constriction | Nausea |
| Constitution, delicate | Nervous exhaustion |
| Fat digestion, poor | Neurotic disorders |
| Flatulence | Passive-aggressive behavior |
| Gallstones | Pneumonia |
| Hepatitis | Psychological boundary issues |
| Emotional instability | Pulmonary tuberculosis |
| Influenza | Stomach pain |
| Irritability | Vertebral subluxation |
| | Vomiting |

**Tongue:** Pale, swollen, with white or yellow coating.
**Pulse:** Wiry (in liver position), weak (in spleen position). May be slippery or floating.

**Note:** Reduce dosage for psychological use.

# BUPLEURUM & TANG KUEI FORMULA

**Bupleurum & Tang Kuei Formula** *(Xiao Yao San)* also known as "Free and Easy Wanderer" or "Rambling Powder," is an important classical prescription used for regulating and harmonizing the energy of the liver and spleen. It is useful for a diverse range of symptoms resulting from constrained liver qi, deficient liver blood, and liver-spleen disharmony. It is an excellent formula for menstrual and premenstrual disorders when strong signs of heat are not present.

## Ingredients

Bupleuri Radix (Bupleurum Root / **Chai Hu**) 16.1%
Angelicae Sinensis Radix (Dong Quai, Tang Kuei / **Dang Gui**) 16.1%
Paeoniae Radix, alba (Chinese White Peony / **Bai Shao**) 16.1%
Atractylodis Macrocephalae Rhizoma (White Atractylodes Rhizome / **Bai Zhu**) 16.1%
Poria (Poria, Hoelen, Tuckahoe / **Fu Ling**) 16.1%
Glycyrrhizae Radix Preparata (Chinese Licorice Root, honey-fried / **Zhi Gan Cao**) 8.1%
Zingiberis Rhizoma (Dried Ginger / **Gan Jiang**) 8.1%
Menthae Haplocalysis Herba (Chinese Mint / **Bo He**) 3.3%

## Chinese Medical Actions

Nourishes liver blood and yin, spreads liver qi, strengthens the spleen, harmonizes the liver and spleen.

## Indications

Abdominal distension or bloating
Allergies, food
Appetite, poor
Breast distension or tenderness
Breast lumps, fibrocystic
Constipation
Depression
Dizziness
Emotional instability
Fatigue
Hay fever, chronic
Headache
Hot flashes
Hypochondriac pain
Irritability
Lactation, insufficient
Menopausal symptoms
Menstrual pain
Menstruation, fatigue after
Menstruation, irregular
Mood swings
Nausea
Palpitation
Premenstrual Syndrome
Stools, erratic
Uterine bleeding, dysfunctional
Weight loss

**Tongue:** Pale body, slightly red, especially on the sides.
**Pulse:** Wiry, thin, rapid.

## Contraindications

When strong heat signs are present, use **Free & Easy Wanderer Plus** instead. Reduce dose if irritability or digestive disturbance increase while taking this formula.

# BUPLEURUM D FORMULA

**Bupleurum D Formula** *(Chai Hu Jia Long Gu Mu Li Tang),* also known as "Bupleurum Plus Dragon Bone and Oyster Shell Formula," is a classical Chinese formula used to clear heat and as a sedative. From the *Shang Han Lun,* this formula is a modification of Minor Bupleurum Formula *(Xiao Chai Hu Tang)* for improperly treated wind-cold disorders. Over centuries of use, this formula has been expanded to treat a variety of internal and emotional patterns, especially those whose symptoms are marked by fullness in the chest, irritability, and palpitations. Altai anemone *(jiu jie chang pu)* has been added to aid in transformation of phlegm. This formula is useful for drug and smoking withdrawal.

## Ingredients

Bupleuri Radix (Bupleurum Root / **Chai Hu**) 17.7%
Codonopsis Pilosae Radix (Codonopsis / **Dang Shen**) 17.7%
Pinelliae Rhizoma Preparatum (Pinellia, ginger-cured / **Zhi Ban Xia**) 8.9%
Scutellariae Radix (Chinese Scullcap, Scutellaria, Scute / **Huang Qin**) 6.7%
Zingiberis Rhizoma Recens (Fresh Ginger / **Sheng Jiang**) 6.7%
Cinnamomi Ramulus (Cassia, Cinnamon Twig / **Gui Zhi**) 6.7%
Poriae Sclerotium Pararadicis (Poria Spirit / **Fu Shen**) 6.7%
Fossilia Ossis Mastodi (Dragon Bone, Fossilized Bone / **Long Gu**) 6.7%
Ostreae Concha (Oyster Shell / **Mu Li**) 6.7%
Rhei Radix et Rhizoma (Chinese Rhubarb / **Da Huang**) 6.7%
Jujubae Fructus (Jujube Fruit, Chinese Red Date / **Hong Zao, Da Zao**) 4.4%
Anemones Altaicae Rhizoma (Altai Anemone Rhizome / **Jiu Jie Chang Pu**) 4.4%

## Chinese Medical Actions

Unblocks the three yang stages, sedates and calms the spirit, moves liver qi, brings down liver yang, clears heat from the liver.

## Indications

Anxiety
Chest, fullness in
Constipation
Convulsions
Delirium
Dream disturbed sleep
Drug withdrawal
Emotional instability
Fright, disorders due to
Headache
Heat sensation in head
Hot flashes
Hypertension
Hypochondriac pain
Insomnia
Irritability
Mania
Menopausal symptoms
Palpitation
Post-concussion syndrome
Post-traumatic Stress Disorder
Restlessness
Smoking withdrawal
Urinary difficulty or incontinence

**Tongue:** Red, with slippery coating. **Pulse:** Wiry, rapid.

## Contraindications

USE CAUTIOUSLY DURING PREGNANCY OR WHILE NURSING. Reduce dose if loose stools occur.

# CHASE WIND, PENETRATE BONE FORMULA

**Chase Wind, Penetrate Bone Formula** *(Zhui Feng Tou Gu Wan)* is a combination of herbs that remove wind, cold, and dampness; herbs that move the blood; and herbs that strengthen qi, blood, yin, and yang. It can be used for various types of acute and chronic joint pain, stiffness, and swelling.

## Ingredients

Taxilli Herba (Loranthus, Chinese Mistletoe / **Sang Ji Sheng**) 5.8%
Cyperi Rhizoma (Cyperus, Nut-Grass / **Xiang Fu**) 5.8%
Phaseoli Semen (Phaseoli Seed, Adzuki Bean / **Chi Xiao Dou**) 5.8%
Notopterygii Rhizoma seu Radix (Notopterygium / **Qiang Huo**) 5.8%
Ligustici Rhizoma (Chinese Lovage, Ligusticum / **Gao Ben**) 5.8%
Eucommiae Cortex (Eucommia Bark / **Du Zhong**) 5.8%
Achyranthis Bidentatae Radix (Achyranthes / **Huai Niu Xi**) 5.8%
Speranskiae Herba (Speranskia / **Tou Gu Cao**) 5.8%
Paeoniae Radix, alba (Chinese White Peony / **Bai Shao**) 5.8%
Angelicae Dahuricae Radix (Purple Angelica / **Bai Zhi**) 5.8%
Dipsaci Radix (Japanese Teasel Root, Dipsacus / **Xu Duan**) 5.8%
Glycyrrhizae Radix (Chinese Licorice Root / **Gan Cao**) 5.8%
Notoginseng Radix (Tienqi Ginseng, Pseudoginseng Root / **San Qi, Tian Qi**) 5%
Myrrha (Myrrh / **Mo Yao**) 4%
Olibanum (Frankincense / **Ru Xiang**) 4%
Poria (Poria, Hoelen, Tuckahoe / **Fu Ling**) 2.9%
Angelicae Pubescentis Radix (Pubescent Angelica Root / **Du Huo**) 2.9%
Cinnamomi Cortex (Cassia Bark, Cinnamon Bark / **Rou Gui**) 2.9%
Nardostachydis Radix seu Rhizoma (Chinese Nardostachys / **Gan Song Xiang**) 2.9%
Gentianae Macrophyllae Radix (Large Leaf Gentian Root / **Qin Jiao**) 2.9%
Saposhnikoviae Radix (Siler / **Fang Feng**) 2.9%

## Chinese Medical Actions

Removes painful obstruction from wind-cold and wind-dampness, reduces swelling, alleviates pain, moves stagnant qi and blood, disperses constrained liver qi, strengthens the muscles, supplements qi and blood, liver yin, and kidney yin and yang.

## Indications

| | |
|---|---|
| Arthritis | Joint pain, swelling, stiffness |
| Back pain | Knees, weak |
| Back stiffness, chronic | Legs, weak and painful |
| Bone degeneration or weakness | Sciatica, chronic |

## Contraindications

DO NOT USE DURING PREGNANCY. Use with caution with excess heat, as this formula is warming. If heat is present (joints swollen or hot to the touch), combine with **Coptis Relieve Toxicity Formula.** Modify to smaller dosages in cases of digestive weakness. In cases of severe deficiency, this formula can be combined with a supplementing formula.

# CHILDREN'S EAR FORMULA

**Children's Ear Formula** *(Hai Er Fang)* is a modern formula developed by Jake Fratkin, OMD, to treat ear infections in infants and young children (to 6 years old). **Children's Ear Formula** has proven itself over many years, with many practitioners. Given orally, it will usually stop the pain of otitis media (middle ear infection) and otitis externa (outer ear infection) within two hours. It is intended for painful ear infection, but is also appropriate for inflamed or bulging eardrum, without pain.

## Ingredients

Agastaches Herba (Chinese Giant Hyssop, Agastache / **Huo Xiang**) 10%
Poria (Poria, Hoelen, Tuckahoe / **Fu Ling**) 10%
Chrysanthemi Flos (Chrysanthemum / **Ju Hua**) 8%
Coptidis Rhizoma (Coptis / **Huang Lian**) 8%
Forsythiae Fructus (Forsythia Fruit / **Lian Qiao**) 8%
Paeoniae Radix, rubra (Chinese Red Peony / **Chi Shao**) 8%
Peucedani Radix (Peucedanum, Hog Fennel / **Qian Hu**) 8%
Angelicae Dahuricae Radix (Purple Angelica / **Bai Zhi**) 7%
Bupleuri Radix (Bupleurum Root / **Chai Hu**) 7%
Fritillariae Thunbergii Bulbus (Sichuan Fritillary / **Zhe Bei Mu**) 7%
Pinelliae Rhizoma Preparatum (Pinellia, ginger-cured / **Zhi Ban Xia**) 7%
Viticis Fructus (Chaste Tree Fruit, Vitex Fruit / **Man Jing Zi**) 7%
Zingiberis Rhizoma Recens (Fresh Ginger / **Sheng Jiang**) 5%

## Chinese Medical Actions

Clears heat, resolves toxin, dispels dampness, relieves pain.

## Indications

Ear infection with pain in infants and young children
Eardrum, inflamed or bulging, without pain
Ears, congested
Fever, in children prone to ear infections
Headache, with phlegm-heat

**Note: This formula is to be taken orally, not put in the ear.** This formula is an alternative to antibiotics, which increase the chance of a recurrence of the ear infection within 6 weeks. If ear infection is not responsive in 24 hours, consult your healthcare provider. **Children's Ear Formula** addresses the branch—the acute symptoms. When pain eases, the root problem should be treated as well.

# CHONG RELEASE FORMULA

**Chong Release Formula** *(Jia Wei Tao Hong Si Wu Tang)* ) is a modification of the classic formula for nourishing and moving blood, *Tao Hong Si Wu Tang*. It is especially effective in treating menstrual blood stagnation. This formula opens the collaterals to eliminate blood stasis and facilitates the complete discharge of the endometrial lining, so that the new endometrial lining can grow on a smooth, clean base.

## Ingredients

Spatholobi Caulis (Spatholobus / **Ji Xue Teng**) 15%
Albiziae Cortex (Mimosa Tree Bark, Silk-Tree Bark / **He Huan Pi**) 15%
Paeoniae Radix, alba (Chinese White Peony / **Bai Shao**) 12%
Codonopsis Pilosae Radix (Codonopsis / **Dang Shen**) 12%
Atractylodis Macrocephalae Rhizoma (White Atractylodes Rhizome / **Bai Zhu**) 12%
Angelicae Sinensis Radix (Dong Quai, Tang Kuei / **Dang Gui**) 10%
Paeoniae Radix, rubra (Chinese Red Peony / **Chi Shao**) 10%
Chuanxiong Rhizoma (Ligusticum Wallichii Rhizome / **Chuan Xiong**) 6%
Persicae Semen (Peach Kernel, Persica Seed / **Tao Ren**) 5%
Carthami Flos (Safflower, Carthamus Flower / **Hong Hua**) 3%

## Chinese Medical Actions

Nourishes and invigorates blood, supplements qi to support the generation and movement of blood, calms the spirit.

**Tongue:** Pale, slightly purple body or sides, may have distended veins.

## Indications

Endometriosis
Infertility w/ lower burner blood stasis
Menstrual bleeding starts and stops
Menstrual blood clots
Menstrual cycles irregular
Menstrual pain
Menstruation with dark blood or dark spotting
Pelvic congestion
Premenstrual syndrome
Uterine bleeding, dysfunctional

**Pulse:** Wiry, thin, or choppy.

**Contraindications**

DO NOT USE DURING PREGNANCY. Use with **Blood Palace Formula** for strong blood stasis causing significant menstrual pain. If menstrual bleeding is prolonged or heavy, discontinue use.

**Note:** When treating infertility, use this formula from day one of menstration until flow has ceased.

# CINNAMON & PORIA FORMULA

**Cinnamon & Poria Formula** is a modification of Cinnamon Twig and Poria Formula *(Gui Zhi Fu Ling Wan),* with red peony *(chi shao),* salvia *(dan shen)*, sparganium *(san leng)* and rhubarb *(da huang)* added to reinforce the actions of the original formula. This formula is used for blood stasis in the lower abdomen, fixed abdominal masses with abdominal pain, tenderness, and tension. **Cinnamon & Poria Formula** can also be used by men for prostate problems.

## Ingredients

Paeoniae Radix, rubra (Chinese Red Peony / **Chi Shao**) 13.9%
Cinnamomi Ramulus (Cassia, Cinnamon Twig / **Gui Zhi**) 11.1%
Poria (Poria, Hoelen, Tuckahoe / **Fu Ling**) 11.1%
Moutan Cortex (Tree Peony Root Bark / **Mu Dan Pi**) 11.1%
Persicae Semen (Peach Kernel, Persica Seed / **Tao Ren**) 11.1%
Paeoniae Radix, alba (Chinese White Peony / **Bai Shao**) 11.1%
Salviae Miltiorrhizae Radix (Chinese Salvia Root / **Dan Shen**) 11.1%
Rhei Radix et Rhizoma (Chinese Rhubarb / **Da Huang**) 11.1%
Sparganii Rhizoma (Sparganium, Bur-Reed Rhizome / **San Leng**) 8.4%

## Chinese Medical Actions

Invigorates the blood, transforms blood stasis, and reduces fixed abdominal masses.

## Indications

Abdominal distension
Abdominal masses, fixed
Abdominal pain, fixed or stabbing
Abdominal tenderness
Amenorrhea, w/ pain or distension
Back pain, (lower) from fullness
Endometriosis
Hemorrhoids
Infertility
Menopausal symptoms
Menstrual pain
Menstruation, irregular
Night sweats
Ovarian cysts
Pelvic Inflammatory Disease, chronic
Prostate enlarged
Uterine fibroids
Uterine bleeding, dysfunctional

**Tongue:** Body dark or with purple spots.
**Pulse:** Choppy, tense, and sunken.

## Contraindications

DO NOT USE DURING PREGNANCY OR WHILE NURSING. With blood deficiency and stasis, use with **Tang Kuei & Salvia Formula**.

# CINNAMON D FORMULA

**Cinnamon D Formula** (*Gui Zhi Jia Long Gu Mu Li Tang)* also known as "Cinnamon plus Dragon Bone and Oyster Shell Formula" is a classical Chinese formula that addresses deficiency of yin and yang, and lack of communication between the heart and kidneys. It is used for physical symptoms arising from chronic constraint, overwork, or sexual excess, as well as for a number of psychological symptoms.

## Ingredients

Cinnamomi Ramulus (Cassia, Cinnamon Twig / **Gui Zhi**) 15%
Paeoniae Radix, alba (Chinese White Peony / **Bai Shao**) 15%
Zingiberis Rhizoma (Dried Ginger / **Gan Jiang**) 15%
Jujubae Fructus (Jujube Fruit, Chinese Red Date / **Hong Zao, Da Zao**) 15%
Fossilia Ossis Mastodi (Dragon Bone, Fossilized Bone / **Long Gu**) 15%
Ostreae Concha (Oyster Shell / **Mu Li**) 15%
Glycyrrhizae Radix Preparata (Chinese Licorice Root, honey-fried / **Zhi Gan Cao**) 10%

## Chinese Medical Actions

Regulates yin and yang, harmonizes heart and kidneys, restrains essence *(jing)*, harmonizes nutritive *(ying)* and protective *(wei)* qi, calms the spirit.

## Indications

Abdominal contraction
Anxiety
Cold extremities
Coldness in genitals
Diarrhea
Dizziness
Dream-disturbed sleep
Emotional instability
Hair loss
Impotence, with exhaustion
Insomnia
Irritability
Mental confusion
Memory, poor
Nervousness
Nervous exhaustion from sexual excess
Neurotic disorders
Night sweats
Nocturnal emissions
Palpitation
Psychological boundary issues
Sexual intercourse, pain with
Sexual dysfunction in women
Sexual exhaustion in men
Sexual dreams

**Tongue:** Pale with a thin, white coating.
**Pulse:** Hollow, forceless, or thready and floating.

**Note:** Ted Kaptchuk, OMD, states that this formula is useful for sexual abuse survivors, as well as patients who have difficulty with intimacy, commitment, and sexual promiscuity.

# CINNAMON TWIG FORMULA

**Cinnamon Twig Formula** *(Gui Zhi Tang).* This is one of the most commonly modified formulas from the *Shang Han Lun.* **Cinnamon Twig Formula** is best used in cases where the protective *(wei)* qi cannot protect the exterior, and the nutritive *(ying)* qi cannot nourish and stabilize the interior. A common presentation is sweating with invasion from wind-cold, where the sweating does not lead to improvement of the condition and renders the patient more sensitive to the environment. In these cases it is inappropriate to use formulas with ephedra *(ma huang)* or other strongly diaphoretic, warm herbs, or formulas with cold and bitter herbs. In small doses, this formula can also be used to address psychological boundary issues seen in easily overwhelmed patients who have difficulty holding qi or nourishment. These patients usually have chronic deficiency patterns and progress very slowly. **Cinnamon Twig Formula** gives them some energetic containment, and helps them make effective therapeutic progress.

## Ingredients

Cinnamomi Ramulus (Cassia, Cinnamon Twig / **Gui Zhi**) 21.4%
Paeoniae Radix, alba (Chinese White Peony / **Bai Shao**) 21.4%
Zingiberis Rhizoma Recens (Fresh Ginger / **Sheng Jiang**) 21.4%
Jujubae Fructus (Jujube Fruit, Chinese Red Date / **Hong Zao, Da Zao**) 21.4%
Glycyrrhizae Radix Preparata (Chinese Licorice Root, honey-fried / **Zhi Gan Cao**) 14.4%

## Chinese Medical Actions

Regulates the nutritive *(ying)* and protective *(wei)* qi, disperses wind-cold from the muscle layer.

### Indications

Allergies
Aversion to wind
Chills
Cold limbs
Common cold
Dry heaves
Eczema
Fever unrelieved by sweating
Flushing up of qi
Headache
Hives
Invasion by wind-cold
Itching
Neck stiffness
Psychological boundary issues
Sinus congestion
Sweating, spontaneous

**Tongue:** Moist, with thin, white coating.
**Pulse:** Floating and weak.

## Contraindications

Do not use in case with exterior cold and interior heat (fever with thirst, sore throat, rapid pulse).

**Note:** Reduce dosage for psychological use.

# CITRUS & PINELLIA FORMULA

**Citrus & Pinellia Formula** *(Er Chen Tang)* This classical formula is the basis for nearly any formula that is used when phlegm-damp is the presenting symptom. It is used when phlegm-damp from the spleen blocks the flow of qi and interferes with the normal functions of the spleen and stomach. It can be used for clear or white, sticky phlegm in the lungs as well as many problems of the stomach and spleen caused by phlegm-damp.

## Ingredients

Pinelliae Rhizoma Preparatum (Pinellia, ginger-cured / **Zhi Ban Xia**) 35%
Citri Reticulatae Pericarpium (Tangerine Peel / **Chen Pi**) 35%
Poria (Poria, Hoelen, Tuckahoe / **Fu Ling**) 20%
Glycyrrhizae Radix Preparata (Chinese Licorice Root, honey-fried / **Zhi Gan Cao**) 10%

## Chinese Medical Actions

Dries dampness, transforms phlegm, regulates qi, harmonizes the spleen and stomach.

## Indications

Bronchitis, chronic
Chest, stifling sensation in
Cough, with clear or white sputum
Diaphragm, stifling sensation in
Dizziness
Hangover
Morning sickness
Nausea
Palpitation
Retention of food or fluids in stomach
Vomiting

**Tongue:** Swollen, with a thick, white, greasy coating.
**Pulse:** Slippery.

## Contraindications

Do not use with lung yin deficiency; use **Lily Preserve Metal Formula** or **Sheng Mai Formula** instead. For phlegm-heat, use **Fritillaria & Pinellia Formula**.

# CLEMATIS & STEPHANIA FORMULA

**Clematis & Stephania Formula** *(Shu Jing Huo Xue Tang)* is a traditional formula also known as "Relax the Channels and Invigorate the Blood Decoction." It is used for pain caused by wind-dampness, and qi and blood stasis in the channels and collaterals.

## Ingredients

Paeoniae Radix, alba (Chinese White Peony / **Bai Shao**) 11.3%
Angelicae Sinensis Radix (Dong Quai, Tang Kuei / **Dang Gui**) 9.0%
Rehmanniae Radix (Rehmannia Root, unprocessed / **Sheng Di Huang**) 7.5%
Persicae Semen (Peach Kernel, Persica Seed / **Tao Ren**) 7.5%
Atractylodis Rhizoma (Cang-Zhu Atractylodes Rhizome / **Cang Zhu**) 7.5%
Achyranthis Bidentatae Radix (Achyranthes / **Huai Niu Xi**) 7.5%
Clematidis Radix (Chinese Clematis / **Wei Ling Xian**) 7.5%
Citri Reticulatae Pericarpium (Tangerine Peel / **Chen Pi**) 7.5%
Poria (Poria, Hoelen, Tuckahoe / **Fu Ling**) 5.3%
Stephaniae Tetrandrae Radix (Stephania / **Han Fang Ji**) 4.6%
Notopterygii Rhizoma seu Radix (Notopterygium / **Qiang Huo**) 4.6%
Saposhnikoviae Radix (Siler/ **Fang Feng**) 4.6%
Gentianae Radix (Manchurian Gentian / **Long Dan Cao**) 4.6%
Angelicae Dahuricae Radix (Purple Angelica / **Bai Zhi**) 4.6%
Chuanxiong Rhizoma (Ligusticum Wallichii Rhizome / **Chuan Xiong**) 3.4%
Glycyrrhizae Radix (Chinese Licorice Root / **Gan Cao**) 3.0%

## Chinese Medical Actions

Dispels wind-dampness, moves blood stasis, moves qi, unblocks and relaxes the channels.

## Indications

| | |
|---|---|
| Back pain, lower | Movement difficulty |
| Edema | Muscle aches |
| Gout | Numbness, lower extremities |
| Hypertension | Pain, in trunk |
| Joint pain | Post-partum pain |
| Leg pain, radiating | Sciatica |

**Tongue:** Swollen.
**Pulse**: Strong, choppy, superficial.

## Contraindications

DO NOT USE DURING PREGNANCY. This formula is for pain with excess; for pain from deficiency, use **Duhuo & Loranthus Formula.**

# COPTIS RELIEVE TOXICITY FORMULA

**Coptis Relieve Toxicity Formula** *(Huang Lian Jie Du Pian)* is based on a classical Chinese formula known as "Coptis and Scute" used to clear heat from the three burners. It is used for symptoms resulting from liver heat, heat in the blood, and heat in the heart. Rhubarb *(da huang)* and lophatherum *(dan zhu ye)* have been added to aid in the formula's ability to drain damp-heat.

## Ingredients

Gardeniae Fructus (Gardenia Fruit / **Zhi Zi**) 26.7%
Coptidis Rhizoma (Coptis / **Huang Lian**) 20%
Lophatheri Herba (Lophatherum / **Dan Zhu Ye**) 20%
Scutellariae Radix (Chinese Scullcap, Scutellaria, Scute / **Huang Qin**) 13.3%
Phellodendri Cortex (Phellodendron Bark / **Huang Bai**) 13.3%
Rhei Radix et Rhizoma (Chinese Rhubarb / **Da Huang**) 6.7%

## Chinese Medical Actions

Drains fire, relieves heat-toxin, cools liver heat, cools the blood, drains damp-heat.

## Indications

- Acne
- Abscess
- Acid reflux
- Bacterial infection
- Bad breath
- Bleeding from excess heat
- Blood in stools or urine
- Boils
- Carbuncle
- Chicken pox
- Coughing up or vomiting blood
- Delirium
- Diarrhea
- Dizziness or vertigo
- Dryness of mouth and throat
- Eczema
- Emotional instability
- Fever
- Gastritis
- Hangover
- Heat rash
- Hypertension
- Incoherent speech
- Insomnia
- Irritability
- Mania
- Mumps
- Nosebleed
- Palpitation
- Strep throat
- Sties
- Stomach acid, excess
- Tonsillitis
- Toothache
- Urinary tract infection
- Urination, painful
- Vaginal discharge, yellow
- Vomiting, with high fever

**Tongue:** Red, with yellow coating. **Pulse:** Rapid and strong.

## Contraindications

DO NOT USE DURING PREGNANCY OR WHILE NURSING. Not intended for long-term use, as this formula can injure the yin. For patients a with strong constitution. Reduce dose if diarrhea occurs.

# CORYDALIS FORMULA

**Corydalis Formula** (*Shao Yao Gan Cao Jia Yan Hu Tang)* is a combination of the classical "Peony and Licorice Formula" *(Shao Yao Gan Cao Tang)* and corydalis *(yan hu suo).* Peony and Licorice Formula is traditionally used for pain, cramping, or muscle spasms caused by injury to the liver blood or yin. Corydalis *(yan hu suo)* is used for pain from stagnation of qi or blood. These herbs together make this a suitable formula for many types of pain, muscle spasms, and cramps.

## Ingredients

Extract of Corydalis Rhizoma (Corydalis Yanhusuo / **Yan Hu Suo**) 33.4%
Paeoniae Radix, alba (Chinese White Peony / **Bai Shao**) 33.3%
Glycyrrhizae Radix (Chinese Licorice Root / **Gan Cao**) 33.3%

## Chinese Medical Actions

Moves blood and qi, soothes the liver, relieves pain, relaxes muscles, relieves spasms.

## Indications

| | |
|---|---|
| Abdominal pain | Menstrual pain |
| Back pain | Muscular aches and spasms |
| Bronchial pain | Pancreatitis, pain from |
| Gallbladder spasms | Sciatica |
| Headache | Stomach pain |
| Herpes zoster (shingles) pain | Toothache |
| Insomnia from pain | Urinary bladder pain |
| Intestinal cramping | Urination, painful |

## Contraindications

DO NOT USE DURING PREGNANCY. Patients may experience drowsiness when taking this formula and should, therefore, use caution when driving or operating heavy machinery. This formula is not appropriate for pain from wind. Use **Chase Wind, Penetrate Bone Formula**, **Du Huo & Loranthus Formula, or Juan Bi Formula** instead.

# CURCUMA LONGA FORMULA

**Curcuma Longa Formula** *(Jiang Huang Wan)* is designed to manage pain, reduce swelling, and alleviate allergic reactions by reducing inflammation. Systemic inflammation has been found to be a factor in such diverse health disorders as arthritis, atherosclerosis, Alzheimer's disease, cancer, allergies, and autoimmune disorders. The herbs in **Curcuma Longa Formula** have been shown to exhibit anti-inflammatory, analgesic, antioxidant, hepatoprotective, and immunomodulatory effects. This formula supports the liver and blood vessels, and promotes circulation of blood and qi.

## Ingredients

Curcurmae Longae Rhizoma (Turmeric Rhizome / **Jiang Huang**) 16%
Polygoni Cuspidati Rhizoma (Japanese Knotweed / **Hu Zhang**) 14%
Ligustri Lucidi Fructus (Ligustrum, Privet Fruit / **Nu Zhen Zi**) 12%
Olibanum (Frankincense / **Ru Xiang**) 12%
Scutellariae Radix (Chinese Scullcap, Scutellaria, Scute / **Huang Qin**) 10%
Prunellae Spica (Prunella, Heal All, Self-Heal Spike / **Xia Ku Cao**) 8%
Zingiberis Rhizoma Recens (Fresh Ginger / **Sheng Jiang**) 8%
Cinnamomi Ramulus (Cassia, Cinnamon Twig / **Gui Zhi**) 8%
Camelliae Folium (Green Tea Leaf / **Lu Cha**) 4%
Citri Reticulatae Pericarpium (Tangerine Peel / **Chen Pi**) 3%
Glycyrrhizae Radix (Chinese Licorice Root / **Gan Cao**) 3%
Coptidis Rhizoma (Coptis / **Huang Lian**) 2%

## Chinese Medical Actions

Activates blood circulation and invigorates the movement of qi, opens channels and collaterals, stops pain and relieves swelling, clears heat and eliminates toxin.

## Indications

Arthritis, rheumatoid
Asthma, with inflammation
Atherosclerosis
Autoimmune disease
Cancer, inflammation from
COPD
Eyes, red, itchy
Fibromyalgia, with inflammation
Gastritis
Gout
Heart disease
Inflammation, systemic
Knee pain
Lymph nodes, enlarged
Neuropathy
Osteoporosis
Sinus inflammation
Traumatic injury w/ inflammation

**Tongue:** Slightly dusky or deep red, possibly with papilla.
**Pulse:** Choppy, thin, or wiry.

**Dosage:** This formula can be taken in larger doses if necessary (4 tablets, 3 times per day). If prescribing larger doses, or for an extended period of time (longer than 120 days), an assisting formula to prevent possible depletion of qi or yin may be needed. Some recommended protective formulas include: **Astragalus & Ligustrum Formula**, **Ji Xue Formula**, **Jing Qi Formula**, or **Sheng Mai Formula**. One tablet per dose of the assisting formula provides sufficient support in most cases.

## Contraindications

DO NOT USE DURING PREGNANCY. Use caution in patients with spleen qi or blood deficiency, or combine with an appropriate tonic formula such as **Ginseng & Longan Formula**.

**Possible Herb-Drug Interactions:**

1. Anticoagulant/Antiplatelet Drugs: Warfarin, Heparin, Aspirin (affecting platelet levels).
2. Antidiabetic Drugs: Insulin, Glipizide, Tolbutamide (affecting blood sugar levels).

# DUHUO & LORANTHUS FORMULA

**Duhuo & Loranthus Formula** *(Du Huo Ji Sheng Tang)* is a classical formula for painful obstruction in the lower body with deficiency of the liver and kidneys. As described in Chapter 43 of *Basic Questions*: "Painful obstruction in the bones causes heaviness; in the blood vessels causes coagulations and loss of flow; in the sinews causes contractions with an inability to extend the joints, and in the muscles causes numbness." This manifests in symptoms such as arthritis, and heavy and painful sensations in the lower back and legs with weakness and stiffness. This formula is based on the strategy of both supporting normal qi and removing obstruction. Safflower *(hong hua)* was added to augment the pain-relieving properties of this formula.

## Ingredients

Taxilli Herba (Loranthus, Chinese Mistletoe / **Sang Ji Sheng**) 13.6%
Angelicae Pubescentis Radix (Pubescent Angelica Root / **Du Huo**) 8.1%
Carthami Flos (Safflower, Carthamus Flower / **Hong Hua**) 8.1%
Speranskiae Herba (Speranskia / **Tou Gu Cao**) 5.4%
Saposhnikoviae Radix (Siler / **Fang Feng**) 5.4%
Gentianae Macrophyllae Radix (Large Leaf Gentian Root / **Qin Jiao**) 5.4%
Eucommiae Cortex (Eucommia Bark / **Du Zhong**) 5.4%
Achyranthis Bidentatae Radix (Achyranthes / **Huai Niu Xi**) 5.4%
Cinnamomi Cortex (Cassia Bark, Cinnamon Bark / **Rou Gui**) 5.4%
Angelicae Sinensis Radix (Dong Quai, Tang Kuei / **Dang Gui**) 5.4%
Paeoniae Radix, alba (Chinese White Peony / **Bai Shao**) 5.4%
Chuanxiong Rhizoma (Ligusticum Wallichii Rhizome / **Chuan Xiong**) 5.4%
Rehmanniae Radix Preparata (Cured Rehmannia Root / **Shu Di Huang**) 5.4%
Ginseng Radix (Asian Ginseng Root / **Ren Shen**) 5.4%
Poria (Poria, Hoelen, Tuckahoe / **Fu Ling**) 5.4%
Glycyrrhizae Radix Preparata (Chinese Licorice Root, honey-fried / **Zhi Gan Cao**) 5.4%

## Chinese Medical Actions

Expels wind-dampness, disperses painful obstruction, supplements deficient qi, kidney yang, and liver blood.

## Indications

Arthritis
Atrophy, in lower limbs
*Bi* syndrome
Back pain lower, chronic
Bone weakness or degeneration
Coldness, in back and knees
Eczema, in children
Joint stiffness
Knee or leg pain or weakness
Pain, in lower body
Poliomyelitis, sequelae of
Shortness of breath
Walking difficulty

**Tongue:** May be pale, with white coating. **Pulse:** Weak, slow, and thin.

## Contraindications

USE WITH CAUTION DURING PREGNANCY.

# EARTH-HARMONIZING FORMULA

**Earth Harmonizing Formula** *(He Tu Pian)* is designed to treat chronic or recurring disorders of the digestive tract caused by a disharmony between earth and wood. Liver qi invading the spleen or stomach can give rise to a variety of symptoms including acid reflux, bloating, abdominal distension, epigastric pain, belching, nausea, lack of appetite, foul taste in the mouth, and constipation or diarrhea. This formula addresses both liver qi constraint and deficiency of the spleen and stomach simultaneously. Bupleurum *(chai hu),* white peony *(bai shao),* barley sprout *(mai ya)* and curcuma *(yu jin)* soothe the liver and relax liver qi constraint. The four herbs, codonopsis *(dang shen),* white atractylodes *(bai zhu),* poria *(fu ling)* and licorice *(gan cao)*—known together as the "Four Gentlemen Decoction" *(si jun zi tang)*—supplement the central burner and harmonize the stomach. Hawthorn *(shan zha)* and barley sprout *(mai ya)* disperse food stagnation and accumulation. Further, since stagnation in the digestive tract can give rise to heat, this formula includes a small amount of coptis *(huang lian)* to clear stomach heat and solomon's seal *(yu zhu)* to nourish stomach yin.

## Ingredients

Paeoniae Radix, alba (Chinese White Peony / **Bai Shao**) 13%
Curcumae Radix (Turmeric, Curcuma Tuber / **Yu Jin**) 12%
Crataegi Fructus (Chinese Hawthorn Fruit / **Shan Zha**) 12%
Hordei Fructus Germinatus (Barley Sprout / **Mai Ya**) 12%
Bupleuri Radix (Bupleurum Root / **Chai Hu**) 10%
Atractylodis Macrocephalae Rhizoma (White Atractylodes Rhizome / **Bai Zhu**) 8%
Poria (Poria, Hoelen, Tuckahoe / **Fu Ling**) 8%
Codonopsis Pilosae Radix (Codonopsis / **Dang Shen**) 8%
Polygonati Odorati Rhizoma (Aromatic Solomon's Seal / **Yu Zhu**) 8%
Glycyrrhizae Radix (Chinese Licorice Root / **Gan Cao**) 7%
Coptidis Rhizoma (Coptis / **Huang Lian**) 2%

## Chinese Medical Actions

Harmonizes liver and stomach, relaxes liver qi constraint, disperses food stagnation, supplements spleen and stomach, clears heat, and regulates the flow of qi.

## Indications

Abdominal distension or bloating
Acid reflux
Appetite, lack of
Bad breath or taste in mouth
Belching
Constipation
Diarrhea
Digestive discomfort, chronic
Food stagnation, chronic
Nausea

**Tongue:** Thick, yellow coating.
**Pulse:** Wiry or slippery.

# EASE DIGESTION FORMULA

**Ease Digestion Formula** *(Jia Wei Kang Ning Wan)*, is a modification of the popular "Pill Curing" or "Healthy Quiet Pills." It is useful in the treatment of stomach flu (gastroenteritis), hangover, sudden turmoil disorder (concurrent vomiting and diarrhea), and a variety of other digestive complaints. The modifications in this version give it stronger action against mild food poisoning. The glutinous substances have been removed from the original formula so that it is a safe option for patients with gluten intolerance or celiac disease. **Ease Digestion Formula** is an excellent choice to bring along while traveling or to keep at home in the medicine cabinet.

## Ingredients

Poria (Poria, Hoelen, Tuckahoe / **Fu Ling**) 15%
Agastaches Herba (Chinese Giant Hyssop, Agastache / **Huo Xiang**) 10%
Raphani Semen (Radish Seed / **Lai Fu Zi**) 9%
Setariae Fructus Germinantus (Rice Sprout / **Gu Ya**) 9%
Magnoliae Officinalis Cortex (Magnolia Bark / **Hou Po**) 9%
Atractylodis Rhizoma (Cang-Zhu Atractylodes Rhizome / **Cang Zhu**) 8%
Perillae Folium (Perilla Leaf / **Zi Su Ye**) 8%
Angelicae Dahuricae Radix (Purple Angelica / **Bai Zhi**) 8%
Dolomiaeae Radix (Costus Root, Vladimiria Root / **Chuan Mu Xiang**) 7%
Pinelliae Rhizoma Preparatum (Pinellia, ginger-cured / **Zhi Ban Xia**) 7%
Menthae Haplocalysis Herba (Chinese Mint / **Bo He**) 4%
Citri Reticulatae Exocarpium Rubrum (Red Tangerine Peel / **Ju Hong**) 4%
Coptidis Rhizoma (Coptis / **Huang Lian**) 2%

## Chinese Medical Actions

Disperses wind and dampness, resolves spleen dampness, regulates the stomach and resolves phlegm.

## Indications

Abdominal distension
Abdominal pain
Belching
Constipation
Concurrent vomiting and diarrhea
Diarrhea
Flatulence
Food poisoning
Food stagnation
Gastroenteritis
Hangover
Intestinal cramping
Loose stools
Morning sickness
Motion sickness
Nausea
Stomach pain
Vomiting

# EIGHT IMMORTALS FORMULA

**Eight Immortals Formula** *(Ba Xian Chang Shou Wan)* is a modification of Rehmannia Six Formula *(Liu Wei Di Huang Wan).* It can be used to treat many kinds of conditions resulting from deficient yin of the lungs, kidneys, and stomach. The traditional formula has been augmented with ephemerantha (*you gua shi hu*), solomon's seal (*yu zhu*), and glehnia *(sha shen)* to strengthen the cooling and moistening effects of the formula. Use for chronic yin deficiency causing tidal fever, night sweats, ringing in the ears, cough, palpitations, and dizziness.

## Ingredients

Rehmanniae Radix (Rehmannia Root, unprocessed / **Sheng Di Huang**) 17.7%
Ophiopogonis Radix (Ophiopogon Tuber / **Mai Men Dong**) 11.0%
Ephemeranthae Herba (Ephemerantha / **You Gua Shi Hu**) 8.9%
Dioscoreae Rhizoma (Chinese Yam / **Shan Yao**) 8.9%
Corni Fructus (Asiatic Dogwood Fruit, Cornelian Cherry / **Shan Zhu Yu**) 8.9%
Polygonati Odorati Rhizoma (Aromatic Solomon's Seal / **Yu Zhu**) 8.9%
Glehniae Radix (Glehnia Root / **Sha Shen**) 8.9%
Alismatis Rhizoma (Asian Water Plantain / **Ze Xie**) 6.7%
Moutan Cortex (Tree Peony Root Bark / **Mu Dan Pi**) 6.7%
Poria (Poria, Hoelen, Tuckahoe / **Fu Ling**) 6.7%
Schisandrae Fructus (Schisandra Fruit / **Wu Wei Zi**) 6.7%

## Chinese Medical Actions

Supplements kidney qi and yin, supplements lung and stomach yin, moistens dryness, cools lungs, stops cough.

## Indications

Asthma
Constipation, from dryness
Cough
Coughing up blood
Diabetes mellitus
Dizziness
Dry mouth
Dry skin
Fever, tidal
Laryngitis, from dryness
Nausea
Nephritis, chronic
Night sweats
Palms, hot
Palpitation
Pulmonary tuberculosis
Ringing in the ears
Throat, dry

**Tongue:** Red, shiny, with little or no coating.
**Pulse:** Thin and rapid.

## Contraindications

Do not use with internal or external cold, as this formula is cooling. In cases with yin deficiency fire and dampness, use **Rehmannia & Scrophularia Formula** instead.

# ELEUTHERO TABLETS

**Eleuthero Tablets** *(Wu Jia Shen Pian)* contain the single ingredient eleuthero root *(wu jia shen)*. Modern clinical research has indicated eleuthero to be anti-inflammatory and analegisic, and to inhibit arthritis. In addition, eleuthero contains potent adaptogens, which enable the body to fight fatigue, increase resistance to disease, counter the effects of stress, and restore the organism to balance. It is considered an immune system enhancer and cardiovascular tonic. Eleuthero protects against altitude sickness and helps counter the side effects of radiation and chemotherapy.

## Ingredient

Acanthopanacis Senticosi Radix et Caulis (Eleuthero Root / **Wu Jia Shen**) 100%

## Chinese Medical Actions

Supplements the spleen, warms the kidneys, invigorates the blood, unblocks the collaterals, supplements heart qi, calms the spirit.

## Indications

- Altitude sickness
- Appetite, poor
- Back weakness and pain
- Chemotherapy, side effects of
- Circulation, poor, w/ blood stasis
- Concentration, poor
- Fatigue
- Immune system, weak
- Impotence
- Joint pain
- Muscle spasm and weakness
- Nervous exhaustion
- Stress

## Contraindications

Use with caution in cases of deficient yin with heat.

# ESSENTIAL YANG FORMULA

**Essential Yang Formula** (*Jia Jian Jin Gui Shen Qi Wan)* is a modification of the classical Rehmannia Eight Formula or Golden Cabinet Kidney Qi Pill *(Jin Gui Shen Qi Wan)* used to supplement kidney yang. The yang of the kidney is the root of yang for the entire body. Yang energy allows us the ability to be active, vital, and assertive, and is responsible for function, warmth, and movement. From the traditional formula, the aconite has been removed. This formula has added lycium fruit *(gou qi zi)* to nourish the yin and supplement the blood, and the yang tonics morinda *(ba ji tian)*, epimedium *(yin yang huo)*, and psoralea *(bu gu zhi)* to add warmth and to strengthen the kidneys.

## Ingredients

Rehmanniae Radix Preparata (Cured Rehmannia Root / **Shu Di Huang**) 19.8%
Dioscoreae Rhizoma (Chinese Yam / **Shan Yao**) 9.9%
Lycii Fructus (Lycium Fruit, Chinese Wolfberry / **Gou Qi Zi**) 9.9%
Morindae Officinalis Radix (Morinda / **Ba Ji Tian**) 9.9%
Corni Fructus (Asiatic Dogwood Fruit, Cornelian Cherry / **Shan Zhu Yu**) 9.9%
Epimedii Herba (Epimedium / **Yin Yang Huo**) 8.4%
Alismatis Rhizoma (Asian Water Plantain / **Ze Xie**) 7.4%
Moutan Cortex (Tree Peony Root Bark / **Mu Dan Pi**) 7.4%
Poria (Poria, Hoelen, Tuckahoe / **Fu Ling**) 7.4%
Psoraleae Fructus (Psoralea Fruit / **Bu Gu Zhi**) 7.4%
Cinnamomi Cortex (Cassia Bark, Cinnamon Bark / **Rou Gui**) 2.6%

## Chinese Medical Actions

Warms and supplements kidney yang.

## Indications

- Anemia
- Arthritis
- Asthma, chronic bronchial
- Back pain and weakness, lower
- Cataracts
- Cold lower back and legs
- Complexion, pale
- Constipation
- Diabetes
- Edema
- Fatigue
- Glaucoma
- Hypertension (kidney yang *xu*)
- Hypotension
- Hypothyroidism
- Impotence
- Libido, low
- Nephritis
- Nocturnal emissions
- PSA elevated
- Scoliosis
- Sweating, spontaneous or at night
- Urethritis
- Urinary incontinence
- Urinary tract infection, chronic
- Urination, excessive or nocturnal

**Tongue:** Pale, may be swollen, with thin, moist, white coating.
**Pulse:** Empty, weak, and submerged in the kidney position.

## Contraindications

Do not use when signs of heat are present (red tongue, rapid pulse). With chronic digestive weakness from yang deficiency use **Sea of Qi Formula.**

# FIVE MUSHROOM FORMULA

**Five Mushroom Formula** *(Wu Gu Fang).* Mushrooms have been used for their healing properties in Asia for thousands of years. In recent years, Japan and China have conducted extensive research on the medicinal properties of mushrooms. Scientists are particularly focused on the polysaccharides (high-molecular-weight complex sugars), more specifically the beta-glucans and their immune-enhancing qualities. Five mushrooms were chosen that contain high levels of beta-glucans, and because of two specific properties that are common to each of them. All five of these mushrooms provide hepatic support in cases of hepatitis (chronic or acute), as well as supporting the immune system by helping the body to produce more NK (Natural Killer) cells, which play a major role in the rejection of tumors. In addition to the above mentioned properties, these mushrooms have other beneficial functions:

**Agaricus blazei** *(ji song reng)*: eases and promotes digestion, fortifies bones, regulates blood pressure and blood glucose levels.
**Trametes versicolor** *(yun zhi)*: treats infection and/or inflammation of the upper respiratory, urinary, and digestive tracts, clears dampness, reduces phlegm.
**Ganoderma lucidum** *(ling zhi / reishi)*: calms the spirit, nourishes qi and blood, stops cough, alleviates wheezing, dispels phlegm, helps to regulate blood glucose levels; antibacterial, anti-inflammatory, antihypertensive.
**Grifola frondosa** *(hui shu hua / maitake)*: anti-viral and antibacterial, supports the immune system specifically by preventing helper T-cells from being destroyed, promotes weight loss, regulates blood glucose levels, reduces hyperlipidemia, aids in the treatment of hypertension.
**Cordyceps sinensis** *(dong chong xia cao):* supports the kidneys and *jing*, supplements yang, augments lung yin, transforms phlegm, stops bleeding, regulates blood glucose levels.

## Ingredients

Agaricus blazei (45% polysaccharide concentrate from fruiting body Himematsutake / **Ji Song Rong**) 22%
Trametes versicolor (30% polysaccharide concentrate from fruiting body Coriolus, Turkey Tail / **Yun Zhi**) 22%
Ganoderma (Reishi, Ganoderma Mushroom / **Ling Zhi**) 22%
Grifola frondosa (Maitake / **Hui Shu Hua**) 22%
Cordyceps Sinensis (Cordyceps Mycelium / **Dong Chong Xia Cao**) 12%

## Chinese Medical Actions

Supplements spleen and kidney qi, promotes *wei qi,* strengthens the lungs, nourishes liver yin and blood, calms the spirit.

## Indications

| | |
|---|---|
| Cancer, adjuvant therapy | Hypertension |
| Chemotherapy, support during | Hypoglycemia |
| Cholesterol, elevated | Immune system, weak |
| Cough from deficiency | Weakness, general or after illness |
| Fatigue | Wheezing, from deficiency |
| Hepatitis (acute or chronic) | |
| Hyperglycemia | |

## Contraindications

Use with caution in patients with excess conditions.

# FOUR MARVEL FORMULA

**Four Marvel Formula** *(Si Miao Wan)* is based on Zhu Dan-Xi's classic damp-heat resolving formula, *Er Miao San*. The original formula contains two herbs: phellodendron bark *(huang bai)*, which treats damp-heat in the lower burner and atractylodes *(cang zhu)*, which dries dampness. Two additional herbs are included: cyathula *(chuan niu xi)*, which leads the formula downward to the legs, and moves and cools blood, and coix *(yi yi ren)*, which supports the damp-dispelling function of the formula.

## Ingredients

Phellodendri Cortex (Phellodendron Bark / **Huang Bai**) 33%
Coicis Semen (Job's Tears Seed, Chinese Pearl Barley, Coix / **Yi Yi Ren**) 33%
Atractylodis Rhizoma (Cang-Zhu Atractylodes Rhizome / **Cang Zhu**) 17%
Cyathulae Radix (Cyathula Root / **Chuan Niu Xi**) 17%

## Chinese Medical Actions

Clears heat, dries damp.

## Indications

Arthritis, rheumatoid
Atrophy, numbness and weakness of lower limbs
Cervicitis from damp-heat
Edema, lower body
Feet, painful and swollen
Genital sores
Gout
Numbness, lower body
Skin rash, from damp-heat
Testicular eczema or swelling
Urinary tract infection
Vaginal discharge, yellow
Vaginitis from damp-heat

**Tongue:** May be swollen, red, with greasy yellow coating.
**Pulse:** Rapid, swollen, tight.

## Contraindications

Not to be used alone in cases of lung heat or with liver and kidney deficiency.

**Note:**
With qi deficiency, combine with **Six Gentlemen Formula**; with blood deficiency, combine with **Tang Kuei & Salvia Formula**. If there is concurrent qi and blood deficiency, use with **Women's Precious Formula**.

In cases of liver and kidney deficiency, use **Astragalus & Ligustrum Formula**, **Rehmannia Six Formula**, or **Nourish Essence Formula** instead. In cases of lung heat use **Mulberry & Lycium Formula**.

# FREE & EASY WANDERER PLUS

**Free & Easy Wanderer Plus** *(Jia Wei Xiao Yao San)* is a modification of the classical Bupleurum and Peony Formula or Augmented Free and Easy Wanderer used for easing liver constraint and encouraging the free-flowing of liver qi. The blood-moving component to this formula has been augmented with motherwort *(yi mu cao),* red peony *(chi shao)*, and curcuma *(yu jin).* Curcuma also clears the heart and is useful for such emotional symptoms as anxiety and agitation. These herbs have made the formula especially useful for premenstrual syndrome with blood stasis, and painful menstruation with concomitant emotional symptoms, in addition to its other uses.

## Ingredients

Bupleuri Radix (Bupleurum Root / **Chai Hu**) 12.5%
Angelicae Sinensis Radix (Dong Quai, Tang Kuei / **Dang Gui**) 12.5%
Paeoniae Radix, alba (Chinese White Peony / **Bai Shao**) 12.5%
Atractylodis Macrocephalae Rhizoma (White Atractylodes Rhizome / **Bai Zhu**) 12.5%
Poria (Poria, Hoelen, Tuckahoe / **Fu Ling**) 12.5%
Glycyrrhizae Radix Preparata (Chinese Licorice Root, honey-fried / **Zhi Gan Cao**) 6.25%
Paeoniae Radix, rubra (Chinese Red Peony / **Chi Shao**) 6.25%
Moutan Cortex (Tree Peony Root Bark / **Mu Dan Pi**) 6.25%
Gardeniae Fructus (Gardenia Fruit / **Zhi Zi**) 6.25%
Curcumae Radix (Turmeric, Curcuma Tuber / **Yu Jin**) 6.25%
Leonuri Herba (Chinese Motherwort / **Yi Mu Cao**) 6.25%

## Chinese Medical Actions

Clears heat, cools blood, relaxes constrained liver qi, nourishes and circulates blood and disperses blood stasis, strengthens spleen and transforms phlegm, harmonizes the liver and spleen.

## Indications

Abdominal distension
Acid reflux
Anger outbursts or irritability
Anxiety
Appetite, poor
Breast distension and pain
Breast lumps, fibrocystic
Cirrhosis of the liver
Constipation
Depression
Dizziness
Emotional instability
Eyes, red
Headache
Hepatitis, chronic
Herpes, genital
Infertility
Menopausal symptoms
Menstruation, irregular
Menstrual pain
Nausea
Nervous exhaustion
Premenstrual syndrome
Restlessness
Skin rash
Vomiting

**Tongue:** Red sides, body may be red or pale. **Pulse:** Wiry, rapid, thin.

## Contraindications

DO NOT USE DURING PREGNANCY. In cases without signs of heat, use **Bupleurum & Tang Kuei Formula** instead.

# FRITILLARIA & PINELLIA FORMULA

**Fritillaria & Pinellia Formula** *(Chuan Bei Ban Xia Tang)* is a modification of the patent formula *Qing Chi Hua Tan Tang* for cough caused by lung heat. The arisaema and trichosanthes were omitted, and fritillary *(zhe bei mu)*, momordica *(luo han guo)*, houttuynia *(yu xing cao)*, and bamboo secretions *(tian zhu huang)* were added—making this formula ideal for treating hot phlegm (with yellow, green, or thick, sticky sputum) conditions such as bronchitis or pneumonia. This formula is also safe and effective for the hot phlegm conditions of children. It is available in both liquid and tablet form.

## Ingredients

Pinelliae Rhizoma Preparatum (Pinellia, ginger-cured / **Zhi Ban Xia**) 11.6%
Fritillariae Thunbergii Bulbus (Sichuan Fritillary / **Zhe Bei Mu**) 11.5%
Mormordicae Fructus (Momordica Fruit / **Luo Han Guo**) 11.5%
Houttuyniae Herba (Houttuynia / **Yu Xing Cao**) 11.5%
Bambusae Concretio Silicea (Bamboo Secretions / **Tian Zhu Huang**) 7.7%
Scutellariae Radix (Chinese Scullcap, Scutellaria, Scute / **Huang Qin**) 7.7%
Citri Reticulatae Pericarpium (Tangerine Peel / **Chen Pi**) 7.7%
Armeniacae Semen (Apricot Seed, Chinese Bitter Almond / **Xing Ren**) 7.7%
Aurantii Fructus Immaturus (Immature Bitter Orange Fruit / **Zhi Shi**) 7.7%
Poria (Poria, Hoelen, Tuckahoe / **Fu Ling**) 7.7%
Glycyrrhizae Radix (Chinese Licorice Root / **Gan Cao**) 7.7%

## Chinese Medical Actions

Clears lung heat, relieves cough, resolves phlegm, transforms phlegm-heat, promotes downward flow of qi.

## Indications

- Cough, w/ yellow or green sputum
- Cough, leading to vomiting
- Chest, fullness in
- Phlegm, thick sticky
- Smoker's cough
- Snoring, with phlegm
- Throat, sore

**Tongue:** Red with sticky, yellow coating.
**Pulse:** Rapid and full.

## Contraindications

Do not use with dry cough without phlegm.

# GAN MAO LING FORMULA

**Gan Mao Ling Formula** *(Gan Mao Ling Pian)* is a commonly used formula for the initial onset of external pathogenic wind-heat. It is considered an especially potent remedy for dispelling external pathogenic wind, so as to prevent it from penetrating more deeply into the body. **Gan Mao Ling Formula** can also be taken preventively for exposure to common cold and flu.

## Ingredients

Ilicis Pubescentis Radix (Pubescent Holly Root, Ilex / **Mao Dong Qing**) 25%
Isatidis seu Baphicacanthis Radix (Isatis Root / **Ban Lan Gen**) 20%
Evodiae Radix (Evodia Root / **San Ya Ku**) 20%
Chrysanthemi Flos (Chrysanthemum / **Ju Hua**) 13%
Viticis Fructus (Chaste Tree Fruit, Vitex Fruit / **Man Jing Zi**) 12%
Lonicerae Flos (Japanese Honeysuckle Flower / **Jin Yin Hua**) 10%

## Chinese Medical Actions

Clears heat, dispels wind-heat, resolves toxin, relieves cough, opens nasal passages.

## Indications

Common cold
Ear infection
Eyes red
Fever
Headache
Influenza
Lymph nodes, enlarged
Measles, early stage
Neck and shoulders, stiff
Sinus congestion or discharge
Sinus infection
Throat sore
Tonsillitis

## Contraindications

Do not use in cases where patient is experiencing strong chills. Use **Cinnamon Twig Formula** instead.

**Note:** Take every 3 hours as needed at the onset of symptoms of wind invasion.

# GASTRODIA & UNCARIA FORMULA

**Gastrodia & Uncaria Formula** *(Tian Ma Gou Teng Yin)* is a traditional formula used to clear heat, extinguish wind, and calm the liver. Water plantain *(ze xie)* was added to further aid the heat-clearing and downward action of the formula. This formula is indicated when liver yin is deficient and unable to restrain the yang of the liver, causing symptoms such as twitching, spasms, dizziness, headaches, etc. This formula can also be used for high blood pressure due to deficiency.

## Ingredients

Polygoni Multiflori Caulis (Fo-ti Stem, Polygonum Vine / **Ye Jiao Teng**) 16.8%
Haliotidis Concha (Abalone Shell / **Shi Jue Ming**) 13.5%
Taxilli Herba (Loranthus, Chinese Mistletoe / **Sang Ji Sheng**) 13.5%
Uncariae Ramulus cum Uncis (Gambir Vine Stems and Thorns / **Gou Teng**) 8.4%
Poriae Sclerotium Pararadicis (Poria Spirit / **Fu Shen**) 8.4%
Cyathulae Radix (Cyathula Root / **Chuan Niu Xi**) 6.7%
Alismatis Rhizoma (Asian Water Plantain / **Ze Xie**) 6.7%
Gastrodiae Rhizoma (Gastrodia / **Tian Ma**) 5.6%
Gardeniae Fructus (Gardenia Fruit / **Zhi Zi**) 5.1%
Scutellariae Radix (Chinese Scullcap, Scutellaria, Scute / **Huang Qin**) 5.1%
Leonuri Herba (Chinese Motherwort / **Yi Mu Cao**) 5.1%
Eucommiae Cortex (Eucommia Bark / **Du Zhong**) 5.1%

## Chinese Medical Actions

Calms the liver, extinguishes internal wind, clears heat, moves the blood, supplements the liver and kidney yin.

## Indications

Convulsions
Dizziness or vertigo
Dream-disturbed sleep
Emotional instability
Eyes, red or dry
Headache
Heat sensation in head
Hypertension
Insomnia
Light-headedness
Muscle spasms in limbs
Numbness
Paralysis
Ringing in the ear
Twitching
Vision, blurred

**Tongue:** Red.
**Pulse:** Wiry, may be thin and superficial.

## Contraindications

USE WITH CAUTION DURING PREGNANCY.

# GENERAL TONIC FORMULA

**General Tonic Formula** *(Shi Quan Da Bu Wan),* also known as "Ginseng and Tang Kuei Ten Formula," is a common modification of Women's Precious Formula *(Ba Zhen Wan).* It has been augmented with Chinese red date *(da zao)* to supplement the spleen and stomach and dried ginger *(gan jiang)* to warm the middle. This formula is used for qi and blood deficiency when the patient also tends to feel cold.

## Ingredients

Codonopsis Pilosae Radix (Codonopsis / **Dang Shen**) 13.6%
Rehmanniae Radix Preparata (Cured Rehmannia Root / **Shu Di Huang**) 13.6%
Paeoniae Radix, alba (Chinese White Peony / **Bai Shao**) 11.4%
Angelicae Sinensis Radix (Dong Quai, Tang Kuei / **Dang Gui**) 11.4%
Poria (Poria, Hoelen, Tuckahoe / **Fu Ling**) 11.4%
Atractylodis Macrocephalae Rhizoma (White Atractylodes Rhizome / **Bai Zhu**) 9.1%
Astragali Radix (Astragalus / **Huang Qi**) 6.8%
Jujubae Fructus (Jujube Fruit, Chinese Red Date / **Hong Zao, Da Zao**) 6.8%
Chuanxiong Rhizoma (Ligusticum Wallichii Rhizome / **Chuan Xiong**) 4.5%
Glycyrrhizae Radix (Chinese Licorice Root / **Gan Cao**) 4.5%
Cinnamomi Cortex (Cassia Bark, Cinnamon Bark / **Rou Gui**) 4.5%
Zingiberis Rhizoma (Dried Ginger / **Gan Jiang**) 2.4%

## Chinese Medical Actions

Warms and supplements qi and blood, supplements yang, benefits the spleen and heart qi.

## Indications

Anemia
Appetite, reduced
Back weakness
Cold aversion
Cold hands and feet
Complexion, pale
Cough, consumptive or chronic
Digestion, poor
Dizziness
Fatigue
Legs, weak
Post-partum weakness
Shortness of breath
Sores, chronic, unhealed
Surgery, debility after
Weakness, generalized, or after surgery or illness

**Tongue:** Pale with thin, white coating.
**Pulse:** Thin, weak, thready.

## Contraindications

Do not use with signs of heat. If abdominal distension occurs while taking this formula, use **Ginseng & Longan Formula** instead.

# GENTIANA DRAIN FIRE FORMULA

**Gentiana Drain Fire Formula** *(Long Dan Xie Gan Tang)* is a modification of a classical formula used to drain fire in the liver and gallbladder channels and damp-heat from the lower burner. The formula was modified by adding coptis *(huang lian)* and tree peony root bark *(mu dan pi),* for their heat-clearing and anti-microbial effects, and substituting lophatherum *(dan zhu ye)* for clematis (*mu tong).* **Gentiana Drain Fire Formula** is useful in the treatment of urinary tract infections and vaginal infections with yellowish discharge.

## Ingredients

Rehmanniae Radix (Rehmannia Root, unprocessed / **Sheng Di Huang**) 13.0%
Scutellariae Radix (Chinese Scullcap, Scutellaria, Scute / **Huang Qin**) 10.3%
Gardeniae Fructus (Gardenia Fruit / **Zhi Zi**) 10.3%
Plantaginis Semen (Asian Plantain Seed, Plantago Seed / **Che Qian Zi**) 10.3%
Alismatis Rhizoma (Asian Water Plantain / **Ze Xie**) 10.3%
Angelicae Sinensis Radix (Dong Quai, Tang Kuei / **Dang Gui**) 10.3%
Moutan Cortex (Tree Peony Root Bark / **Mu Dan Pi**) 8.6%
Gentianae Radix (Manchurian Gentian / **Long Dan Cao**) 7.8%
Bupleuri Radix (Bupleurum Root / **Chai Hu**) 6.9%
Glycyrrhizae Radix (Chinese Licorice Root / **Gan Cao**) 6.2%
Lophatheri Herba (Lophatherum / **Dan Zhu Ye**) 3.4%
Coptidis Rhizoma (Coptis / **Huang Lian**) 2.6%

## Chinese Medical Actions

Drains fire from the liver and gallbladder, clears and drains damp-heat from the lower burner.

## Indications

- Bitter taste in mouth
- Conjunctivitis
- Dizziness
- Ear infection with pus
- Eczema
- Eyes, red and sore
- Gallbladder inflammation
- Gallstones
- Genital itching, swelling, and pain
- Hangover
- Headache
- Herpes Simplex
- Herpes Zoster (shingles)
- Hyperthyroidism
- Hypochondriac pain
- Irritability
- Jaundice
- Menstrual cycle shortened
- Migraine headache
- Pelvic Inflammatory Disease
- Prostatitis
- Skin rash
- Tonsillitis
- Urinary tract infection
- Urination, painful
- Vaginal discharge, foul-smelling
- Vaginal yeast infection
- Vaginitis, non-specific

**Tongue:** Red with yellow coating. **Pulse:** Wiry, rapid, forceful.

## Contraindications

DO NOT USE DURING PREGNANCY. Not for long-term use. Use with caution in cases with spleen deficiency.

# GINKGO FORMULA

**Ginkgo Formula** *(Yin Guo Ye Wan)* is a modification of Healthy Brain Pills *(Jian Nao Wan)*. Cinnabar (which contains mercury) has been omitted and ginkgo leaf *(yin guo ye)* added. Ginkgo is a cardiovascular and nervous restorative. It is combined in this formula with other herbs that nourish and support mental functions.

## Ingredients

Ginkgo Folium (Ginkgo Leaf / **Yin Guo Ye**) 23.8%
Ziziphi Spinosa Semen (Sour Date Seed, Jujube Seed / **Suan Zao Ren**) 15.3%
Angelicae Sinensis Radix (Dong Quai, Tang Kuei / **Dang Gui**) 10.2%
Dioscoreae Rhizoma (Chinese Yam / **Shan Yao**) 8.5%
Cistanches Herba (Broomrape, Cistanches / **Rou Cong Rong**) 6.7%
Lycii Fructus (Lycium Fruit, Chinese Wolfberry / **Gou Qi Zi**) 6.7%
Schisandrae Fructus (Schisandra Fruit / **Wu Wei Zi**) 6.7%
Alpiniae Oxyphyllae Fructus (Black Cardamom, Alpinia Fruit / **Yi Zhi Ren**) 5.1%
Succinum Resina (Amber / **Hu Po**) 3.4%
Fossilia Ossis Mastodi (Dragon Bone, Fossilized Bone / **Long Gu**)3.4%
Ginseng Radix (Asian Ginseng Root / **Ren Shen**) 3.4%
Anemones Altaicae Rhizoma (Altai Anemone Rhizome / **Jiu Jie Chang Pu**) 3.4%
Platycladi Semen (Oriental Arborvitae Seed, Biota Seed / **Bai Zi Ren**) 3.4%

## Chinese Medical Actions

Supplements heart and liver blood, calms the spirit, sedates liver fire and wind.

## Indications

Amnesia
Concentration, poor
Dizziness
Dream-disturbed sleep
Insomnia
Memory, poor
Mental confusion
Mental fatigue
Palpitation
Restlessness

## Contraindications

Use caution when using coumadin and other blood thinners concurrently with **Ginkgo Formula**.

# GINSENG & ASTRAGALUS FORMULA

**Ginseng & Astragalus Formula** (*Bu Zhong Yi Qi Wan)* also known as "Support Central Qi Pills" is a classical formula used to supplement spleen and stomach qi and to raise yang.

## Ingredients

Astragali Radix (Astragalus / **Huang Qi**) 32%
Atractylodis Macrocephalae Rhizoma (White Atractylodes Rhizome / **Bai Zhu**) 14%
Bupleuri Radix (Bupleurum Root / **Chai Hu**) 12%
Angelicae Sinensis Radix (Dong Quai, Tang Kuei / **Dang Gui**) 10%
Glycyrrhizae Radix (Chinese Licorice Root / **Gan Cao**) 8%
Citri Reticulatae Pericarpium (Tangerine Peel / **Chen Pi**) 8%
Ginseng Radix (Asian Ginseng Root / **Ren Shen**) 8%
Cimicifugae Rhizoma (Chinese Cimicifuga / **Sheng Ma**) 8%

## Chinese Medical Actions

Replenishes the qi, supplements the qi of the middle burner and raises sunken yang.

## Indications

Abdominal distension or bloating
Abdominal pain
Appetite, reduced
Bronchitis, chronic
Cold aversion
Complexion, pale
Constitution, delicate
Curl up, tendency to
Diarrhea, chronic
Digestion, weak
Dizziness
Fatigue
Fever, chronic, intermittent or worse with exertion
Flatulence
Headache
Hypoglycemia
Hypotension
Limbs weak or tired
Memory, poor
Miscarriage, recurrent
Night sweats
Postpartum weakness
Prolapse (deficient qi and yang)
Shortness of breath
Sores, slow to heal
Sweating, spontaneous
Stools, loose and watery
Thirst for warm drinks
Uterine bleeding, dysfunctional
Weakness, generalized, or after surgery or illness
Weight loss

**Tongue:** Pale, slightly swollen, with white coating.
**Pulse:** Deficient, especially in the spleen position.

## Contraindications

Do not use in cases of fever (heat) from yin deficiency. If abdominal distension occurs while taking this formula, use **Ginseng & Longan Formula** instead.

# GINSENG & LONGAN FORMULA

**Ginseng & Longan Formula** *(Gui Pi Tang),* also known as "Restore the Spleen Decoction," is a popular formula that is used when excessive or obsessive mental activity injures both the spleen and the heart causing insomnia, palpitations, inability to concentrate, memory loss, anxiety and phobias. Injury to the spleen impairs its ability to generate and control blood. When the blood is deficient, the heart is not nourished. This affects the heart's ability to store the *shen* (spirit) and the spleen's ability to store the *yi* (intelligence). This formula can be used in place of **Ginseng & Astragalus Formula** or **General Tonic Formula** in patients who experience abdominal distension when taking those formulas.

## Ingredients

Astragali Radix (Astragalus / **Huang Qi**) 11.2%
Atractylodis Macrocephalae Rhizoma (White Atractylodes Rhizome / **Bai Zhu**) 11.2%
Poria (Poria, Hoelen, Tuckahoe / **Fu Ling**) 11.2%
Ziziphi Spinosa Semen (Sour Date Seed, Jujube Seed / **Suan Zao Ren**) 11.2%
Longan Arillis (Longan Fruit / **Long Yan Rou**) 11.2%
Angelicae Sinensis Radix (Dong Quai, Tang Kuei / **Dang Gui**) 11.2%
Polygalae Radix (Polygala, Chinese Senega Root / **Yuan Zhi**) 11.2%
Ginseng Radix (Asian Ginseng Root / **Ren Shen**) 5.6%
Dolomiaeae Radix (Costus Root, Vladimiria Root / **Chuan Mu Xiang**) 5.6%
Jujubae Fructus (Jujube Fruit, Chinese Red Date / **Hong Zao, Da Zao**) 5.6%
Glycyrrhizae Radix Preparata (Chinese Licorice Root, honey-fried / **Zhi Gan Cao**) 2.7%
Zingiberis Rhizoma Recens (Fresh Ginger / **Sheng Jiang**) 2.1%

## Chinese Medical Actions

Supplements qi, supplements heart blood, strengthens spleen and heart qi.

## Indications

Anxiety
Appetite poor
Bruises, easily
Concentration poor
Constitution, delicate
Dream-disturbed sleep
Fever, from deficiency
Fright
Insomnia
Memory, poor
Menstrual bleeding, excessive
Nervous exhaustion
Night sweats
Palpitation
Phobias
Post-concussion syndrome
Post-traumatic Stress Disorder
Uterine bleeding
Vaginal discharge
Weakness, generalized, or after surgery or illness
Weight loss

**Tongue:** Pale with a thin, white coating. May be swollen.
**Pulse:** Thin or thready and weak.

# GINSENG ENDURANCE FORMULA

**Ginseng Endurance Formula** *(Ren Shen Pian)* is designed to enhance athletic performance and improve stamina. Ginseng *(ren shen),* astragalus *(huang qi),* atractylodes *(bai zhu),* and licorice *(gan cao)* are used to supplement qi. Eleuthero root *(wu jia shen)* is an adaptogenic tonic. Schisandra *(wu wei zi)* supports the lung and heart functions and retains the essence. Rhodiola *(hong jing tian)* invigorates the blood and has been shown to increase arterial oxygen. Tang kuei *(dang gui)* supplements and invigorates the blood. Ganoderma *(ling zhi)* is used to supplement blood and vital qi. Cordyceps *(dong chong xia cao)* is a famous yang tonic that has been used by Olympic athletes to enhance performance.

## Ingredients

Astragali Radix (Astragalus / **Huang Qi**) 18%
Acanthopanacis Senticosi Radix et Caulis (Eleuthero Root / **Wu Jia Shen**) 16%
Rhodiola Herba (Rhodiola / **Hong Jing Tian**) 15%
Ginseng Radix (Asian Ginseng Root / **Ren Shen**) 9%
Angelicae Sinensis Radix (Dong Quai, Tang Kuei / **Dang Gui**) 8%
Schisandrae Fructus (Schisandra Fruit / **Wu Wei Zi**)7%
Atractylodis Macrocephalae Rhizoma (White Atractylodes Rhizome / **Bai Zhu**) 7%
Ganoderma (Reishi, Ganoderma Mushroom / **Ling Zhi**) 7%
Poria (Poria, Hoelen, Tuckahoe / **Fu Ling**) 5%
Glycyrrhizae Radix (Chinese Licorice Root / **Gan Cao**) 4%
Cordyceps Sinensis (Cordyceps Mycelium / **Dong Chong Xia Cao**) 4%

## Chinese Medical Actions

Supplements qi, blood, and yang, invigorates blood.

## Indications

Appetite, loss of
Breathing labored upon exertion
Breathing shallow
Fatigue
Immune system weak
Recovery after illness
Shortness of breath
Weakness, generalized or after surgery or illness

## Contraindications

Not to be taken with fever or an acute wind condition, or with heat from yin deficiency.

**Note:** This formula can be taken 30 minutes to 1 hour prior to a workout or sports event.

# GINSENG NOURISHING FORMULA

**Ginseng Nourishing Formula** *(Ren Shen Yang Ying Wan)* is also known as "Ginseng Nutritive Formula." Nutritive or tonic formulas are used to supplement weak qi and are useful in preventing disease. This formula is especially good for the elderly and for people who are chronically fatigued, anxious, lacking in vitality, or recovering from surgery or a long illness.

## Ingredients

Paeoniae Radix, alba (Chinese White Peony / **Bai Shao**) 19.9%
Angelicae Sinensis Radix (Dong Quai, Tang Kuei / **Dang Gui**) 6.9%
Citri Reticulatae Pericarpium (Tangerine Peel / **Chen Pi**) 6.9%
Astragali Radix (Astragalus / **Huang Qi**) 6.9%
Cinnamomi Cortex (Cassia Bark, Cinnamon Bark / **Rou Gui**) 6.9%
Ginseng Radix (Asian Ginseng Root / **Ren Shen**) 6.9%
Atractylodis Macrocephalae Rhizoma (White Atractylodes Rhizome / **Bai Zhu**) 6.9%
Glycyrrhizae Radix Preparata (Chinese Licorice Root, honey-fried / **Zhi Gan Cao**) 6.9%
Jujubae Fructus (Jujube Fruit, Chinese Red Date / **Hong Zao, Da Zao**) 6.9%
Schisandrae Fructus (Schisandra Fruit / **Wu Wei Zi**) 6.9%
Poriae Sclerotium Pararadicis (Poria Spirit / **Fu Shen**) 5.5%
Rehmanniae Radix Preparata (Cured Rehmannia Root / **Shu Di Huang**) 5.5%
Polygalae Radix (Polygala, Chinese Senega Root / **Yuan Zhi**) 4.2%
Zingiberis Rhizoma Recens (Fresh Ginger / **Sheng Jiang**) 2.8%

## Chinese Medical Actions

Supplements qi and blood, nourishes the heart, calms the spirit, sharpens the memory.

## Indications

Amnesia
Anemia
Anxiety
Appetite poor
Constitution, delicate
Diarrhea, chronic
Digestion, weak
Emotional instability
Fatigue
Hair loss, from injury to the blood
Hypothyroidism
Insomnia
Memory, poor
Mental fatigue or exhaustion
Muscle spasms
Nervousness
Night sweats
Palpitation
Post-partum fatigue
Premature ejaculation
Restlessness
Shortness of breath
Sleep, restless
Sores, chronic non-healing
Stools, loose
Sweating, spontaneous or profuse
Weakness, chronic
Weakness after surgery or illness
Weight loss

**Tongue:** Pale. **Pulse:** Weak, soft.

# HAWTHORN & FENNEL FORMULA

**Hawthorn & Fennel Formula** *(Shan Zha Xiao Hui Xiang Fang)* is designed to promote safe and healthy weight loss. This formula aims to increase metabolism, adjust the digestive system, promote the metabolism of fats and lipids, and aid water metabolism. It is appropriate for all types of overweight persons and safe for long-term use. Coix *(yi yi ren)* supplements the spleen, transforms dampness, and regulates water metabolism. Astragalus *(huang qi)* supplements qi and blood, promotes urination, and reduces edema. Immature bitter orange *(zhi shi)* regulates qi in the digestive system, directs qi downward, and disperses food accumulation. It is currently used as a "fat buster" in the natural foods industry. Hawthorn *(shan zha)*, another "fat buster," disperses stagnation, improves digestion of fat, and reduces cholesterol. Lotus leaf *(he ye)* is a digestive stimulant and, in modern times, is used as a safe diuretic that mildly clears heat. Atractylodes *(bai zhu)* supplements qi, transforms phlegm and dampness, and disperses water retention. Fennel *(xiao hui xiang)* reduces the appetite and regulates digestive function. Cassia *(jue ming zi)* moistens and unblocks the intestines and improves lipid metabolism. Water plantain *(ze xie)* promotes urination and lowers cholesterol. Rhubarb *(da huang)* purges the intestines and lowers cholesterol. Radish seed *(lai fu zi)* transforms phlegm and disperses accumulations of stagnant food. Green tea *(lu cha)* increases lipid metabolism and stimulates the central nervous system. It also contains anti-oxidants and is considered a tool in cancer prevention. Cinnamon twig *(gui zhi)* promotes circulation and is used for edema. Licorice root *(gan cao)* is included to supplement qi and harmonize the characteristics of the other ingredients.

## Ingredients

Coicis Semen (Job's Tears Seed, Chinese Pearl Barley, Coix / **Yi Yi Ren**) 14%
Astragali Radix (Astragalus / **Huang Qi**) 12%
Aurantii Fructus Immaturus (Immature Bitter Orange Fruit / **Zhi Shi**) 10%
Crataegi Fructus (Chinese Hawthorn Fruit / **Shan Zha**) 9%
Nelumbinis Folium (Lotus Leaf / **He Ye**) 8%
Atractylodis Macrocephalae Rhizoma (White Atractylodes Rhizome / **Bai Zhu**) 8%
Foeniculi Fructus (Fennel Fruit / **Xiao Hui Xiang**) 7%
Cassiae Semen (Cassia Seed, Sickle-pod Senna / **Jue Ming Zi**) 6%
Alismatis Rhizoma (Asian Water Plantain / **Ze Xie**) 6%
Rhei Radix et Rhizoma (Chinese Rhubarb / **Da Huang**) 5%
Raphani Semen (Radish Seed / **Lai Fu Zi**) 5%
Camelliae Folium (Green Tea Leaf / **Lu Cha**) 4%
Cinnamomi Ramulus (Cassia, Cinnamon Twig / **Gui Zhi**) 3%
Glycyrrhizae Radix (Chinese Licorice Root / **Gan Cao**) 3%

## Chinese Medical Actions

Drains dampness, moves qi and blood, disperses food stagnation, moves stool, supplements the spleen, clears liver heat, regulates the appetite, adjusts metabolism.

## Indications

| | |
|---|---|
| Abdominal distension or bloating | Food stagnation |
| Cholesterol, elevated | Obesity |
| Constipation | Phlegm |
| Digestion, weak | Stagnation, in digestive system |
| Edema | Toxicity, feeling of |

## Contraindications

DO NOT USE DURING PREGNANCY OR WHILE NURSING. Discontinue use or decrease dose if diarrhea occurs.

**Note:** Can be combined with the appropriate constitutional formula (**Women's Precious Formula, Sea of Qi Formula, Tang Kuei & Salvia Formula, Free & Easy Wanderer Plus, Essential Yang Formula,** etc.). Best taken 30 minutes before meals. More effective weight loss will be experienced if the patient drinks 8 glasses of water per day. Healthy weight loss occurs gradually. It is important to recommend that patients establish a routine of consistent and regular aerobic exercise and to make healthy choices in their eating habits.

# HE SHOU WU TABLETS

**He Shou Wu Tablets** *(Shou Wu Pian)* contain the single ingredient radix polygoni multiflori *(he shou wu* or *fo ti)*, which supplements the liver and kidneys and nourishes the blood and essence *(jing)*.

## Ingredient

Polygoni Multiflori Radix Preparata (Polygonum Root, Fo Ti / **Zhi He Shou Wu**) 100%

## Chinese Medical Actions

Supplements the liver and kidneys, nourishes the blood and yin, benefits and retains the essence, stops leakage, detoxifies, moistens the intestines and moves the stool, expels wind from the skin by nourishing the blood.

## Clinical Research

Decreases blood cholesterol levels, antibacterial—has an *in vitro* inhibitory effect on *Mycobacterium tuberculosis* and *Shigella flexneri*, raises serum glucose levels, increases liver glycogen content.

## Indications

- Back weakness, lower
- Blood deficiency patterns
- Carbuncle
- Cholesterol elevated
- Constipation w/ blood deficiency
- Dizziness
- Dryness
- Eczema
- Hair, premature graying
- Hypertension
- Hypoglycemia
- Insomnia
- Knees, weak
- Limbs, sore
- Nocturnal emissions
- Skin rash from blood deficiency
- Sores
- Vaginal discharge
- Vision, blurred or spots in

**Tongue:** Pale, may be dry.
**Pulse:** Weak, thin.

## Contraindications

Do not use in cases with phlegm, or with diarrhea from spleen deficiency.

# HEAD RELIEF FORMULA

**Head Relief Formula** *(Tou Tong Pian)* was created by Jake Fratkin, OMD, as an herbal alternative to over-the-counter analgesics such as aspirin and acetaminophen. It is indicated for headache, and can also be used for sinus pain, toothache, and pain due to TMJ (temporomandibular joint) disorder. Over-the-counter analgesics carry a price: acetaminophen can be toxic to the liver, especially when combined with alcohol. Aspirin and ibuprofen damage the lining of the small intestine, aggravating leaky gut syndrome or causing intestinal bleeding. **Head Relief Formula** is safe and can be used as needed.

## Ingredients

Saposhnikoviae Radix (Siler / **Fang Feng**) 10%
Ligustici Rhizoma (Chinese Lovage, Ligusticum / **Gao Ben**) 10%
Menthae Haplocalysis Herba (Chinese Mint / **Bo He**) 10%
Carthami Flos (Safflower, Carthamus Flower / **Hong Hua**) 10%
Angelicae Dahuricae Radix (Purple Angelica / **Bai Zhi**) 9%
Salviae Miltiorrhizae Radix (Chinese Salvia Root / **Dan Shen**) 9%
Uncariae Ramulus cum Uncis (Gambir Vine Stems and Thorns / **Gou Teng**) 9%
Viticis Fructus (Chaste Tree Fruit, Vitex Fruit / **Man Jing Zi**) 9%
Bupleuri Radix (Bupleurum Root / **Chai Hu**) 8%
Scutellariae Radix (Chinese Scullcap, Scutellaria, Scute / **Huang Qin**) 8%
Paeoniae Radix, rubra (Chinese Red Peony / **Chi Shao**) 8%

## Chinese Medical Actions

Dispels pathogenic wind, warms the channels and collaterals, moves blood, frees the collaterals, relieves pain.

## Indications

Headache due to wind-cold, muscle tension, or trauma
Hangover
Sinus pain
Toothache

## Contraindications

DO NOT USE DURING PREGNANCY. Not effective for headache due to deficiency of qi, blood, or yin.

**Dosage:** This formula can be taken every three hours as needed. Reduce dose in children.

# HEAVENLY EMPEROR'S FORMULA

**Heavenly Emperor's Formula** (*Tian Wang Bu Xin Dan),* also known as "Emperor's Tea" or "Ginseng and Zizyphus Formula," is used to treat yin deficiency of the heart and kidneys. It is an excellent herbal alternative to tranquilizers or sleeping pills. This version of the formula does **not** contain cinnabar *(zhu sha).*

## Ingredients

Rehmanniae Radix (Rehmannia Root, unprocessed / **Sheng Di Huang**) 29.7%
Codonopsis Pilosae Radix (Codonopsis / **Dang Shen**) 7.4%
Asparagi Radix (Chinese Asparagus Tuber / **Tian Men Dong**) 7.4%
Ophiopogonis Radix (Ophiopogon Tuber / **Mai Men Dong**) 7.4%
Angelicae Sinensis Radix (Dong Quai, Tang Kuei / **Dang Gui**) 7.4%
Schisandrae Fructus (Schisandra Fruit / **Wu Wei Zi**) 7.4%
Platycladi Semen (Oriental Arborvitae Seed, Biota Seed / **Bai Zi Ren**) 7.4%
Ziziphi Spinosa Semen (Sour Date Seed, Jujube Seed / **Suan Zao Ren**) 7.4%
Scrophulariae Radix (Scrophularia, Figwort Root / **Xuan Shen**) 3.7%
Salviae Miltiorrhizae Radix (Chinese Salvia Root / **Dan Shen**) 3.7%
Poriae Sclerotium Pararadicis (Poria Spirit / **Fu Shen**) 3.7%
Polygalae Radix (Polygala, Chinese Senega Root / **Yuan Zhi**) 3.7%
Platycodi Radix (Platycodon Root, Balloon Flower Root / **Jie Geng**) 3.7%

## Chinese Medical Actions

Nourishes yin, nourishes blood, supplements the heart, calms the spirit, strengthens the will.

## Indications

Anxiety
Concentration, poor
Conjunctivitis, chronic
Dream-disturbed sleep
Emotional instability
Hives
Hyperthyroidism
Insomnia
Irritability
Itching, painful
Memory, poor
Mental confusion
Menopausal symptoms
Nervousness
Nocturnal emissions
Palpitation
Sleep, restless

**Tongue:** Red, with little coating.
**Pulse:** Thin, rapid.

## Contraindications

Do not use in cases of spleen deficiency with dampness.

# IMMORTAL VALLEY FORMULA

**Immortal Valley Formula** *(Xian Gu Fang)* treats a variety of gynecological problems, such as cervical dysplasia and vaginal discharge with dampness and heat in the lower burner. Lonicera *(jin yin hua)*, oldenlandia *(bai hua she she cao),* and phellodendron *(huang bai)* clear heat and toxin and are effective in treating the human papillomavirus (HPV) infection often associated with cervical cancer. Oldenlandia *(bai hua she she cao)* and paris *(chong lou)* clear heat-toxin and are anti-neoplastic herbs. Coix *(yi yi ren),* smilax *(tu fu ling)*, and polyporus *(zhu ling)* also have anti-neoplastic properties, and together clear dampness and heat-toxin. Dioscorea *(shan yao)* supplements the spleen and kidney, while white peony *(bai shao)* softens and nourishes the liver. Zedoary *(e zhu)* is anti-neoplastic and works synergistically with achyranthes *(huai niu xi)* to invigorate and enliven, where stagnation of blood and congestion of dampness and heat lead to poor blood circulation and unhealthy tissue.

## Ingredients

Hedyotis Diffusae Herba (Hedyotis, Oldenlandia / **Bai Hua She She Cao**) 12%
Coicis Semen (Job's Tears Seed, Chinese Pearl Barley, Coix / **Yi Yi Ren**) 10%
Smilacis Glabrae Rhizoma (Chinese Smilax Rhizome / **Tu Fu Ling**) 10%
Lonicerae Flos (Japanese Honeysuckle Flower / **Jin Yin Hua**) 10%
Dioscoreae Rhizoma (Chinese Yam / **Shan Yao**) 9%
Paeoniae Radix, alba (Chinese White Peony / **Bai Shao**) 9%
Phellodendri Cortex (Phellodendron Bark / **Huang Bai**) 8%
Polyporus (Polyporus Sclerotium / **Zhu Ling**) 8%
Achyranthis Bidentatae Radix (Achyranthes / **Huai Niu Xi**) 7%
Paridis Rhizoma (Paris Rhizome / **Chong Lou**) 7%
Curcumae Rhizoma (Zedoary Rhizome / **E Zhu**) 5%
Sargentodoxae Caulis (Sargentodoxa Caulis / **Hong Teng**) 5%

## Chinese Medical Actions

Soothes and relaxes the liver, mildly supplements spleen, clears damp-heat and heat-toxin in lower burner, dispels blood stasis.

## Indications

| | |
|---|---|
| Abdominal distension, lower | Pelvic Inflammatory Disease |
| Cervical dysplasia | Uterine bleeding, dysfunctional |
| Cervicitis | Vaginal discharge, yellow, odorous |
| Herpes outbreaks, genital | Vaginitis |
| HPV | Vulvar itching and pain |
| Menstrual bleeding, abnormal | Yeast infections |

**Tongue:** Pale, purple, or reddish body; may have red sides and yellow coating at the back. **Pulse**: Slippery, maybe slightly rapid, often wiry.

## Contraindications

DO NOT USE DURING PREGNANCY. Do not use with cold signs of yang deficiency. For heat in the blood (with post-coital or heavy menstrual bleeding, or bleeding during ovulation), use **Yin Valley Formula** instead.

# INTESTINAL FUNGUS FORMULA

**Intestinal Fungus Formula** *(Chang Mei Jun Fang)* was developed by Jake Fratkin, OMD, to treat candida fungal infection in the large and small intestines. *Candida albicans* and other opportunistic fungi develop and grow in the intestines following antibiotic therapy, or ingestion of antibiotics from meat sources. These fungi disrupt the normal bacterial flora, as well as irritate and inflame the intestinal lining, contributing to "Leaky Gut Syndrome"—the infiltration of intestinal toxins into the blood. Leaky gut contributes to many health problems, including fatigue, fibromyalgia, headache, and lowered immunity. This formula directly attacks heat-toxin (fungal, viral, bacterial and protozoan) with the herbs coptis *(huang lian)*, phellodendron *(huang bai)*, pulsatilla *(bai tou weng)* and capillaris *(yin chen hao)*. The other herbs, poria *(fu ling)*, coix *(yi yi ren)* and pinellia *(ban xia)* dispel dampness and mucus. The formula can also be used for acute food poisoning, giardia, and stomach flu.

## Ingredients

Poria (Poria, Hoelen, Tuckahoe / **Fu Ling**) 15%
Coicis Semen (Job's Tears Seed, Chinese Pearl Barley, Coix / **Yi Yi Ren**) 15%
Pinelliae Rhizoma Preparatum (Pinellia, ginger-cured / **Zhi Ban Xia**) 14%
Coptidis Rhizoma (Coptis / **Huang Lian**) 14%
Phellodendri Cortex (Phellodendron Bark / **Huang Bai**) 14%
Pulsatillae Radix (Chinese Pulsatilla Root / **Bai Tou Weng**) 14%
Artemisiae Scopariae Herba (Capillaris / **Yin Chen Hao**) 14%

## Chinese Medical Actions

Clears heat, resolves toxin, dispels dampness.

## Indications

| | |
|---|---|
| Abdominal distension or bloating | Immunity, lowered |
| Candida infection in intestines | Intestinal cramping |
| Diarrhea | Irritable Bowel Syndrome |
| Flatulence | Parasites |
| Food poisoning | Rectal itching |
| Gastroenteritis | Stool, loose or erratic |
| Giardia | Skin problems |

**Tongue:** A white or yellow, greasy coating at proximal root.
**Pulse:** Normal, or rapid and slippery.

## Contraindications

Can cause loose stools, if so, reduce dose.

**Note:** When intestinal epithelia have been damaged or inflamed, combine with **Pulsatilla Intestinal Formula.** When treating patients diagnosed with candida, it is recommended to change herbal therapies every 30 days. Alternate with **Oregano Oil Formula**.

# JADE SCREEN & XANTHIUM FORMULA

**Jade Screen & Xanthium Formula** *(Yu Ping Feng Jia Cang Er San)* is an augmentation of the classical formula "Jade Windscreen Powder" *(Yu Ping Feng San),* used to supplement the *wei* or protective qi, which defends the body from invasion by external pathogens. To this formula, magnolia flower *(xin yi hua)*, xanthium *(cang er zi)*, and angelica dahurica *(bai zhi)* have been added to address symptoms of chronic or allergic rhinitis, open the sinuses, relieve sinus headache, and disperse wind and dampness. In addition, red peony *(chi shao)* and forsythia *(lian qiao)* have been included. These herbs, according to modern research in China, address the allergic reaction. **Jade Screen & Xanthium Formula** is extremely effective for airborne or environmental allergies. It both stabilizes the exterior and supplements the qi to strengthen the body's defenses. It is an excellent choice for hypertensive patients with allergies or other persons who cannot tolerate formulas that contain ephedra *(ma huang)*.

## Ingredients

Astragali Radix (Astragalus / **Huang Qi**) 16.8%
Atractylodis Macrocephalae Rhizoma (White Atractylodes Rhizome/ **Bai Zhu**) 13.3%
Saposhnikoviae Radix (Siler / **Fang Feng**) 13.3%
Paeoniae Radix, rubra (Chinese Red Peony / **Chi Shao**) 13.3%
Forsythiae Fructus (Forsythia Fruit / **Lian Qiao**) 11.1%
Xanthii Fructus (Xanthium Fruit, Siberian Cocklebur / **Cang Er Zi**) 11.1%
Magnoliae Flos (Magnolia Flower / **Xin Yi Hua**) 11.1%
Angelicae Dahuricae Radix (Purple Angelica / **Bai Zhi**) 10.0%

## Chinese Medical Actions

Supplements qi, stops sweating, stabilizes the exterior, expels wind and dampness, reduces swelling, opens and clears nasal passages.

## Indications

| | |
|---|---|
| Allergies | Sinus discharge |
| Eyes, red, dry, or itchy | Sinus inflammation |
| Facial swelling | Sinus pain |
| Headache | Skin rashes from allergies |
| Sinus congestion | Throat, sore |

**Pulse:** Floating and weak.

## Contraindications

Patients with yin or blood deficiency may require the additional use of an appropriate tonic formula.

# JADE SOURCE FORMULA

**Jade Source Formula** *(Jia Jian Yu Quan Wan)* is a modification of *Yu Quan Wan* used to treat yin deficiency fire causing extreme thirst (a pattern commonly seen in diabetes). This version of the formula contains Chinese yam *(shan yao)* to strengthen the spleen and stomach and lung yin, and Solomon's seal *(yu zhu)* to nourish yin and moisten dryness. The name of this formula, "Jade Source," refers to the fluids of the mouth and the function of making fluids flow. Diabetes is considered a disorder of consumptive fire of the three burners. While this formula is designed to treat disorders of any of the three burners, it is most effective for upper burner patterns, or in cases that are not yet extreme.

## Ingredients

Astragali Radix (Astragalus / **Huang Qi**) 15%
Ophiopogonis Radix (Ophiopogon Tuber / **Mai Men Dong**) 12%
Trichosanthis Radix (Trichosanthes Root / **Tian Hua Fen**) 12%
Puerariae Radix (Kudzu Root, Pueraria / **Ge Gen**) 12%
Dioscoreae Rhizoma (Chinese Yam / **Shan Yao**) 10%
Polygonati Odorati Rhizoma (Aromatic Solomon's Seal / **Yu Zhu**) 10%
Poria (Poria, Hoelen, Tuckahoe / **Fu Ling**) 10%
Ginseng Radix, dried (White Ginseng Root / **Bai Ren Shen**) 8%
Mume Fructus (Mume Fruit, Japanese Apricot / **Wu Mei**) 6%
Glycyrrhizae Radix (Chinese Licorice Root / **Gan Cao**) 5%

## Chinese Medical Actions

Boosts qi, clears heat, generates fluids, supplements yin.

## Indications

Appetite, increased
Diabetes insipidus
Diabetes mellitus
Dryness of mouth and tongue
Thirst, extreme
Urination, frequent
Weight loss

**Tongue:** Dry, red, may have red spots.
**Pulse:** Rapid.

**Note:** This formula can help patients taking insulin to reduce their dosage, and aid those attempting to control their glucose levels with diet and exercise. This should be done only under the supervision of a qualified health-care provider.

# JADE WINDSCREEN FORMULA

**Jade Windscreen Formula** *(Yu Ping Feng San)* is a classical formula used to increase the protective *(wei)* qi. It is used for people whose immune system is weak, leaving them susceptible to catching colds. It can also be used for acute attacks of wind-cold in patients who are too weak to tolerate dispersing formulas. When taken in advance of the cold season, it can prevent colds, or in extremely weak patients, result in less frequent or less severe colds.

## Ingredients

Atractylodis Macrocephalae Rhizoma (White Atractylodes Rhizome / **Bai Zhu**) 40%
Saposhnikoviae Radix (Siler / **Fang Feng**) 40%
Astragali Radix (Astragalus / **Huang Qi**) 20%

## Chinese Medical Actions

Supplements qi, stabilizes the exterior, stops sweating.

## Indications

- Bronchitis, mild, in children
- Constitution, delicate
- Common cold in weak patients
- Common cold, recurrent
- Complexion, pale
- Immune system weakness
- Sinus discharge, chronic
- Sinus inflammation, chronic
- Sweating, spontaneous or profuse

**Tongue:** Pale, with thin, white coating.
**Pulse:** Floating, weak.

**Note:** Patients taking this formula to prevent colds should take for one to five months in advance of the cold season.

# JI XUE FORMULA

**Ji Xue Formula*** *(Huang Qi Ji Xue Wan)* is a major restorative formula that protects the blood from damage and helps to restore circulation to the microvessels, while supplementing the middle and gently eliminating toxin. It is especially effective in the treatment of various senile diseases and as an aid to patients undergoing chemotherapy. The formula is based on two branches of modern Chinese research. The first, *fu zheng pei ben* theory, demonstrates that when the qi and blood are properly supported, strength and vitality return, organ function is restored, and *zheng qi* (upright or righteous qi) is restored. The second, *heng fa*, "balancing method," emphasizes stasis transformation as an essential component of any treatment for aging or debilitation. Millettia or spatholobus (*ji xue teng*) builds both red and white blood cells while transforming stasis and invigorating blood flow in the minute collaterals. Astragalus (*huang qi*) is widely studied for increasing immunity and building spleen and lung qi. The rest of the formula includes substances to promote digestion, support the kidneys and liver, and gently guide out accumulations of damp, food, and toxin.

## Ingredients

Spatholobi Caulis (Spatholobus / **Ji Xue Teng**) 20%
Astragali Radix (Astragalus / **Huang Qi**) 14%
Coicis Semen (Job's Tears Seed, Chinese Pearl Barley, Coix / **Yi Yi Ren**) 11%
Polygoni Multiflori Radix Preparata (Polygonum Root, Fo Ti / **Zhi He Shou Wu**) 8%
Angelicae Sinensis Radix (Dong Quai, Tang Kuei / **Dang Gui**) 8%
Cordyceps Sinensis (Cordyceps Mycelium / **Dong Chong Xia Cao**) 8%
Paeoniae Radix, rubra (Chinese Red Peony / **Chi Shao**) 8%
Massa Fermentata (Fermented Leaven / **Shen Qu**) 8%
Rehmanniae Radix Preparata (Cured Rehmannia Root / **Shu Di Huang**) 5%
Schisandrae Fructus (Schisandra Fruit / **Wu Wei Zi**) 4%
Aurantii Fructus (Bitter Orange / **Zhi Ke**) 3%
Gardeniae Fructus (Gardenia Fruit / **Zhi Zi**) 3%

## Chinese Medical Actions

Supplements blood and qi, nourishes blood and essence, invigorates blood and promotes the smooth flow of qi, promotes healthy digestion, drains damp, resolves toxin, secures qi and essence.

### Indications

Appetite, poor
Blood damage from toxic exposure
Body temperature, elevated
Complexion, pale
Concentration, poor
Depression
Digestion, weak
Dizziness
Exhaustion, after long illness
Fatigue, chronic
Fibromyalgia
Hair loss, from chemotherapy
Neuropathy
Weakness, after illness or chemo

**Tongue:** Pale or light purple, may have papilla.
**Pulse:** Deficient, thin, may be rapid and/or choppy.


*This formula was formerly called **Chemo Blood Support Formula***

# JING QI FORMULA

**Jing Qi Formula** *(Jing Qi Pian)* is designed for persons who have depleted themselves through excessive stress, work, or sexual activity and who present with kidney and liver yin deficiency, spleen qi deficiency, and slight liver qi constraint. It can be used over a long term to rebuild exhausted qi and *jing.*

## Ingredients

Ligustri Lucidi Fructus (Ligustrum, Privet Fruit / **Nu Zhen Zi**) 13%
Ecliptae Herba (Eclipta / **Han Lian Cao**) 13%
Dioscoreae Rhizoma (Chinese Yam / **Shan Yao**) 13%
Codonopsis Pilosae Radix (Codonopsis / **Dang Shen**) 13%
Poria (Poria, Hoelen, Tuckahoe / **Fu Ling**) 9%
Atractylodis Macrocephalae Rhizoma (White Atractylodes Rhizome / **Bai Zhu**) 6%
Lycii Fructus (Lycium Fruit, Chinese Wolfberry / **Gou Qi Zi**) 6%
Schisandrae Fructus (Schisandra Fruit / **Wu Wei Zi**) 5%
Glycyrrhizae Radix (Chinese Licorice Root / **Gan Cao**) 5%
Bupleuri Radix (Bupleurum Root / **Chai Hu**) 4%
Citri Reticulatae Pericarpium (Tangerine Peel / **Chen Pi**) 4%
Cyperi Rhizoma (Cyperus, Nut-Grass / **Xiang Fu**) 3%
Dolomiaeae Radix (Costus Root, Vladimiria Root / **Chuan Mu Xiang**) 2%
Zingiberis Rhizoma Recens (Fresh Ginger / **Sheng Jiang**) 2%
Amomi Fructus (Chinese Cardamom / **Bai Dou Kou**) 2%

## Chinese Medical Actions

Nourishes *jing* (essence), supplements and regulates qi, moves constrained liver qi, nourishes kidney and liver yin.

## Indications

Anxiety
Appetite, lack of
Chemotherapy, recovery from
Digestive weakness
Dizziness
Fatigue
Impotence
Insomnia
Mental fatigue
Nervous exhaustion
Night sweats
Sperm count, low
Sweating, spontaneous
Vision, blurred
Visual acuity, decreased
Weakness, general or after illness

**Tongue:** Peeled, shiny, slightly red.
**Pulse:** Thin, rapid.

## Contraindications

Do not use with signs of heat or acute wind invasion. With deficiency fire symptoms, use **Rehmannia & Scrophularia Formula** instead.

# JUAN BI FORMULA

**Juan Bi Formula** *(Juan Bi Tang)* or "Remove Painful Obstruction Decoction," is a modification of the traditional formula. This version of the formula has added turmeric *(jiang huang)* and acanthopanax stem bark *(hong mao wu jia pi)*, and omitted caulis piperis. Used for pain caused by wind, dampness, cold, and blood stasis, this formula is specific for pain, heaviness, or numbness in the upper body.

## Ingredients

Notopterygii Rhizoma seu Radix (Notopterygium / **Qiang Huo**) 14.8%
Curcurmae Longae Rhizoma (Turmeric Rhizome / **Jiang Huang**) 14.8%
Mori Ramulus (White Mulberry Twig / **Sang Zhi**) 14.8%
Angelicae Sinensis Radix (Dong Quai, Tang Kuei / **Dang Gui**) 14.8%
Acanthopanax Giraldii Cortex (Acanthopanax Stem Bark / **Hong Mao Wu Jia Pi**) 14.8%
Angelicae Pubescentis Radix (Pubescent Angelica Root / **Du Huo**) 4.9%
Gentianae Macrophyllae Radix (Large Leaf Gentian Root / **Qin Jiao**) 4.9%
Olibanum (Frankincense / **Ru Xiang**) 3.9%
Dolomiaeae Radix (Costus Root, Vladimiria Root / **Chuan Mu Xiang**) 3.9%
Chuanxiong Rhizoma (Ligusticum Wallichii Rhizome / **Chuan Xiong**) 3.4%
Cinnamomi Ramulus (Cassia, Cinnamon Twig / **Gui Zhi**) 2.5%
Glycyrrhizae Radix Preparata (Chinese Licorice Root, honey-fried / **Zhi Gan Cao**) 2.5%

## Chinese Medical Actions

Removes wind-dampness in the upper body, alleviates painful obstruction.

## Indications

| | |
|---|---|
| Arthritis | Pain, upper body, moving |
| Bursitis | Pain, worse with cold |
| Joint pain in the upper body | Shoulder pain |

**Tongue:** White coating, may have purple body.
**Pulse:** Slow, possibly slippery.

## Contraindications

DO NOT USE DURING PREGNANCY. For pain in the lower body, use **Duhuo & Loranthus Formula.**

# LILY PRESERVE METAL FORMULA

**Lily Preserve Metal Formula** *(Bai He Gu Jin Tang)* is used for treating dryness of the lungs caused by damage to lung and kidney yin. American ginseng root *(xi yang shen)* has been added to the traditional formula to further nourish the lungs and to clear fire from deficiency.

## Ingredients

Lilii Bulbus (Lily Bulb / **Bai He**) 22.2%
Rehmanniae Radix Preparata (Cured Rehmannia Root / **Shu Di Huang**) 16.6%
Rehmanniae Radix (Rehmannia Root, unprocessed / **Sheng Di Huang**) 11.0%
Panacis Quinquefolii Radix (American Ginseng Root / **Xi Yang Shen**) 8.3%
Ophiopogonis Radix (Ophiopogon Tuber / **Mai Men Dong**) 8.3%
Fritillariae Cirrhosae Bulbus (Sichuan Fritillary Bulb / **Chuan Bei Mu**) 5.6%
Angelicae Sinensis Radix (Dong Quai, Tang Kuei / **Dang Gui**) 5.6%
Paeoniae Radix, alba (Chinese White Peony / **Bai Shao**) 5.6%
Glycyrrhizae Radix (Chinese Licorice Root / **Gan Cao**) 5.6%
Scrophulariae Radix (Scrophularia, Figwort Root / **Xuan Shen**) 5.6%
Platycodi Radix (Platycodon Root, Balloon Flower Root / **Jie Geng**) 5.6%

## Chinese Medical Actions

Nourishes the yin, moistens the lungs, transforms phlegm, stops cough.

## Indications

Asthma
Bronchitis, chronic
Cough, blood-streaked or sticky sputum
Cough, dry
Dry mouth
Influenza, post-illness w/ damage to yin
Lips, dry
Night sweats
Nose, dry
Palms and soles, hot
Pharyngitis
Pneumothorax, spontaneous
Throat, sore and dry
Wheezing

**Tongue:** Red with little coating.
**Pulse:** Thin and rapid.

## Contraindications

This formula is used for chronic conditions or conditions which arise from external invasion, but do not resolve. For the acute stages of exterior conditions, use an appropriate surface-relieving formula. Do not use in cases of dampness or copious phlegm. In cases with accompanying diarrhea and indigestion, add a formula to strengthen the spleen and regulate the qi such as **Six Gentlemen Formula.**

# LING ZHI LUNG FORMULA

**Ling Zhi Lung Formula** *(Ling Zhi Fei Pian)* is the result of multiple trials comparing different formulations to effectively treat asthma without using ephedra *(ma huang)*. This formula helps to calm breathing, resolve phlegm, and descend lung qi. Especially effective for rectifying wheezing from allergies, **Ling Zhi Lung Formula** can be used in combination with other formulas to treat most forms of asthma. This formula is primarily supplementing and secondarily sedating, making it effective after just one or two doses, yet safe for long-term (seasonal) application.

## Ingredients

Ganoderma (Reishi, Ganoderma Mushroom / **Ling Zhi**) 46%
Sophorae Flavescentis Radix (Sophora Root / **Ku Shen**) 21%
Lepidii / Descurainiae Semen (Lepidium, Descurainia Seed / **Ting Li Zi**) 13%
Jujubae Fructus (Jujube Fruit, Chinese Red Date / **Hong Zao, Da Zao**) 13%
Glycyrrhizae Radix (Chinese Licorice Root / **Gan Cao**) 7%

## Chinese Medical Actions

Rectifies lung qi, supplements lungs, assists kidneys in grasping the qi, resolves phlegm, stops cough, arrests wheezing, calms *shen*.

## Indications

Asthma
Breathing labored with exertion
Cough
Influenza, post-illness w/ damage to qi
Wheezing

**Tongue:** Normal or thick coating.
**Pulse:** May be superficial, slightly rapid or slightly tight and slow.

## Contraindications

Do not use if condition is due to lung fire, or if the wheezing is due to pneumonia.

**Dosage:** This formula is safer to take in larger doses than those containing ephedra *(ma huang)*.

Acute Conditions: For adults, 3-4 tablets as needed, up to five doses in 24 hours. Reduce frequency to three times daily after symptoms have abated by 50% or more. If condition does not noticeably improve within the first 24 hours, re-evaluate the diagnosis or refer to appropriate medical professional.

Sub-acute or Chronic Conditions: At the first signs of a developing asthmatic condition, take 2-4 tablets as needed, 2-3 times per day, until resolved (up to three weeks).

**Note:**
Use **Ling Zhi Lung Formula** by itself to treat most types of asthmatic breathing without fever.

Combine with **Lily Preserve Metal Formula** if symptoms began as an acute febrile condition and the wheezing is due to yin damage sustained during the acute stage, which has developed into a chronic condition. When this combination is appropriate, there is likely to be dry throat with thirst, a geographic or scanty tongue coating, and a fine slightly rapid pulse. Cough is often more prominent than wheezing, and may be streaked with blood. Use 2 tablets of each formula as a starting point for dosage.

Combine with **Yin Chiao Formula**, **Viola Clear Fire Formula**, or **Zhong Gan Ling Formula** if triggered by a sudden viral invasion in the wind-cold or wind-heat stage of penetration. This combination works best if administered within the first day of an external invasion.

Combine with **Poria Five Formula** if wheezing is due primarily to water retention. This condition is not common, but if the water metabolism problem leads to wheezing, this combination will work well. In such cases, **Poria Five Formula** will be the main formula and **Ling Zhi Lung Formula** will act as assistant. Accompanying signs and symptoms include urinary difficulty or retention, possible mild fever, and some clear sign of water metabolism dysfunction. (See **Poria Five Formula**.)

# LINKING FORMULA

**Linking Formula** *(Yi Guan Jian)*. This classic formula gently spreads the liver qi while it nourishes the yin of the kidney and liver. Yin deficiency by itself can diminish the liver's ability to regulate the qi, but when the lack of yin has allowed the development of constrained fire, the coursing and regulating function of the liver becomes even more compromised. This can create a cycle of yin deficiency-stagnation-fire-yin deficiency. The resulting fire constraint can eventually cause the liver to transversely attack the stomach causing pain, acid regurgitation, and ulceration. To the classic formula, white peony *(bai shao)* and licorice *(gan cao)* have been added, to further enhance its ability to reduce pain, especially resulting from ulcers. Today, **Linking Formula** is often used to treat stomach and duodenal ulcers and chronic hepatitis. It is, however, appropriate whenever the patient presents with yin deficiency signs concurrent with qi stagnation.

## Ingredients

Rehmanniae Radix (Rehmannia Root, unprocessed / **Sheng Di Huang**) 26%
Lycii Fructus (Lycium Fruit, Chinese Wolfberry / **Gou Qi Zi**) 14%
Glehniae Radix (Glehnia Root / **Bei Sha Shen**) 14%
Ophiopogonis Radix (Ophiopogon Tuber / **Mai Men Dong**) 14%
Angelicae Sinensis Radix (Dong Quai, Tang Kuei / **Dang Gui**) 12%
Toosendan Fructus (Melia Fruit, Chinaberry / **Chuan Lian Zi**) 10%
Paeoniae Radix, alba (Chinese White Peony / **Bai Shao**) 5%
Glycyrrhizae Radix (Chinese Licorice Root / **Gan Cao**) 5%

## Chinese Medical Actions

Nourishes the yin and spreads liver qi.

## Indications

Abdominal distension or pain
Acid regurgitation
Bitter taste in mouth
Epigastric pain
Flank pain
Gastritis, chronic
Hepatitis, chronic
Hypochondriac pain
Insomnia
Intercostal neuralgia
Mouth, dry
Palms and soles, hot
Stomach ache
Thirst
Throat, dry
Ulcer stomach and duodenal
Vomiting, of sour fluid

**Tongue:** Red, with dry or scanty coating.
**Pulse:** Thin, weak or wiry, may be rapid.

## Contraindications

Do not use with pain due to dampness or phlegm.

# LIVER C FORMULA

**Liver C Formula** *(Gan C Pian)* was created by Jake Paul Fratkin, OMD, based on current research in China regarding the treatment of middle-stage Hepatitis C. In this stage, patients exhibit elevated liver enzymes on blood tests and may have the associated symptoms of fatigue, headache, fibromyalgia, and darkening spots on the skin. The formula helps to promote natural immunity, inhibit viral growth, reduce symptoms of fatigue and poor appetite, and is effective for lowering liver enzymes back into the normal range.

## Ingredients

Ganoderma (Reishi, Ganoderma Mushroom / **Ling Zhi**) 9%
Paeoniae Radix, rubra (Chinese Red Peony / **Chi Shao**) 9%
Astragali Radix (Astragalus / **Huang Qi**) 8%
Lycii Fructus (Lycium Fruit, Chinese Wolfberry / **Gou Qi Zi**) 8%
Salviae Miltiorrhizae Radix (Chinese Salvia Root / **Dan Shen**) 8%
Artemisiae Scopariae Herba (Capillaris / **Yin Chen Hao**) 8%
Hedyotis Diffusae Herba (Hedyotis, Oldenlandia / **Bai Hua She She Cao**) 8%
Bupleuri Radix (Bupleurum Root / **Chai Hu**) 8%
Gardeniae Fructus (Gardenia Fruit / **Zhi Zi**) 8%
Curcumae Radix (Turmeric, Curcuma Tuber / **Yu Jin**) 8%
Polygoni Multiflori Radix Preparata (Polygonum Root, Fo Ti / **Zhi He Shou Wu**) 7%
Schisandrae Fructus (Schisandra Fruit / **Wu Wei Zi**) 6%
Toosendan Fructus (Melia Fruit, Chinaberry / **Chuan Lian Zi**) 5%

## Chinese Medical Actions

Supplements qi and blood, clears damp-heat, dredges the liver, invigorates blood, clears heat and resolves toxins, relieves pain.

## Indications

| | |
|---|---|
| Cirrhosis of liver, early stage | Hepatomegaly |
| Fatigue, from chronic hepatitis | Jaundice |
| Hepatitis, chronic | Liver enzymes elevated |

## Contraindications

DO NOT USE DURING PREGNANCY OR WHILE NURSING.

**Note:** This formula is not effective for end-stage liver cirrhosis.

# LUO BU MA FORMULA

**Luo Bu Ma Formula** *(Luo Bu Ma Pian).* This formula is commonly used to treat high blood pressure due to the excitation of liver fire. The chief herb of this formula, apocynum *(luo bu ma)*, comprising almost half of the formula, is sometimes used as a stand-alone herb for its ability to lower the blood pressure and reduce cholesterol. **Luo Bu Ma Formula** is designed to treat excess patterns, as opposed to **Gastrodia & Uncaria Formula** *(Tian Ma Gou Teng Yin),* which treats high blood pressure by nourishing the yin to anchor the yang. Cassia *(jue ming zi)* has been substituted for the *zhen zhu mu* to further promote the cholesterol lowering aspect of the formula.

## Ingredients

Apocyni Veneti Folium (Dogbane leaf / **Luo Bu Ma**) 45%
Prunellae Spica (Prunella, Heal All, Self-Heal Spike / **Xia Ku Cao**) 10%
Uncariae Ramulus cum Uncis (Gambir Vine Stems and Thorns / **Gou Teng**) 10%
Cassiae Semen (Cassia Seed, Sickle-pod Senna / **Jue Ming Zi**) 10%
Chrysanthemi Flos (Chrysanthemum / **Ju Hua**) 7%
Alismatis Rhizoma (Asian Water Plantain / **Ze Xie**) 6%
Cyathulae Radix (Cyathula Root / **Chuan Niu Xi**) 6%
Crataegi Fructus (Chinese Hawthorn Fruit / **Shan Zha**) 6%

## Chinese Medical Actions

Calms the liver and extinguishes wind, clears liver heat, eliminates damp by promoting urination, transforms phlegm, subdues yang, benefits the heart, slightly moistens the intestine.

## Indications

Cholesterol, elevated
Dizziness or vertigo
Edema
Eyes, painful, red, swollen, or pressure behind
Face, flushed
Headache
Hypertension
Insomnia
Irritability
Restlessness
Stool, dry
Urination, difficult

**Tongue:** Red, swollen, may have a thick, yellow coating.
**Pulse:** Rapid, full.

### Contraindications

Do not use if patient has low blood pressure, diarrhea from spleen qi deficiency, or is taking diuretic drugs.

# LYSIMACHIA GB FORMULA

**Lysimachia GB Formula** *(Xiao Chai Hu Jia Jin Qian Cao Fang)* is a modification of Minor Bupleurum Formula *(Xiao Chai Hu Tang)*, designed to address gallstones and gallbladder inflammation. The formula contains lysimachia *(jin qian cao)* to clear damp-heat from the liver and gallbladder and expel gallstones, curcuma *(yu jin)* to invigorate qi and blood, clear heat, cool blood and benefit the gallbladder, capillaris *(yin chen hao)* to clear damp-heat from the liver and gallbladder. In addition, bamboo shavings *(zhu ru)* cool blood, clear heat and phlegm-heat; gardenia fruit *(zhi zi)* drains damp-heat and moves constrained liver and gallbladder qi; white peony *(bai shao)* softens the liver to stop painful spasms in the abdomen; and melia fruit *(chuan lian zi)* moves constrained liver qi and stops pain. These modifications make this formula specific for gallbladder inflammation, damp-heat, and gallstones.

## Ingredients

Lysimachiae Herba (Lysimachia / **Jin Qian Cao**) 15%
Curcumae Radix (Turmeric, Curcuma Tuber / **Yu Jin**) 10%
Bupleuri Radix (Bupleurum Root / **Chai Hu**) 9%
Scutellariae Radix (Chinese Scullcap, Scutellaria, Scute / **Huang Qin**) 9%
Codonopsis Pilosae Radix (Codonopsis / **Dang Shen**) 8%
Artemisiae Scopariae Herba (Capillaris / **Yin Chen Hao**) 8%
Bambusae Caulis in Taeniam (Bamboo Shavings / **Zhu Ru**) 8%
Gardeniae Fructus (Gardenia Fruit / **Zhi Zi**) 8%
Paeoniae Radix, alba (Chinese White Peony / **Bai Shao**) 8%
Toosendan Fructus (Melia Fruit, Chinaberry / **Chuan Lian Zi**) 5%
Jujubae Fructus (Jujube Fruit, Chinese Red Date / **Hong Zao, Da Zao**) 5%
Glycyrrhizae Radix Preparata (Chinese Licorice Root, honey-fried / **Zhi Gan Cao**) 4%
Zingiberis Rhizoma Recens (Fresh Ginger / **Sheng Jiang**) 3%

## Chinese Medical Actions

Drains damp-heat in the liver and gallbladder, cools blood, expels gallstones, moves constrained liver and gallbladder qi and blood, harmonizes the middle burner.

## Indications

| | |
|---|---|
| Cholecystitis | Hepatitis |
| Gallbladder inflammation | Jaundice |
| Gallstones | Vomiting |
| Gallbladder spasms | |

**Tongue:** May be red or have red spots, scalloped sides, yellow coating.
**Pulse:** Wiry and/or tight.

## Contraindications

Do not use in the absence of damp-heat. Patients suspected of having gallstones require close medical supervision.

# MARGARITA COMPLEXION FORMULA

**Margarita Complexion Formula** *(Zhen Zhu Yu Rong Fang).* Margarita *(zhen zhu)* is considered a beauty tonic for the skin, especially the face. This formula is used for facial acne in adolescents and adults. It addresses the main causes of acne by clearing heat from the blood, and drying dampness. It can also be used for red rashes, pimples, itchiness, eczema, and hives from heat in the blood or stomach heat.

## Ingredients

Hedyotis Diffusae Herba (Hedyotis, Oldenlandia / **Bai Hua She She Cao**) 13%
Scrophulariae Radix (Scrophularia, Figwort Root / **Xuan Shen**) 10%
Paeoniae Radix, rubra (Chinese Red Peony / **Chi Shao**) 10%
Margarita (Pearl / **Zhen Zhu**) 9%
Lonicerae Flos (Japanese Honeysuckle Flower / **Jin Yin Hua**) 9%
Eriobotryae Folium (Loquat Leaf / **Pi Pa Ye**) 9%
Rhei Radix et Rhizoma (Chinese Rhubarb / **Da Huang**) 8%
Rehmanniae Radix (Rehmannia Root, unprocessed / **Sheng Di Huang**) 8%
Glehniae Radix (Glehnia Root / **Sha Shen**) 7%
Phellodendri Cortex (Phellodendron Bark / **Huang Bai**) 7%
Ginseng Radix, dried (White Ginseng Root / **Bai Ren Shen**) 5%
Sophorae Flavescentis Radix (Sophora Root / **Ku Shen**) 5%

## Chinese Medical Actions

Clears heat, cools blood, resolves toxin, breaks accumulations, dries dampness.

## Indications

| | |
|---|---|
| Acne, adolescent and adult | Furuncles |
| Boils | Hives |
| Cysts | Pimples, raised |
| Eczema | Skin rashes, red or itchy |

**Tongue:** Red and scalloped, red on the edge or tip, yellow or white coating. **Pulse:** Big, rapid, rolling.

## Contraindications

DO NOT USE DURING PREGNANCY OR WHILE NURSING. With constrained liver qi, use in combination with **Free & Easy Wanderer Plus**.

**Note:** Patients should avoid spicy foods or foods with a high content of fats and sugars. These foods create dampness and heat, which can exacerbate acne.

# MING MU FORMULA

**Ming Mu Formula** *(Ming Mu Di Huang Wan),* also known as "Improve Vision Pill with Rehmannia," is an augmented formula based on "Rehmannia Six Formula" *(Liu Wei Di Huang Wan).* This formula is used to treat eye disorders and improve vision in cases where there is liver and kidney weakness or liver heat and internal wind.

## Ingredients

Rehmanniae Radix Preparata (Cured Rehmannia Root / **Shu Di Huang**) 14.9%
Bupleuri Radix (Bupleurum Root / **Chai Hu**) 7.4%
Angelicae Sinensis Radix (Dong Quai, Tang Kuei / **Dang Gui**) 7.4%
Lycii Fructus (Lycium Fruit, Chinese Wolfberry / **Gou Qi Zi**) 7.4%
Rehmanniae Radix (Rehmannia Root, unprocessed / **Sheng Di Huang**) 7.4%
Dioscoreae Rhizoma (Chinese Yam / **Shan Yao**) 7.4%
Corni Fructus (Asiatic Dogwood Fruit, Cornelian Cherry / **Shan Zhu Yu**) 7.4%
Alismatis Rhizoma (Asian Water Plantain / **Ze Xie**) 7.4%
Moutan Cortex (Tree Peony Root Bark / **Mu Dan Pi**)7.4%
Poria (Poria, Hoelen, Tuckahoe / **Fu Ling**) 7.4%
Schisandrae Fructus (Schisandra Fruit / **Wu Wei Zi**) 7.4%
Tribuli Fructus (Tribulus, Puncture-Vine Fruit, Caltrop Fruit / **Bai Ji Li**) 7.4%
Chrysanthemi Flos (Chrysanthemum / **Ju Hua**) 3.7%

## Chinese Medical Actions

Nourishes the liver and kidneys, nourishes liver blood, sedates liver fire, dispels liver wind, improves vision, benefits the eyes.

## Indications

| | |
|---|---|
| Cataracts | Glaucoma |
| Eyes, excessive tearing | Palms and soles, hot |
| Eyes, dry, red, or itchy | Vision, blurred |
| Eyes, sensitive to light | Vision, weak |

**Tongue:** Red, may have red spots.

**Pulse:** Thin, rapid, may be tight.

## Contraindications

Patients taking this formula should avoid eating turnips (Scheid, Bensky, Ellis, and Barolet, 2009).

# MINOR BUPLEURUM FORMULA

**Minor Bupleurum Formula** *(Xiao Chai Hu Tang)* is a classical formula used to harmonize shao yang-stage disorders (where the pathogenic qi is half-exterior, half-interior). It is helpful in cases where the symptoms of a cold or flu may linger for weeks after the initial acute phase of the illness is over. This formula helps the patient resolve the illness more quickly. It is highly effective for the treatment of ear infections, mumps, and tonsillitis in children. In Japan, this formula is used as an immune system stimulant to prevent the common cold.

## Ingredients

Bupleuri Radix (Bupleurum Root / **Chai Hu**) 22%
Pinelliae Rhizoma Preparatum (Pinellia, ginger-cured / **Zhi Ban Xia**) 21%
Codonopsis Pilosae Radix (Codonopsis / **Dang Shen**) 17%
Scutellariae Radix (Chinese Scullcap, Scutellaria, Scute / **Huang Qin**) 12%
Zingiberis Rhizoma Recens (Fresh Ginger / **Sheng Jiang**) 12%
Glycyrrhizae Radix Preparata (Chinese Licorice Root, honey-fried / **Zhi Gan Cao**) 8%
Jujubae Fructus (Jujube Fruit, Chinese Red Date / **Hong Zao, Da Zao**) 8%

## Chinese Medical Actions

Harmonizes and releases shao yang-stage disorders. Clears heat, releases pathogenic qi, transforms phlegm, harmonizes the middle burner, supports normal qi.

## Indications

Asthma
Bitter or sour taste in mouth
Bronchitis, acute or chronic
Chest, fullness in
Chills and fever, alternating
Common cold, lingering
Constipation
Cough
Diaphragm, fullness in
Diarrhea
Dizziness
Ear infection
Fatigue, chronic, w/ latent pathogen
Fever, lingering
Gallbladder inflammation or spasms
Headache
Head cold that goes to chest
Heartburn
Irritability
Jaundice
Liver enzymes elevated
Lymph nodes, enlarged
Nausea
Pancreatitis
Stomach ache
Throat, dry
Tonsillitis
Vomiting
Vision, blurred

**Tongue:** Thin, with white or yellow coating. **Pulse:** Wiry, especially in the liver/gallbladder positions. Spleen position may be weak.

## Contraindications

Do not use in cases of liver fire rising with yin deficiency. Not for long-term use. Discontinue if headache, dizziness or gum bleeding occur.

# MOBILIZE ESSENCE FORMULA

**Mobilize Essence Formula** *(Fu Ren Bu Yin Pian)* is commonly used during the ovulation phase of the menstrual cycle to support fertility. Once the follicle ruptures, a quick transition from yin to yang must occur. The earlier phase requires a build up of yin and blood. During the second phase, the yin still requires gentle support, but the yang is engaged and the blood mobilized so that the follicle can undergo its rapid transformation. Ligustrum *(nu zhen zi)* supports the yin without being cloying; cuscuta *(tu si zi)* and dipsacus *(xu duan)* encourage proper movement of the yang. The scope of this formula is not restricted to treating infertility. It is appropriate whenever gentle yin-yang balancing is needed while invigorating the blood.

## Ingredients

Albiziae Cortex (Mimosa Tree Bark, Silk-Tree Bark / **He Huan Pi**) 12%
Spatholobi Caulis (Spatholobus / **Ji Xue Teng**) 11%
Angelicae Sinensis Radix (Dong Quai, Tang Kuei / **Dang Gui**) 9%
Salviae Miltiorrhizae Radix (Chinese Salvia Root / **Dan Shen**) 9%
Ligustri Lucidi Fructus (Ligustrum, Privet Fruit / **Nu Zhen Zi**) 9%
Cuscutae Semen (Chinese Dodder Seed, Chinese Cuscuta / **Tu Si Zi**) 9%
Dipsaci Radix (Japanese Teasel Root, Dipsacus / **Xu Duan**) 9%
Paeoniae Radix, alba (Chinese White Peony / **Bai Shao**) 8%
Poria (Poria, Hoelen, Tuckahoe / **Fu Ling**) 7%
Paeoniae Radix, rubra (Chinese Red Peony / **Chi Shao**) 7%
Chuanxiong Rhizoma (Ligusticum Wallichii Rhizome / **Chuan Xiong**) 5%
Carthami Flos (Safflower, Carthamus Flower / **Hong Hua**) 5%

## Chinese Medical Actions

Invigorates blood, opens collaterals, tonifies the yin, blood, and yang, calms the spirit.

## Indications

Abdominal pain, premenstrual
Basal body temperature, slow rise at ovulation
Headaches, mid-menstrual cycle
Infertility caused by dysfunction during ovulation
Menopausal symptoms
Menstrual pain
Menstruation, scanty or absent
Ovarian cysts
Ovulation, late
Ovulation, pain with

**Tongue:** Pale, slightly purple, may have distended veins.
**Pulse:** Thin or weak, wiry.

## Contraindications

DO NOT USE DURING PREGNANCY.

**Note**: Use with **Cinnamon & Poria Formula** or **Phlegm-Transforming Formula**, for phlegm-damp accumulation. Use with **Nourish Ren & Chong Formula** for concurrent yin and blood deficiency. When treating ovulation, begin 3 days before ovulation and take for 6 days.

# MULBERRY & LYCIUM FORMULA

**Mulberry & Lycium Formula** *(Xie Bai San)* is a modified version of what Li Shi-zhen referred to as the exemplar formula for draining the lung. Its primary action is to disperse constrained heat or smoldering fire in the lung. Originally designed as a pediatric formula to treat cough and wheezing due to lung heat, this version is made stronger through the omission of the large percentage of rice, and is widely used to treat both children and adults. Lophatherum *(dan zhu ye)* has been added to augment the heat-clearing action and to address the restlessness that often accompanies this pattern. Anemarrhena *(zhi mu)* and prepared soya *(dan dou qi)* have been added to intensify the heat dispersing action, to help protect the lung yin, and to restore the vital essence.

## Ingredients

Mori Cortex (White Mulberry Root Bark / **Sang Bai Pi**) 25%
Lycii Cortex (Lycium Root Bark, Chinese Wolfberry Root Bark / **Di Gu Pi**) 25%
Lophatheri Herba (Lophatherum / **Dan Zhu Ye**) 14%
Glycyrrhizae Radix (Chinese Licorice Root / **Gan Cao**) 13%
Sojae Semen Preparatum (Prepared Soybean / **Dan Dou Chi**) 13%
Anemarrhenae Rhizoma (Anemarrhena Rhizome / **Zhi Mu**) 10%

## Chinese Medical Actions

Drains and disperses lung heat and fire.

## Indications

- Bronchial asthma
- Bronchitis
- Chest, stifling sensation in
- Cough
- Coughing up blood
- Dry mouth
- Fever, afternoon
- Flu-like symptoms, from lung heat or lung fire
- Influenza
- Measles, initial stage
- Nosebleeds
- Pneumonia
- Pulmonary tuberculosis
- Shortness of breath
- Skin, steaming heat in
- Wheezing

**Tongue:** Red body or tip, possibly with yellow fur.
**Pulse:** Rapid, fine.

## Contraindications

Do not use in cases of wind-cold invasion or in the early-stage of wind-heat.

**Note:** If there is high fever or wind-heat skin lesions, use **Siler & Platycodon Formula** instead.

# NOURISH ESSENCE FORMULA

**Nourish Essence Formula** *(Zi Jing Di Huang Wan)* is an augmented formula based on "Rehmannia Six" *(Liu Wei Di Huang Wan),* a classical formula for deficient kidney and liver yin. Added to this are polygonum *(zhi he shou wu)* and lycium *(gou qi zi)*, yin herbs that nourish the blood; cistanches *(rou cong rong)*, cynomorium *(suo yang)*, and cuscuta *(tu si zi)*, herbs that supplement yang and *jing* (essence); and schisandra *(wu wei zi)* and palm leaf raspberry *(fu pen zi)*, astringent herbs that help retain *jing* (essence).

## Ingredients

Rehmanniae Radix Preparata (Cured Rehmannia Root / **Shu Di Huang**) 14%
Dioscoreae Rhizoma (Chinese Yam / **Shan Yao**) 9%
Polygoni Multiflori Radix Preparata (Polygonum Root, Fo Ti / **Zhi He Shou Wu**) 9%
Cistanches Herba (Broomrape, Cistanches / **Rou Cong Rong**) 9%
Cuscutae Semen (Chinese Dodder Seed, Chinese Cuscuta / **Tu Si Zi**) 8%
Lycii Fructus (Lycium Fruit, Chinese Wolfberry / **Gou Qi Zi**) 8%
Corni Fructus (Asiatic Dogwood Fruit, Cornelian Cherry / **Shan Zhu Yu**) 7%
Poria (Poria, Hoelen, Tuckahoe / **Fu Ling**) 7%
Rubi Fructus (Palm-leaf Raspberry / **Fu Pen Zi**) 7%
Moutan Cortex (Tree Peony Root Bark / **Mu Dan Pi**) 6%
Schisandrae Fructus (Schisandra Fruit / **Wu Wei Zi**) 6%
Alismatis Rhizoma (Asian Water Plantain / **Ze Xie**) 5%
Cynomorii Herba (Cynomorium / **Suo Yang**) 5%

## Chinese Medical Actions

Supplements kidney yin and yang, supplements liver yin, builds blood and qi, benefits and retains *jing* (essence).

## Indications

Back (lower), weak and sore
Constipation (from deficiency)
Dizziness
Dry mouth
Exhaustion
Fatigue
Hair, premature graying
Hearing loss
Hypothyroidism
Infertility
Kidney function, weak
Knees weak
Light-headedness
Miscarriage, habitual
Night sweats
Nocturnal emissions
Post-nasal drip, chronic
Premature ejaculation
Ringing in ear
Sexual energy low
Urination, frequent or nocturnal

**Tongue:** Pale or normal.
**Pulse:** Weak or thin in kidney position.

## Contraindications

Decrease dose if diarrhea or stomach upset occur.

# NOURISH REN & CHONG FORMULA

**Nourish Ren & Chong Formula** *(Jia Wei Gui Shao Di Huang Wan)* nourishes the yin and blood to support the reproductive functions of the *ren* and *chong* vessels during the first phase of a woman's menstrual cycle. During the first phase of the cycle, it is important to support follicle growth and to prepare for ovulation. This support is accomplished by strongly nourishing the yin and blood, and by gently removing heat in the heart and liver that might lead to stasis or emotional imbalance. The scope of the formula extends beyond its application for infertility. It is an appropriate formula whenever there is a pattern of blood and yin deficiency with mild build up of heat.

## Ingredients

Dioscoreae Rhizoma (Chinese Yam / **Shan Yao**) 12%
Angelicae Sinensis Radix (Dong Quai, Tang Kuei / **Dang Gui**) 12%
Paeoniae Radix, alba (Chinese White Peony / **Bai Shao**) 12%
Rehmanniae Radix Preparata (Cured Rehmannia Root / **Shu Di Huang**) 10%
Corni Fructus (Asiatic Dogwood Fruit, Cornelian Cherry / **Shan Zhu Yu**) 9%
Lycii Fructus (Lycium Fruit, Chinese Wolfberry / **Gou Qi Zi**) 9%
Salviae Miltiorrhizae Radix (Chinese Salvia Root / **Dan Shen**) 8%
Gardeniae Fructus (Gardenia Fruit / **Zhi Zi**) 8%
Moutan Cortex (Tree Peony Root Bark / **Mu Dan Pi**) 5%
Poria (Poria, Hoelen, Tuckahoe / **Fu Ling**) 5%
Alismatis Rhizoma (Asian Water Plantain / **Ze Xie**) 5%
Citri Reticulatae Pericarpium (Tangerine Peel / **Chen Pi**) 5%

## Chinese Medical Actions

Nourishes blood and yin, clears heat and stagnation in the heart and liver, mildly invigorates the blood.

### Indications

Amenorrhea, post OCP
Cervical mucus, scanty or dry
Endometrial lining, poor
Fatigue, general or after menses
Follicular phase problems,
Infertility w/ yin and blood deficiency
Light-headedness, after menses
Menarche, late
Menopause, premature
Menstrual blood, pale
Menstrual cycle, long
Menstruation, light
Ovarian follicle quality, poor
Ovulation, late
Post-menstrual headaches
Post-miscarriage deficiencies
Premature ovarian failure

**Tongue:** Pale or slightly reddish body, scanty or no coating, may have red tip or sides. **Pulse:** Thin or weak in liver and kidney positions.

**Note:** In cases of spleen deficiency, use in conjunction with an appropriate formula. Use in conjunction with **True Yin Formula** if stronger kidney/liver yin support is desired. Use with **Salvia Ten Formula** for concurrent spleen qi deficiency with liver-heart stagnation.

# OREGANO OIL FORMULA

**Oregano Oil Formula** *(Jia Wei Tu Yin Chen You Jiao Nang)* is a liquid concentrate in vegetable cellulose capsules. This formula combines wild Mediterranean oregano oil extract *(tu yin chen)*—standardized to a minimum of 70% carvacrol—with coptis *(huang lian)*, quisqualis *(shi jun zi)*, and mume *(wu me)*. Oregano oil has a history of medical use that dates back to ancient Greece. The essential oil is a blend of phenolic compounds with broad-spectrum, anti-microbial action and immune-building properties. It is combined with Chinese herbs to increase effectiveness for bacterial infection, Candida, worms, and other parasites. **Oregano Oil Formula** can also be used externally. This is an excellent formula to take while traveling in places where intestinal parasites are common.

## Ingredients

Quisqualis Fructus (Quisqualis Fruit / **Shi Jun Zi**) 48%
Oil of Origanum Vulgare (Oregano Oil / **Tu Yin Chen**) 25%
Mume Fructus (Mume Fruit, Japanese Apricot / **Wu Mei**) 19%
Coptidis Rhizoma (Coptis / **Huang Lian**) 8%

## Chinese Medical Actions

Clears damp-heat, resolves heat-toxin, expels parasites.

## Indications

- Athlete's foot (use topically)
- Bacterial Infection
- Candida
- Dysentery
- Food poisoning
- Giardia
- Nail fungus (use topically)
- Parasites
- Skin infection (use topically)
- Throat, sore
- Ulcer (from helicobacter pylori)
- Worms

**Note:** It is recommended when treating patients diagnosed with candida to change herbal therapies every 30 days. This formula is ideal to alternate with **Intestinal Fungus Formula**.

# PEACEFUL SPIRIT FORMULA

**Peaceful Spirit Formula** is known in China as *Yang Xin Ning Shen Wan*. It is an excellent formula for nervous exhaustion, anxiety, and for emotional disorders due to stress.

## Ingredients

Codonopsis Pilosae Radix (Codonopsis / **Dang Shen**) 21.3%
Jujubae Fructus (Jujube Fruit, Chinese Red Date / **Hong Zao, Da Zao**) 14.3%
Dioscoreae Rhizoma (Chinese Yam / **Shan Yao**) 10.9%
Longan Arillis (Longan Fruit / **Long Yan Rou**) 10.9%
Salviae Miltiorrhizae Radix (Chinese Salvia Root / **Dan Shen**) 9.9%
Poriae Sclerotium Pararadicis (Poria Spirit / **Fu Shen**) 7.9%
Ginseng Radix (Asian Ginseng Root / **Ren Shen**) 6.9%
Atractylodis Macrocephalae Rhizoma (White Atractylodes Rhizome / **Bai Zhu**) 5.5%
Ziziphi Spinosa Semen (Sour Date Seed, Jujube Seed / **Suan Zao Ren**) 5.5%
Polygalae Radix (Polygala, Chinese Senega Root / **Yuan Zhi**) 2.9%
Citri Reticulatae Pericarpium (Tangerine Peel / **Chen Pi**) 2.5%
Anemones Altaicae Rhizoma (Altai Anemone Rhizome / **Jiu Jie Chang Pu**) 1.5%

## Chinese Medical Actions

Nourishes the heart, calms the spirit, nourishes blood, supplements qi.

## Indications

Anxiety
Dizziness
Insomnia
Irritability
Melancholy, excessive
Memory, poor
Mental fatigue
Nervous exhaustion
Palpitation
Post-Traumatic Stress Disorder
Restlessness

**Tongue:** Pale, may be shaky, with thin, white coating.
**Pulse:** Weak or thin, especially in upper and middle positions.

## Contraindications

Do not use in excess conditions or with signs of heat. In cases where there are also signs of heat from deficient yin, use **Heavenly Emperor's Formula** or **Zizyphus Formula** instead.

# PERSICA & CISTANCHES FORMULA

**Persica & Cistanches Formula** *(Tao Ren Cong Rong Wan)* This formula moistens the intestines to encourage regular bowel movements. It is used for constipation from exhaustion of fluids or dryness. Good for patients who are weak or debilitated.

## Ingredients

Cistanches Herba (Broomrape, Cistanches / **Rou Cong Rong**) 16.2%
Rhei Radix et Rhizoma (Chinese Rhubarb / **Da Huang**) 13.5%
Angelicae Sinensis Radix (Dong Quai, Tang Kuei / **Dang Gui**) 13.5%
Platycladi Semen (Oriental Arborvitae Seed, Biota Seed / **Bai Zi Ren**) 10.9%
Aurantii Fructus Immaturus (Immature Bitter Orange Fruit / **Zhi Shi**) 8.1%
Magnoliae Officinalis Cortex (Magnolia Bark / **Hou Po**) 8.1%
Persicae Semen (Peach Kernel, Persica Seed / **Tao Ren**) 8.1%
Armeniacae Semen (Apricot Seed, Chinese Bitter Almond / **Xing Ren**) 5.4%
Paeoniae Radix, alba (Chinese White Peony / **Bai Shao**) 5.4%
Aurantii Fructus (Bitter Orange / **Zhi Ke**) 5.4%
Glycyrrhizae Radix (Chinese Licorice Root / **Gan Cao**) 5.4%

## Chinese Medical Actions

Moistens and unblocks the intestines, promotes the movement of qi.

## Indications

Bowel movement, incomplete or painful
Constipation
Stool, hard or difficult to pass

**Tongue:** Dry, with yellow coating.
**Pulse:** Submerged, rapid, floating or choppy.

## Contraindications

DO NOT USE DURING PREGNANCY OR WHILE NURSING. Use cautiously with patients with spleen qi deficiency or spleen-damp conditions. Not recommended for children under age six.

# PHLEGM-TRANSFORMING FORMULA

**Phlegm-Transforming Formula** *(Xia Ku Hua Tan Pian)* is a modern formula for patterns of phlegm accumulation. It addresses the qi stagnation, blood stasis, heat-toxin, spleen/kidney deficiency, and yin/blood deficiency that often accompany chronic phlegm patterns. Originally developed as a gynecological formula for ovarian cysts, this formula may also be used for any long-term phlegm-accumulation disorder.

## Ingredients

Prunellae Spica (Prunella, Heal All, Self-Heal Spike / **Xia Ku Cao**)12%
Salviae Miltiorrhizae Radix (Chinese Salvia Root / **Dan Shen**) 10%
Astragali Radix (Astragalus / **Huang Qi**) 10%
Coicis Semen (Job's Tears Seed, Chinese Pearl Barley, Coix / **Yi Yi Ren**) 10%
Patriniae Herba (Patrinia, Snow Thistle / **Bai Jiang Cao**) 10%
Gleditsiae Spina (Gleditsia Thorn / **Zao Jiao Ci**) 7%
Eckloniae Thallus (Kelp, Kombu, Laminaria / **Kun Bu**) 5%
Scrophulariae Radix (Scrophularia, Figwort Root / **Xuan Shen**) 5%
Scutellariae Radix (Chinese Scullcap, Scutellaria, Scute / **Huang Qin**) 5%
Citri Reticulatae Pericarpium (Tangerine Peel / **Chen Pi**) 5%
Cyperi Rhizoma (Cyperus, Nut-Grass / **Xiang Fu**) 5%
Paeoniae Radix, alba (Chinese White Peony / **Bai Shao**) 5%
Angelicae Sinensis Radix (Dong Quai, Tang Kuei / **Dang Gui**) 5%
Cinnamomi Cortex (Cassia Bark, Cinnamon Bark / **Rou Gui**) 3%
Dipsaci Radix (Japanese Teasel Root, Dipsacus / **Xu Duan**) 3%

## Chinese Medical Actions

Transforms phlegm, disperses phlegm nodules, moves blood, regulates qi, clears heat and toxin, eliminates dampness, nourishes yin and blood, supports the spleen and kidneys.

## Indications

| | |
|---|---|
| Abdominal masses, from phlegm | Infertility |
| Breast lumps | Lymph nodes, enlarged |
| Bronchitis, chronic | Menopausal symptoms |
| Endometriosis w/ phlegm patterns | Ovarian cysts |
| Ganglionic cysts | Thyroid tumors, benign |
| Goiter | Uterine bleeding, dysfunctional |
| | Uterine fibroids |

**Tongue:** Swollen, with thick, greasy coating.
**Pulse:** Slippery.

## Contraindications

DO NOT USE DURING PREGNANCY.

# PINELLIA & MAGNOLIA BARK FORMULA

**Pinellia & Magnolia Bark Formula** *(Ban Xia Hou Po Tang)* is a classical Chinese formula. This version has been augmented with cyperus *(xiang fu)* and green tangerine peel *(qing pi)* to aid in the movement of stagnant qi. This formula is appropriate in cases of constrained qi with phlegm. This condition is classically known as "plum pit qi" *(mei he qi),* which usually results from emotional upset. The patient will most commonly experience a sensation of something caught in the throat that can neither be coughed up nor swallowed, or a stifling feeling in the chest and hypochondriac region.

## Ingredients

Zingiberis Rhizoma Recens (Fresh Ginger / **Sheng Jiang**) 23.1%
Pinelliae Rhizoma Preparatum (Pinellia, ginger-cured / **Zhi Ban Xia**) 18.5%
Poriae Sclerotium Pararadicis (Poria Spirit / **Fu Shen**) 18.5%
Magnoliae Officinalis Cortex (Magnolia Bark / **Hou Po**) 13.8%
Perillae Folium (Perilla Leaf / **Zi Su Ye**) 9.2%
Citri Reticulatae Viride Pericarpium (Green Tangerine Peel / **Qing Pi**) 9.2%
Cyperi Rhizoma (Cyperus, Nut-Grass / **Xiang Fu**) 7.7%

## Chinese Medical Actions

Promotes the movement of qi, directs rebellious qi downward, dissipates clumps, transforms phlegm.

## Indications

Acid regurgitation or reflux
Breathing difficulty
Bronchitis
Chest, stifling sensation in
Cough with profuse sputum
Emotional instability
Gastrointestinal disorders, functional
Laryngitis, chronic
Morning sickness
Motion sickness
Snoring
Swallowing, difficulty
Throat, feeling of something caught in
Wheezing
Vomiting

**Tongue:** Moist or greasy, with white coating.
**Pulse:** Wiry and slow or slippery.

## Contraindications

Do not use with patients with a flushed face, bitter taste in mouth, or red tongue with scanty coating. This formula contains drying and dispersing herbs, which can injure the yin and fluids if not used correctly.

# POLYPORUS & DIANTHUS FORMULA

**Polyporus & Dianthus Formula** *(Zhu Ling Qu Mai Tang*) is a modification of Polyporus Formula, a traditional *Shang Han Lun* formula, used to treat pathogenic influences which have transformed into heat in the interior. It is commonly used for urinary tract infections. The traditional formula was modified by adding lophatherum *(dan zhe ye)*, dianthus *(qu mai)*, anemarrhena *(zhi mu)*, andrographis *(chuan xin lian)*, and phellodendron *(huang bai)*. These herbs augment the heat-clearing and dampness-removing properties of the formula. The talcum in the original formula has been replaced with pyrrosia leaf *(shi wei)*.

## Ingredients

Lophatheri Herba (Lophatherum / **Dan Zhu Ye**) 16%
Dianthi Herba (Chinese Pink, Dianthus / **Qu Mai**) 16%
Poria (Poria, Hoelen, Tuckahoe / **Fu Ling**) 12%
Polyporus (Polyporus Sclerotium / **Zhu Ling**) 10%
Alismatis Rhizoma (Asian Water Plantain / **Ze Xie**) 10%
Anemarrhenae Rhizoma (Anemarrhena Rhizome / **Zhi Mu**) 10%
Andrographitis Herba (Andrographis / **Chuan Xin Lian**) 10%
Phellodendri Cortex (Phellodendron Bark / **Huang Bai**) 10%
Pyrrosiae Folium (Pyrrosia Leaf / **Shi Wei**) 6%

## Chinese Medical Actions

Promotes urination, clears heat, nourishes yin, drains damp-heat.

## Indications

Abdominal pain (lower), acute
Blood in urine
Cystitis, w/ fever and thirst w/ desire to drink
Irritability
Nephritis, acute
Urinary tract infections
Urination, painful or difficult
Urine, dark, hot
Uterine bleeding

**Tongue:** Dry, red, may have dark, yellow coating.
**Pulse:** Superficial and rapid.

## Contraindications

DO NOT USE DURING PREGNANCY.

# PORIA & BAMBOO FORMULA

**Poria & Bamboo Formula** *(Wen Dan Tang)* dates back to the 7th century. It was originally intended for treatment of post-wind-cold exterior patterns leading to stomach-gallbladder disharmony. This results in accumulation of phlegm that stagnates qi and combines with heat. Phlegm-heat and stagnation hinder the rising of clear yang, resulting in dizziness or vertigo. Also, phlegm-heat can become rebellious causing nausea or vomiting. Furthermore, phlegm-heat can disturb the chest and heart, manifesting as irritability, insomnia, palpitations, and anxiety. Because stomach-gallbladder disharmony can produce such varying symptoms, this formula can treat many different disorders. The patient will present with phlegm in the middle burner, resulting in symptoms such as heart or *shen* disturbance or counterflow of stomach qi. Polygala *(yuan zhi)* has been added to further assist in dispelling phlegm and calming the spirit.

## Ingredients

Citri Reticulatae Pericarpium (Tangerine Peel / **Chen Pi**) 21%
Bambusae Caulis in Taeniam (Bamboo Shavings / **Zhu Ru**)17%
Pinelliae Rhizoma Preparatum (Pinellia, ginger-cured / **Zhi Ban Xia**) 14%
Aurantii Fructus Immaturus (Immature Bitter Orange Fruit / **Zhi Shi**) 14%
Poria (Poria, Hoelen, Tuckahoe / **Fu Ling**) 11%
Glycyrrhizae Radix (Chinese Licorice Root / **Gan Cao**) 6%
Zingiberis Rhizoma Recens (Fresh Ginger / **Sheng Jiang**) 6%
Polygalae Radix (Polygala, Chinese Senega Root / **Yuan Zhi**) 5%
Jujubae Fructus (Jujube Fruit, Chinese Red Date / **Hong Zao, Da Zao**) 4%
Coptidis Rhizoma (Coptis / **Huang Lian**) 2%

## Chinese Medical Actions

Regulates qi, transforms phlegm, clears the gallbladder, harmonizes the stomach, calms the spirit.

## Indications

Anxiety or fright
Appetite, loss of
Bitter taste in mouth
Bronchitis, chronic
Chemotherapy, thoracic oppression and nausea from
Convulsions
Depression
Dizziness or vertigo
Gallbladder inflammation
Gallstones
Gastritis
Hiccough
Hepatitis, chronic
Insomnia
Irritability
Mania
Morning Sickness
Nausea
Palpitations
Ulcer, duodenal
Vomiting

**Tongue:** Greasy, yellow coating. **Pulse:** Rapid and slippery or wiry.

## Contraindications

Use only with clear signs of phlegm. This formula is drying; use caution with yin deficiency.

# PORIA FIFTEEN FORMULA

**Poria Fifteen Formula** *(Shi Wu Wei Fu Ling Pian)* is designed to help treat obesity. It improves digestion, increases elimination, aids in lipid metabolism, and reduces serum cholesterol, phlegm, and water excess. Suitable for all types of overweight persons, this formula is balanced and safe for long-term use.

## Ingredients

Alismatis Rhizoma (Asian Water Plantain / **Ze Xie**) 11%
Cassiae Semen (Cassia Seed, Sickle-pod Senna / **Jue Ming Zi**) 9.2%
Atractylodis Macrocephalae Rhizoma (White Atractylodes Rhizome / **Bai Zhu**) 9.2%
Poria (Poria, Hoelen, Tuckahoe / **Fu Ling**) 9.2%
Cinnamomi Ramulus (Cassia, Cinnamon Twig / **Gui Zhi**) 7.3%
Aurantii Fructus Immaturus (Immature Bitter Orange Fruit / **Zhi Shi**) 7.3%
Citri Reticulatae Pericarpium (Tangerine Peel / **Chen Pi**) 7.3%
Crataegi Fructus (Chinese Hawthorn Fruit / **Shan Zha**) 7.3%
Rhei Radix et Rhizoma (Chinese Rhubarb / **Da Huang**) 7.3%
Raphani Semen (Radish Seed / **Lai Fu Zi**) 6.1%
Cistanches Herba (Broomrape, Cistanches / **Rou Cong Rong**) 6.1%
Glycyrrhizae Radix (Chinese Licorice Root / **Gan Cao**) 5.4%
Dolomiaeae Radix (Costus Root, Vladimiria Root / **Chuan Mu Xiang**) 4.9%
Pharbitidis Semen (Morning Glory Seed / **Qian Niu Zi**) 2.4%

## Chinese Medical Actions

Drains dampness, moves qi and blood, relieves food stagnation, moves stool, benefits the spleen and kidneys, clears the liver.

## Indications

Abdominal distension or bloating
Cholesterol, elevated
Constipation
Edema
Food stagnation
Heaviness, generalized body
Obesity
Phlegm
Toxicity, feeling of
Urination, difficult

## Contraindications

DO NOT USE DURING PREGNANCY OR WHILE NURSING. Decrease dose if diarrhea occurs.

**Note:** Can be combined with the appropriate constitutional formula (**Women's Precious Formula, Sea of Qi Formula, Tang Kuei & Salvia Formula,** etc.)

# PORIA FIVE FORMULA

**Poria Five Formula** *(Wu Ling San),* also known as "Hoelen Five Formula," is a classical formula from the *Shang Han Lun.* It is used when there is an accumulation of water in the urinary bladder and the qi is unable to transform fluids resulting in urinary difficulty or fluid retention. The causes of this condition can be varied: pathogenic influences from a tai yang stage disorder which have penetrated into the urinary bladder, spleen deficiency which results in accumulation of water in the muscles and skin, or retention of congested fluids in the lower burner.

## Ingredients

Alismatis Rhizoma (Asian Water Plantain / **Ze Xie**) 32.4%
Poria (Poria, Hoelen, Tuckahoe / **Fu Ling**) 18.5%
Polyporus (Polyporus Sclerotium / **Zhu Ling**) 18.5%
Atractylodis Macrocephalae Rhizoma (White Atractylodes Rhizome / **Bai Zhu**) 18.5%
Cinnamomi Ramulus (Cassia, Cinnamon Twig / **Gui Zhi**) 12.1%

## Chinese Medical Actions

Dispels dampness, promotes urination, warms yang, strengthens the spleen, transforms qi.

## Indications

Ascites
Cough
Diarrhea
Dizziness or vertigo
Edema
Fever
Gastroenteritis, with congested fluids
Headache
Heaviness, generalized
Motion sickness
Nephritis
Premenstrual water retention
Scrotal edema
Shortness of breath
Toxemia of pregnancy
Umbilicus, throbbing sensations below
Urination, difficult
Vomiting

**Tongue:** Swollen, wet.
**Pulse:** Slippery, may be superficial and rapid.

## Contraindications

Use with caution in patients with spleen and kidney qi deficiency. Overuse may cause dizziness, vertigo, lack of appetite, and a bland taste in the mouth. In cases of urinary difficulty with yin deficiency, use with **True Yin Formula.**

# PROSTATE FORMULA

**Prostate Formula** *(Qiang Lie Xian Fang)* is designed to promote healthy function of the prostate. From the perspective of Oriental medicine, the prostate gland is primarily nourished by the spleen, kidney, and liver channels. With modern lifestyles and advancing years, certain patterns occur which affect the prostate gland. Decline of spleen yang can bring about an accumulation of dampness in the lower burner. Further decline of kidney yang, a normal occurrence with aging and stress, diminishes urinary function and sexual energy. This formula treats dampness and stasis in the lower burner brought about by deficiency of spleen and kidney yang. This condition is characterized by sexual dysfunction, or frequent or inhibited urination. In western medicine, this often corresponds to Benign Prostatic Hypertrophy (BPH) or enlarged prostate. For many men, these symptoms begin around age 40. **Prostate Formula** supplements the yang and drains accumulated dampness to protect against the effects of aging on the prostate.

## Ingredients

Cuscutae Semen (Chinese Dodder Seed, Chinese Cuscuta / **Tu Si Zi**) 11.9%
Epimedii Herba (Epimedium / **Yin Yang Huo**) 11.9%
Serenoae Fructus (Saw Palmetto Berry) 11.9%
Codonopsis Pilosae Radix (Codonopsis / **Dang Shen**) 11.9%
Angelicae Sinensis Radix (Dong Quai, Tang Kuei / **Dang Gui**) 9.6%
Dioscoreae Hypoglaucae Rhizoma (Tokoro Yam Rhizome / **Bei Xie**) 9.6%
Poria (Poria, Hoelen, Tuckahoe / **Fu Ling**) 7.1%
Paeoniae Radix, rubra (Chinese Red Peony / **Chi Shao**) 7.1%
Alpiniae Oxyphyllae Fructus (Black Cardamom, Alpinia Fruit / **Yi Zhi Ren**) 7.1%
Linderae Radix (Lindera Tuber, Chinese Allspice / **Wu Yao**) 7.1%
Glycyrrhizae Radix (Chinese Licorice Root / **Gan Cao**) 4.8%

## Chinese Medical Actions

Supports spleen and kidney yang, drains dampness, moves blood.

## Indications

Backache
Erectile dysfunction
Libido, loss of
Prostate, throbbing in
Urination, frequent, or difficulty starting and stopping

## Contraindications

If heat is present, clear heat before using this formula. With yin deficiency fire, use **Rehmannia & Scrophularia Formula**. With yin deficiency, use **True Yin Formula**. For acute prostatitis, use the **Gentiana Drain Fire Formula**. For severe swelling, use **Cinnamon & Poria Formula**.

**Note:** The American Institute for Cancer Research considers diets high in fat, salt, animal products, alcohol, and tobacco to be detrimental to prostate health.

# PULSATILLA INTESTINAL FORMULA

**Pulsatilla Intestinal Formula** *(Bai Tou Weng Li Chang Fang)* is a modern formula developed by Jake Fratkin, OMD, to treat epithelial inflammation in the small intestine. This inflammation is due to microbial infection (bacterial, viral, fungal, or protozoan) or to food allergies, and contributes to "Leaky Gut Syndrome." In prolonged intestinal inflammation, chemical and physical toxins are absorbed into the blood stream, and can cause lowered immunity, chronic fatigue, and fibromyalgia. It is often the underlying cause of a number of disorders, including eczema, asthma, sinusitis, dysmenorrhea, and premenstrual syndrome.

## Ingredients

Poria (Poria, Hoelen, Tuckahoe / **Fu Ling**) 17%
Pulsatillae Radix (Chinese Pulsatilla Root / **Bai Tou Weng**) 15%
Phellodendri Cortex (Phellodendron Bark / **Huang Bai**) 14%
Atractylodis Rhizoma (Cang-Zhu Atractylodes Rhizome / **Cang Zhu**) 14%
Paeoniae Radix, alba (Chinese White Peony / **Bai Shao**) 12%
Coptidis Rhizoma (Coptis / **Huang Lian**) 12%
Dolomiaeae Radix (Costus Root, Vladimiria Root / **Chuan Mu Xiang**) 8%
Glycyrrhizae Radix (Chinese Licorice Root / **Gan Cao**) 8%

## Chinese Medical Actions

Clears heat, resolves toxin, dispels dampness, and promotes tissue growth.

## Indications

Abdominal pain or cramping
Crohn's Disease
Diarrhea
Fatigue
Food allergies
Intestinal inflammation
Irritable Bowel Syndrome
Stool, loose or erratic
Skin problems

**Tongue:** Normal or red, with a yellow, greasy coating.
**Pulse:** Normal, or rapid and slippery.

## Contraindications

Reduce dose if loose stools occur while taking this formula.

**Note**: In leaky gut syndrome, attention should also be paid to liver stagnation. Chronic cases may need kidney support. In cases of irritation due to fungal, bacterial, or protozoan sources, combine with **Intestinal Fungus Formula** or **Oregano Oil Formula.**

# RABDOSIA PROSTATE FORMULA

**Rabdosia Prostate Formula** (*Dong Ling Cao Fang).* A number of the herbs in this formula have been used in China in recent years to treat patients with prostate cancer. Rabdosia *(dong ling cao)*, barbed scullcap *(ban zhi lian)*, oldenlandia *(bai hua she she cao)*, isatis *(da qing ye)*, moutan *(mu dan pi)*, zedoary *(e zhu)*, and amber *(hu po)* are used in traditional Chinese herbal medicine to treat cancer and tumors. Licorice *(gan cao)* and ganoderma *(ling zhi)* support qi and the body's immune function. Lindera *(wu yao)* and cyathula *(chuan niu xi)* relieve pain in the lower abdomen. According to modern research, saw palmetto reduces inflammation and supports prostate health.

## Ingredients

Rhabdosiae Herba (Rabdosia / **Dong Ling Cao**) 24.1%
Hedyotis Diffusae Herba (Hedyotis, Oldenlandia / **Bai Hua She She Cao**) 13.8%
Isatidis Folium (Isatis Leaf, Indigo Woad Leaf / **Da Qing Ye**) 6.9%
Scutellaria barbatae Herba (Barbed Scullcap / **Ban Zhi Lian**) 6.2%
Moutan Cortex (Tree Peony Root Bark / **Mu Dan Pi**) 6.2%
Paridis Rhizoma (Paris Rhizome / **Chong Lou**) 6.2%
Glycyrrhizae Radix (Chinese Licorice Root / **Gan Cao**) 6.2%
Cyathulae Radix (Cyathula Root / **Chuan Niu Xi**) 6.2%
Curcumae Rhizoma (Zedoary Rhizome / **E Zhu**) 6.2%
Linderae Radix (Lindera Tuber, Chinese Allspice / **Wu Yao**) 6.2%
Serenoae Fructus (Saw Palmetto Berry) 5.6%
Succinum Resina (Amber / **Hu Po**) 3.4%
Ganoderma (Reishi, Ganoderma Mushroom / **Ling Zhi**) 2.8%

## Chinese Medical Actions

Clears heat and damp-heat, cools and invigorates blood, disperses swelling, resolves toxin.

## Indications

| | |
|---|---|
| Elevated PSA (Prostate Specific Antigen) count | Urogenital dampness and pain |

**Tongue:** May be swollen, purple, or red, with yellow coating.
**Pulse:** Rapid, wiry.

## Contraindications

Use in caution in cases where there is an absence of heat.

# REHMANNIA & SCROPHULARIA FORMULA

**Rehmannia & Scrophularia Formula** *(Zhi Bai Di Huang Wan)* is a modification of Anemarrhena, Phellodendron, and Rehmannia Formula, with the addition of lycium root bark *(di gu pi)* and scrophularia *(xuan shen)*. Based on Rehmannia Six Formula *(Liu Wei Di Huang Wan)*, a kidney yin tonic, this formula is used specifically to address yin deficiency with fire, internal heat, or "bone-steaming" heat. It is excellent for feelings of "burn out" or exhaustion with heat.

## Ingredients

Rehmanniae Radix (Rehmannia Root, unprocessed / **Sheng Di Huang**) 20.3%
Scrophulariae Radix (Scrophularia, Figwort Root / **Xuan Shen**) 14.6%
Dioscoreae Rhizoma (Chinese Yam / **Shan Yao**) 9.8%
Alismatis Rhizoma (Asian Water Plantain / **Ze Xie**) 9.8%
Moutan Cortex (Tree Peony Root Bark / **Mu Dan Pi**) 9.8%
Poria (Poria, Hoelen, Tuckahoe / **Fu Ling**) 9.8%
Lycii Cortex (Lycium Root Bark, Chinese Wolfberry Root Bark / **Di Gu Pi**) 9.8%
Corni Fructus (Asiatic Dogwood Fruit, Cornelian Cherry / **Shan Zhu Yu**) 6.5%
Phellodendri Cortex (Phellodendron Bark **/ Huang Bai**) 4.8%
Anemarrhenae Rhizoma (Anemarrhena Rhizome / **Zhi Mu**) 4.8%

## Chinese Medical Actions

Nourishes the yin and the kidneys, clears heat, quells fire.

## Indications

Back pain
Dizziness or vertigo
Face, red
Fever, low grade, afternoon, or tidal
Hot flashes
Hyperthyroidism
Insomnia
Impotence
Night sweats
Palms and soles, hot
Pain, in back or at midline
Premature ejaculation
Restlessness
Spermatorrhea
Toothache, from deficiency fire
Throat, sore and dry
Urinary difficulty

**Tongue:** Dry, red or red sides, glossy.
**Pulse:** Rapid and thin, may be large in the kidney position.

## Contraindications

Do not use with internal or external cold. If heat signs are not present, use **Rehmannia Six** or **True Yin Formula** instead.

# REHMANNIA COOL BLOOD FORMULA

**Rehmannia Cool Blood Formula** *(Tu Fu Ling Sheng Di Huang Wan).* This formula clears heat from the blood without the use of animal parts, such as rhinoceros horn or its substitute, water buffalo horn. The blood level is the deepest of the four levels of disease. Heat in the blood causes bleeding disorders such as nosebleed, vomiting blood, or blood in the urine and stools, and various types of skin rashes.

## Ingredients

Smilacis Glabrae Rhizoma (Chinese Smilax Rhizome / **Tu Fu Ling**) 14.5%
Rehmanniae Radix (Rehmannia Root, unprocessed / **Sheng Di Huang**) 14.5%
Nelumbinis Folium (Lotus Leaf / **He Ye**) 7.5%
Lonicerae Flos (Japanese Honeysuckle Flower / **Jin Yin Hua**) 7.5%
Sanguisorbae Radix (Sanguisorba, Long-Leaf Burnet Root / **Di Yu**) 7%
Gypsum Fibrosum (Gypsum / **Shi Gao**) 7%
Glauberitum (Calcitum / **Han Shui Shi**) 7%
Dictamni Cortex (Dictamnus Root Bark, Dense-Fruit Dittany / **Bai Xian Pi**) 5%
Moutan Cortex (Tree Peony Root Bark / **Mu Dan Pi**) 5%
Paeoniae Radix, rubra (Chinese Red Peony / **Chi Shao**) 5%
Carthami Flos (Safflower, Carthamus Flower / **Hong Hua**) 5%
Glehniae Radix (Glehnia Root / **Sha Shen**) 5%
Ophiopogonis Radix (Ophiopogon Tuber / **Mai Men Dong**) 5%
Scrophulariae Radix (Scrophularia, Figwort Root / **Xuan Shen**) 5%

## Chinese Medical Actions

Clears heat and cools blood, drains fire, removes toxin, nourishes yin, moves blood stasis, stops bleeding.

## Indications

Blood in stool or urine
Boils
Carbuncles
Chicken pox
Delirium
Eczema
Heat aversion
Hives
Incoherent speech
Irritability
Itching
Mania
Mouth sores
Nosebleed
Psoriasis
Restlessness
Skin rash, red with intense itching
Sores, painful
Stools, dry
Thirst, with no desire to swallow
Throat, sore or dry
Urine, yellow or scanty

**Tongue:** Red or purplish, with thin, yellow, or white coating.
**Pulse:** Rapid.

## Contraindications

DO NOT USE DURING PREGNANCY. Do not use in cases with cold, or with fire from deficiency.

# REHMANNIA SIX FORMULA

**Rehmannia Six Formula** *(Liu Wei Di Huang Wan)* is the famous, classical Chinese herbal formula used to treat kidney and liver yin deficiency. By supplementing the yin of the kidney and liver, this formula helps to support the root yin of the whole body. Originally from a pediatric text, **Rehmannia Six Formula** was developed to treat children with slow development or failure to thrive. Essence-building herbs, rehmannia *(shu di huang)* and corni *(shan zhu yu),* are combined with alismatis *(ze xie)* and moutan *(mu dan pi)* to drain fire, poria *(fu ling)* to drain dampness, and dioscorea *(shan yao)* to strengthen the spleen. Thus, it is a well-balanced formula, appropriate for long-term use to build yin and drain deficiency fire.

## Ingredients

Rehmanniae Radix Preparata (Cured Rehmannia Root / **Shu Di Huang**) 32%
Corni Fructus (Asiatic Dogwood Fruit, Cornelian Cherry / **Shan Zhu Yu**) 16%
Dioscoreae Rhizoma (Chinese Yam / **Shan Yao**) 16%
Cortex Moutan Radicis (Tree Peony Root / **Mu Dan Pi**) 12%
Poria (Poria, Hoelen, Tuckahoe / **Fu Ling**) 12%
Alismatis Rhizoma (Asian Water Plantain / **Ze Xie**) 12%

## Chinese Medical Actions

Supplements yin, nourishes kidneys and liver, builds and stabilizes essence.

## Indications

Back (lower), weak and sore
Children, slow development in
Constitution, delicate
Diabetes mellitus
Dizziness or vertigo
Dry mouth or throat (chronic)
Fatigue
Hearing loss
Impotence
Knees weak
Menopause, premature
Night sweats
Nocturnal emissions
Palms and soles, hot
Premature ejaculation
Ringing in the ear
Tidal fever
Urinary tract infection, chronic
Vision blurred

**Tongue:** Red, with thin coating, dry.
**Pulse:** Thready and rapid.

## Contraindications

**Rehmannia Six Formula** should be used with caution in cases where the patient has weak digestion, loose stools due to spleen deficiency, or a white, greasy tongue coating.

# RESOLVE THE MIDDLE FORMULA

**Resolve the Middle Formula** *(Jia Wei Ping Wei Fang)* is a modified version of *Ping Wei San,* which treats damp turbidity causing stagnation in the middle burner. This formula is best applied when spleen qi deficiency is secondary to the accumulation of damp. The spleen is easily susceptible to the encumbrance of damp from the occasional overindulgence in food or alcohol, or from the long-standing habit of an improper diet. This causes the spleen to become compromised in its transportation and transformation function, leading to damp stagnation with pain, indigestion, bloating and abdominal discomfort after meals, chronic loose or irregular stools, irregular appetite, dulling of taste, and lethargy. The traditional formula has been modified to include coix (*yi yi ren*), poria *(fu ling)*, and amomum *(sha ren)* to help disinhibit dampness and support the spleen; immature bitter orange *(zhi shi)* and hawthorn *(shan zha)* to disperse digestive stagnation; and vladimiria *(chuan mu xiang)* to promote the downward flow of qi through the digestive tract and relieve abdominal distension. Codonopsis *(dang shen)* is included to supplement the qi of the spleen and stomach. This formula can be helpful in patients on a weight loss regimen who are experiencing damp encumbrance. Often, these patients will have such an overwhelming amount of dampness that it is necessary to use this formula initially before the root conditions can be addressed.

## Ingredients

Atractylodis Rhizoma (Cang-Zhu Atractylodes Rhizome / **Cang Zhu**) 14%
Coicis Semen (Job's Tears Seed, Chinese Pearl Barley, Coix / **Yi Yi Ren**) 12%
Crataegi Fructus (Chinese Hawthorn Fruit / **Shan Zha**) 11%
Magnoliae Officinalis Cortex (Magnolia Bark / **Hou Po**) 9%
Citri Reticulatae Pericarpium (Tangerine Peel / **Chen Pi**) 8%
Aurantii Fructus Immaturus (Immature Bitter Orange Fruit / **Zhi Shi**) 8%
Dolomiaeae Radix (Costus Root, Vladimiria Root / **Chuan Mu Xiang**) 7%
Fructus Amomi (Cardamom Fruit / **Sha Ren**) 7%
Codonopsis Pilosae Radix (Codonopsis / **Dang Shen**) 6%
Poria (Poria, Hoelen, Tuckahoe / **Fu Ling**) 6%
Zingiberis Rhizoma Recens (Fresh Ginger / **Sheng Jiang**) 4%
Glycyrrhizae Radix Preparata (Chinese Licorice Root, honey-fried / **Zhi Gan Cao**) 4%
Jujubae Fructus (Jujube Fruit, Chinese Black Date / **Hei Zao**) 4%

## Chinese Medical Actions

Dries dampness, promotes the spleen's transportation and transformation functions, moves qi and transforms accumulation, harmonizes the stomach, promotes digestion.

## Indications

- Acid regurgitation or reflux
- Abdominal and epigastric distension and fullness
- Acid regurgitation
- Appetite, loss of
- Belching
- Constipation
- Diarrhea
- Fatigue, with increased desire to sleep
- Flatulence
- Food stagnation
- Gastritis
- Hangover
- Heaviness, in limbs
- Indigestion
- Intestinal cramping
- Nausea
- Stools, erratic
- Taste, loss of
- Vomiting

**Tongue:** Swollen, possibly with tooth marks; thick, white, greasy coating.
**Pulse:** Moderate or slippery.

## Contraindications

USE WITH CAUTION DURING PREGNANCY. This is a drying formula and should not be used with those who are severely yin or blood deficient unless coupled with an appropriate formula.

**Note:** This formula is best applied in the short term to overcome damp encumbrance.

# RESTFUL SLEEP FORMULA

**Restful Sleep Formula** *(An Xin Pian)* is a modification of Baked Licorice Decoction *(Zhi Gan Cao Tang)*, traditionally used for heart qi and blood deficiency. This version has been modified with biota *(bai zi ren)* to nourish the heart and calm the spirit; longan *(long yan rou)* to supplement the heart and spleen, nourish the blood, and calm the spirit; mimosa *(he huan hua)* to calm the spirit; and cassia *(jue ming zi)* to clear liver heat. This formula is used for chronic sleep disorders. The state of the *shen* (spirit) is responsible for the quantity and quality of sleep. The *shen* is housed in the heart and is supported by heart blood. After a sleepless night, the qi becomes depleted. A pattern of chronic sleeplessness leads to a deficiency of heart blood and yin. As the deficiency becomes more pronounced, it becomes increasingly more difficult to sleep. **Restful Sleep Formula** helps to break this cycle and restore normal sleep patterns. This is an excellent formula for insomnia in older patients with chronic deficiency patterns.

## Ingredients

Platycladi Semen (Oriental Arborvitae Seed, Biota Seed / **Bai Zi Ren**) 18%
Longan Arillis (Longan Fruit / **Long Yan Rou**) 13%
Albiziae Flos (Mimosa Flower, Silk-Tree Flower / **He Huan Hua**) 13%
Cassiae Semen (Cassia Seed, Sickle-pod Senna / **Jue Ming Zi**) 9%
Ophiopogonis Radix (Ophiopogon Tuber / **Mai Men Dong**) 9%
Glycyrrhizae Radix Preparata (Chinese Licorice Root, honey-fried / **Zhi Gan Cao**) 8%
Jujubae Fructus (Jujube Fruit, Chinese Red Date / **Hong Zao, Da Zao**) 6%
Rehmanniae Radix (Rehmannia Root, unprocessed / **Sheng Di Huang**) 6%
Ginseng Radix (Asian Ginseng Root / **Ren Shen**) 6%
Zingiberis Rhizoma Recens (Fresh Ginger / **Sheng Jiang**) 6%
Cinnamomi Ramulus (Cassia, Cinnamon Twig / **Gui Zhi**) 6%

## Chinese Medical Actions

Supplements qi and heart blood, calms the spirit, clears heat.

| Indications | |
|---|---|
| Appetite, poor | Insomnia |
| Complexion, pale | Memory, poor |
| Constipation, with dry stool | Palpitation |
| Fatigue, from sleeplessness | Sleep, restless or disturbed |

**Tongue:** Pale. **Pulse:** Thin and weak.

**Note:** This formula should be taken consistently over a period of time to address deficiency of qi and heart blood created by a pattern of sleeplessness. It will be important to address other possible causes for insomnia, such as pain or other patterns of disharmony. For insomnia due to liver yin deficiency, use **Zizyphus Formula**. In cases with liver fire, use **Bupleurum D Formula**. For heart and kidney yin deficiency, use **Heavenly Emperor's Formula**. For insomnia with depression, use **Salvia Ten Formula**. With liver wind and liver yin deficiency, use **Gastrodia & Uncaria Formula**.

# RESTORATIVE FORMULA

**Restorative Formula** *(Yang Xue Zhuang Jin Jian Bu Wan).* Most formulas that are designed to treat pain primarily use herbs that regulate and invigorate qi and blood. **Restorative Formula** differs in that it not only moves blood and qi, but also focuses on supplementing qi, blood, yin, and yang. This makes it ideal for patients whose presentation is more related to deficiency than stasis. The balanced nature of the formula allows it to transform damp without damaging yin, thus making it ideal as a general tonic for aging patients.

## Ingredients

Rehmanniae Radix Preparata (Cured Rehmannia Root / **Shu Di Huang**) 9.4%
Achyranthis Bidentatae Radix (Achyranthes / **Huai Niu Xi**) 6%
Eucommiae Cortex (Eucommia Bark / **Du Zhong**) 6%
Angelicae Sinensis Radix (Dong Quai, Tang Kuei / **Dang Gui**) 6%
Phellodendri Cortex (Phellodendron Bark / **Huang Bai**) 6%
Atractylodis Rhizoma (Cang-Zhu Atractylodes Rhizome / **Cang Zhu**) 6%
Codonopsis Pilosae Radix (Codonopsis / **Dang Shen**) 6%
Psoraleae Fructus (Psoralea Fruit / **Bu Gu Zhi**) 5.2%
Dioscoreae Rhizoma (Chinese Yam / **Shan Yao**) 5.2%
Schisandrae Fructus (Schisandra Fruit / **Wu Wei Zi**) 5.2%
Lycii Fructus (Lycium Fruit, Chinese Wolfberry / **Gou Qi Zi**) 5.2%
Cuscutae Semen (Chinese Dodder Seed, Chinese Cuscuta / **Tu Si Zi**) 5.2%
Atractylodis Macrocephalae Rhizoma (White Atractylodes Rhizome / **Bai Zhu**) 5.2%
Paeoniae Radix, alba (Chinese White Peony / **Bai Shao**) 5.2%
Astragali Radix (Astragalus / **Huang Qi**) 5.2%
Saposhnikoviae Radix (Siler / **Fang Feng**) 2.6%
Notopterygii Rhizoma seu Radix (Notopterygium / **Qiang Huo**) 2.6%
Spatholobi Caulis (Spatholobus / **Ji Xue Teng**) 2.6%
Plantaginis Semen (Asian Plantain Seed, Plantago Seed / **Che Qian Zi**) 2.6%
Trachelospermi Caulis (Star Jasmine Stem / **Luo Shi Teng**) 2.6%

## Chinese Medical Actions

Nourishes qi and blood, dispels wind and dampness, frees the connecting vessels to relieve pain.

### Indications

Arthritis
Chronic pain in the elderly or in patients weakened by illness
Fibromyalgia
Limbs, tired or aching
Nerve pain
Pain in the muscles, tendons, and joints

**Tongue:** Pale, with a thin, white coating.
**Pulse:** Weak and thin.

# RESTORE THE LUNG FORMULA

**Restore the Lung Formula** *(Bu Fei Tang)* treats chronic cough that has arisen from depleted lung qi following an acute or prolonged illness. The original formulation is a modification of Sheng Mai Formula, which is for restoring the pulse after prolonged or severe illness. Instead of ophiopogon *(mai men dong)*, **Restore the Lung Formula** contains prepared rehmannia *(shu di huang)* because the emphasis is not so much on moistening as it is on restoring a strong relationship between lung and kidney. The source formula includes mulberry bark *(sang bai pi)* and aster *(zi wan)* to relieve cough. The source formula has been modified by adding platycodon *(jie geng)* to enhance its ability to resolve phlegm and stop cough.

## Ingredients

Astragali Radix (Astragalus / **Huang Qi**) 20%
Rehmanniae Radix Preparata (Cured Rehmannia Root / **Shu Di Huang**) 20%
Codonopsis Pilosae Radix (Codonopsis / **Dang Shen**) 15%
Mori Cortex (White Mulberry Root Bark / **Sang Bai Pi**) 15%
Asteris Radix (Tartarian Aster Root / **Zi Wan**) 12%
Platycodi Radix (Platycodon Root, Balloon Flower Root / **Jie Geng**) 10%
Schisandrae Fructus (Schisandra Fruit / **Wu Wei Zi**) 8%

## Chinese Medical Actions

Revitalizes the lung qi, harmonizes lung and kidney, resolves phlegm, relieves cough.

## Indications

| | |
|---|---|
| Bronchitis, chronic or post-acute | Fatigue |
| Cough, chronic (dry or phlegmatic) | Shortness of breath |
| | Sweating, spontaneous |

**Tongue:** Pale, may be slightly red at tip.
**Pulse:** Large, empty.

**Note:** The application of this formula is similar to that of **Lily Preserve Metal Formula**.The main difference is that **Lily Preserve Metal Formula** restores the lung that has sustained damage primarily to its fluids; **Restore the Lung Formula** vitalizes the lung qi that has been depleted.

# SALVIA TEN FORMULA

**Salvia Ten Formula** (*Dan Shen Jia Si Jun Zi Pian)* is based on a formula used in modern China for the treatment of depression. To the basic formula, the traditional Six Gentlemen Formula *(Liu Jun Zi Wan)* has been added to support the general vitality, which is often diminished in chronic depression. When appropriate, this formula can be useful for patients who are undergoing psychotherapy, as it helps lighten and free the emotions while providing support.

## Ingredients

Salviae Miltiorrhizae Radix (Chinese Salvia Root / **Dan Shen**) 13.3%
Curcumae Radix (Turmeric, Curcuma Tuber / **Yu Jin**) 13.3%
Paeoniae Radix, rubra (Chinese Red Peony / **Chi Shao**) 10.6%
Albiziae Flos (Mimosa Flower, Silk-Tree Flower / **He Huan Hua**) 10.6%
Codonopsis Pilosae Radix (Codonopsis / **Dang Shen**) 10.6%
Poria (Poria, Hoelen, Tuckahoe / **Fu Ling**) 10.6%
Atractylodis Macrocephalae Rhizoma (White Atractylodes Rhizome / **Bai Zhu**) 10.6%
Citri Reticulatae Pericarpium (Tangerine Peel / **Chen Pi**) 8.9%
Glycyrrhizae Radix (Chinese Licorice Root / **Gan Cao**) 6.2%
Pinelliae Rhizoma Preparatum (Pinellia, ginger-cured / **Zhi Ban Xia**) 5.3%

## Chinese Medical Actions

Circulates qi and blood, cools the blood, resolves phlegm, builds qi, supplements the spleen and stomach, calms the spirit, soothes the nerves.

## Indications

Anxiety
Appetite, loss of
Depression
Digestion, weak
Fatigue
Insomnia
Irritability
Melancholy, excessive
Mental disorders
Palpitation
Restlessness
Weight loss

## Contraindications

DO NOT USE DURING PREGNANCY. Use cautiously in cases of deficient blood. With blood deficiency and the proper presentation, use **Peaceful Spirit Formula** or **Ginseng Nourishing Formula**.

# SAN QI FORMULA

**San Qi Formula** *(San Qi Pian)* This formula combines several potent blood-stanching herbs to treat bleeding from internal disharmony or external trauma.

## Ingredients

Notoginseng Radix (Tienqi Ginseng, Pseudoginseng Root / **San Qi, Tian Qi**) 45%
Agrimoniae Herba (Agrimony / **Xian He Cao**) 20%
Celosiae Cristatae Flos (Cockscomb Flower / **Ji Guan Hua**) 15%
Imperatae Rhizoma (Imperata Rhizome / **Bai Mao Gen**) 10%
Platycladi Cacumen (Oriental Arborvitae Leaf and Stem / **Ce Bai Ye**) 10%

## Chinese Medical Actions

Stops bleeding, dispels blood stasis.

## Indications

- Bleeding, internal or external, from trauma
- Blood in the urine or stool
- Coughing up blood
- Crohn's disease, acute
- Gums bleeding
- Hemorrhoids
- Menstrual bleeding, excessive
- Nosebleed
- Phlebitis
- Rectal bleeding
- Ulcers, bleeding
- Uterine bleeding
- Vomiting blood

## Contraindications

DO NOT USE DURING PREGNANCY.

**Note:** For bleeding from a constitutional imbalance, it may be appropriate to combine with a formula to treat the root disorder. For example, bleeding due to heat in the blood can be addressed with **Rehmannia Cool Blood Formula**. Qi deficiency bleeding can be addressed by using **San Qi Formula** with **Ginseng & Astragalus Formula**. Bleeding from blood-heat (especially uterine bleeding) precipitated by constrained liver qi can be treated by combining **San Qi Formula** with **Free & Easy Wanderer Plus**.

# SAN QI TABLETS

**San Qi Tablets** *(San Qi Wan)* contain the single ingredient pseudoginseng root, which is effective in controlling bleeding, transforming blood stasis, and dispersing clots and deposits in the blood vessels. It is also good for pain and swelling from traumatic injury.

## Ingredient

Notoginseng Radix (Tienqi Ginseng, Pseudoginseng Root / **San Qi, Tian Qi**) 100%

## Chinese Medical Actions

Stops bleeding and transforms blood stasis, reduces pain and swelling.

## Clinical Research

Hemostatic, decreases blood pressure, relieves pain from angina pectoris, decreases serum lipids and cholesterol, aids in relieving acute attacks of Crohn's disease.

| Indications | |
|---|---|
| Abdominal pain w/ blood stasis | Menstrual pain with blood stasis |
| Bleeding, internal and external | Nosebleed |
| Blood in stools or urine | Pain from injury |
| Bruises | Rectal bleeding |
| Chest pain w/ blood stasis | Swelling from injury |
| Crohn's disease, acute | Traumatic injury |
| Gums bleeding | Uterine bleeding |
| Hemorrhoids | Varicose veins |
| Menstural bleeding, abnormal | Vomiting blood |

## Contraindications

DO NOT USE DURING PREGNANCY. Use cautiously with patients with deficient blood.

# SEA OF QI FORMULA

**Sea of Qi Formula** *(Qi Hai Yao Fang)* is designed to strengthen the *dantien* or *hara* by vitalizing the yang of the kidney and spleen. It is useful for patients with kidney deficiency who also have weak spleen yang and lack the digestive fire to process kidney tonics alone.

## Ingredients

Cuscutae Semen (Chinese Dodder Seed, Chinese Cuscuta / **Tu Si Zi**) 11.5%
Atractylodis Macrocephalae Rhizoma (White Atractylodes Rhizome / **Bai Zhu**) 9.2%
Poria (Poria, Hoelen, Tuckahoe / **Fu Ling**) 9.2%
Dioscoreae Rhizoma (Chinese Yam / **Shan Yao**) 9.2%
Corni Fructus (Asiatic Dogwood Fruit, Cornelian Cherry / **Shan Zhu Yu**) 9.2%
Alismatis Rhizoma (Asian Water Plantain / **Ze Xie**) 9.2%
Zingiberis Rhizoma (Dried Ginger / **Gan Jiang**) 7.6%
Psoraleae Fructus (Psoralea Fruit / **Bu Gu Zhi**) 7.6%
Citri Reticulatae Pericarpium (Tangerine Peel / **Chen Pi**) 6.9%
Ginseng Radix (Asian Ginseng Root / **Ren Shen**) 5.3%
Glycyrrhizae Radix (Chinese Licorice Root / **Gan Cao**) 5.3%
Dolomiaeae Radix (Costus Root, Vladimiria Root / **Chuan Mu Xiang**) 5.3%
Cinnamomi Cortex (Cassia Bark, Cinnamon Bark / **Rou Gui**) 4.5%

## Chinese Medical Actions

Warms and supplements the middle burner, warms the kidneys, supplements qi and yang, strengthens spleen and kidney yang.

## Indications

Abdomen, cold sensation in
Appetite, loss of
Cold hands and feet
Cold, sensitivity to
Complexion, pale
Cough with white sputum
Diarrhea
Dizziness
Fatigue
Impotence
Lassitude
Menstruation, prolonged
Urinary incontinence
Urination, excessive
Vaginal discharge, white or clear
Weak limbs
Weakness, generalized

**Tongue:** Pale, may be swollen.
**Pulse:** Slow and weak.

## Contraindications

USE WITH CAUTION DURING PREGNANCY. Do not use in the absence of deficient yang.

# SEVEN TREASURES FORMULA

**Seven Treasures Formula** *(Jin Hua Mei Ran Wan).* The traditional formula upon which this tablet is based treats a broad range of symptoms that result from deficient kidney yin and essence *(jing)*, and deficient liver blood and yin. The Chinese name of this formula can be translated as "Seven Treasures Elixir for Beautiful Hair." In contemporary times, it has been commonly used to treat thinning or graying hair—even though the source text makes only a passing reference to this symptom. The formula presented here has been modified with drynaria *(gu sui bu)* to further supplement the kidney and liver, red peony *(chi shao)* to cool and invigorate blood, and licorice root *(gan cao)* to harmonize and supplement qi.

## Ingredients

Polygoni Multiflori Radix Preparata (Polygonum Root, Fo Ti / **Zhi He Shou Wu**) 20%
Drynariae Rhizoma (Drynaria Rhizome / **Gu Sui Bu**) 12%
Lycii Fructus (Lycium Fruit, Chinese Wolfberry / **Gou Qi Zi**) 11%
Achyranthis Bidentatae Radix (Achyranthes / **Huai Niu Xi**) 10%
Angelicae Sinensis Radix (Dong Quai, Tang Kuei / **Dang Gui**) 10%
Cuscutae Semen (Chinese Dodder Seed, Chinese Cuscuta / **Tu Si Zi**) 10%
Psoraleae Fructus (Psoralea Fruit / **Bu Gu Zhi**) 10%
Poria (Poria, Hoelen, Tuckahoe / **Fu Ling**) 8%
Paeoniae Radix, rubra (Chinese Red Peony / **Chi Shao**) 6%
Glycyrrhizae Radix (Chinese Licorice Root / **Gan Cao**) 3%

## Chinese Medical Actions

Replenishes the yin and essence *(jing)* of the kidney, nourishes liver blood and yin.

## Indications

Back (lower), weak and sore
Hair, premature graying
Hair loss or thinning
Infertility, from kidney deficiency
Knees, weak and sore
Nocturnal emissions
Thirst
Vaginal discharge, profuse

**Tongue:** Pale, thin, shiny, or lacking a tongue coating.
**Pulse:** Thin, weak, may also be tight.

## Contraindications

Use with caution with patients who have thick tongue coating or loose stools. May be combined with qi-supplementing formulas when appropriate. Do not use during the course of an external wind invasion.

# SHENG MAI FORMULA

**Sheng Mai Formula** *(Sheng Mai San),* also known as "Generate the Pulse Powder," is a classical formula used to strengthen the pulse by strengthening the qi and yin of the lungs. It is used for injury to the yin from summer heat or in cases of chronic weakness caused by lung qi or yin deficiency. It can also be used after trauma or shock.

## Ingredients

Ginseng Radix (Asian Ginseng Root / **Ren Shen**) 37.5%
Ophiopogonis Radix (Ophiopogon Tuber / **Mai Men Dong**) 37.5%
Schisandrae Fructus (Schisandra Fruit / **Wu Wei Zi**) 25%

## Chinese Medical Actions

Builds qi and yin, replenishes fluids, stops excessive sweating.

## Indications

- Chest, stifling sensation in
- Cough, chronic w/ difficult to expectorate sputum
- Dizziness
- Dryness
- Fatigue
- Heart disease
- Heat exhaustion
- Palpitation
- Shock
- Shortness of breath
- Sweating, profuse
- Thirst
- Weakness

**Tongue:** Dry, or red with dry coating.
**Pulse:** Weak and rapid, or weak and thin.

## Contraindications

Do not use with a high fever, or in initial stages of summer flu, or with unresolved conditions from external pathogenic factors.

# SHU GAN FORMULA

**Shu Gan Formula** *(Shu Gan Wan)*, also known as "Soothe Liver Pill," is a popular formula used to treat congestion of liver qi which affects the digestion.

## Ingredients

Cyperi Rhizoma (Cyperus, Nut-Grass / **Xiang Fu**) 10%
Paeoniae Radix, alba (Chinese White Peony / **Bai Shao**) 10%
Bupleuri Radix (Bupleurum Root / **Chai Hu**) 8%
Crataegi Fructus (Chinese Hawthorn Fruit / **Shan Zha**) 8%
Aurantii Fructus (Bitter Orange / **Zhi Ke**) 7%
Amomi Fructus (Cardamom Fruit / **Sha Ren**) 7%
Citri Reticulatae viride Pericarpium (Green Tangerine Peel / **Qing Pi**) 6%
Citri Reticulatae Pericarpium (Tangerine Peel / **Chen Pi**) 6%
Magnoliae Officinalis Cortex (Magnolia Bark / **Hou Po**) 6%
Curcumae Radix (Turmeric, Curcuma Tuber / **Yu Jin**) 6%
Amomi Fructus Rotundus (Chinese Cardamom / **Bai Dou Kou**) 6%
Dolomiaeae Radix (Costus Root, Vladimiria Root / **Chuan Mu Xiang**) 6%
Citri Sarcodactylis Fructus (Fresh-Finger Citron Fruit / **Fo Shou**) 5%
Glycyrrhizae Radix (Chinese Licorice Root / **Gan Cao**) 4%
Curcurmae Longae Rhizoma (Turmeric Rhizome / **Jiang Huang**) 3%
Zingiberis Rhizoma Recens (Dried Ginger / **Sheng Jiang**) 2%

## Chinese Medical Actions

Soothes the liver, regulates the stomach, moves qi, breaks up stagnation, dries dampness, and transforms phlegm.

## Indications

Abdominal distension or bloating
Abdominal pain
Acid regurgitation
Appetite, poor
Bitter or sour taste in mouth
Belching
Digestion, poor
Flatulence
Hepatitis
Hiccoughs
Hypoglycemia
Hypochondriac pain
Indigestion
Intestinal cramping
Irritable Bowel Syndrome
Stomach ache
Stools, erratic
Vomiting

**Tongue:** Normal, or with a thin, greasy coating.
**Pulse:** Excess or wiry in liver and stomach positions.

# SILER & PLATYCODON FORMULA

**Siler & Platycodon Formula** *(Fang Feng Tong Sheng San)* was designed to treat excess heat simultaneously occurring in the interior and the exterior. The two most common patterns are of 1) an exterior heat pathogen that has penetrated to the interior without leaving the exterior, and 2) an exterior heat pattern that attacks where there is a preexisting internal heat pattern. The most common applications today are the resolution of heat-type influenza and acute, hot skin disorders. The formula is balanced between purgative/heat-clearing substances and exterior-releasing substances. In addition, **Siler & Platycodon Formula** supplements qi and blood.

## Ingredients

Glycyrrhizae Radix (Chinese Licorice Root / **Gan Cao**) 21%
Alismatis Rhizoma (Asian Water Plantain / **Ze Xie**) 12%
Platycodi Radix (Platycodon Root, Balloon Flower Root / **Jie Geng**) 10%
Malvae Semen (Malva Seed, Whorled Mallow Fruit / **Dong Kui Zi**) 10%
Scutellariae Radix (Chinese Scullcap, Scutellaria, Scute / **Huang Qin**) 8%
Saposhnikoviae Radix (Siler / **Fang Feng**) 4%
Rhei Radix et Rhizoma (Chinese Rhubarb / **Da Huang**) 4%
Menthae Haplocalysis Herba (Chinese Mint / **Bo He**) 4%
Forsythiae Fructus (Forsythia Fruit / **Lian Qiao**) 4%
Schizonepetae Herba (Schizonepeta / **Jing Jie**) 4%
Anemarrhenae Rhizoma (Anemarrhena Rhizome / **Zhi Mu**) 4%
Chuanxiong Rhizoma (Ligusticum Wallichii Rhizome / **Chuan Xiong**) 3%
Angelicae Sinensis Radix (Dong Quai, Tang Kuei / **Dang Gui**) 3%
Paeoniae Radix, alba (Chinese White Peony / **Bai Shao**) 3%
Atractylodis Macrocephalae Rhizoma (White Atractylodes Rhizome/ **Bai Zhu**) 2%
Gardeniae Fructus (Gardenia Fruit / **Shan Zhi Zi**) 2%
Zingiberis Rhizoma Recens (Fresh Ginger / **Sheng Jiang**) 2%

## Chinese Medical Actions

Expels exogenous wind-heat, drains heat from the interior, supplements qi and blood.

## Indications

Bitter taste in mouth
Boils
Bronchitis
Common cold, with high fever
Conjunctivitis
Constipation
Cough
Eyes, red and painful
Fever
Hives
Itching
Infection, viral
Influenza
Sinus infections, with fever
Skin rashes, hot
Sores, red, hot
Sties
Urination, dark, rough
Warts, flat

**Tongue:** Red at tip, with yellow coating.
**Pulse:** Rapid and flooding, rapid and wiry, or rapid and rolling.

## Contraindications

This formula is designed for acute conditions and is contraindicated for long-term use.

**Note:** In respiratory disorders with no exterior heat signs, such as simultaneous chills and fever, or aversion to wind or cold, **Mulberry & Lycium Formula** may be a more appropriate strategy.

# SIX GENTLEMEN FORMULA

**Six Gentlemen Formula** *(Liu Jun Zi Tang)*, also known as "Major Six Formula," is a classical Chinese formula used to supplement the qi. It is a combination of the "Four Gentleman Formula" for spleen qi deficiency with "Two-Cured Decoction," a formula to dry dampness and transform phlegm.

## Ingredients

Codonopsis Pilosae Radix (Codonopsis / **Dang Shen**) 19.7%
Poria (Poria, Hoelen, Tuckahoe / **Fu Ling**) 19.7%
Atractylodis Macrocephalae Rhizoma (White Atractylodes Rhizome/ **Bai Zhu**) 19.7%
Pinelliae Rhizoma Preparatum (Pinellia, ginger-cured / **Zhi Ban Xia**) 14.7%
Citri Reticulatae Pericarpium (Tangerine Peel / **Chen Pi**) 14.7%
Glycyrrhizae Radix (Chinese Licorice Root / **Gan Cao**) 11.5%

## Chinese Medical Actions

Supplements the qi, strengthens the spleen, transforms phlegm and dampness.

## Indications

Acid regurgitation
Appetite, loss of
Cough with thin white sputum
Diarrhea
Digestion, weak
Dizziness
Fatigue
Mental disorders from phlegm
Nausea
Nervous exhaustion
Shortness of breath
Vomiting

**Tongue:** Pale, slightly swollen.
**Pulse:** Weak, especially in the spleen position.

## Contraindications

The overuse of this formula can lead to dry mouth and excessive thirst. Unless used in conjunction with another appropriate formula, this formula should not be used in cases where there is deficiency heat, high fever, or irritability, thirst, and constipation.

# STASIS-TRANSFORMING FORMULA

**Stasis Transforming Formula** *(Dan Shen Hua Yu Pian)* is a modern formula for treating patterns of blood stasis. Since chronic blood stasis usually presents with qi stagnation, phlegm nodulation, heat-toxin, and/or spleen/kidney deficiency, this formula addresses each of these. Originally developed as a gynecology formula for endometriosis and dysmenorrhea, this formula may also be used for men's health, and for any long-term blood stasis disorder. Tang Kuei *(dang gui)*, cnidium *(chuan xiong)*, myrrh *(mo yao)*, sparganium *(san leng)*, zedoary *(e zhu)*, and salvia *(dan shen)* all move the blood. Myrrh *(mo yao)* relieves pain. Cyperus *(xiang fu)* regulates the qi and stops pain. Sargentodoxa *(hong teng)* and patrinia *(bai jiang cao)* clear heat, dispel toxin, and move the blood. Prunella *(xia ku cao)* clears heat and disperses nodules. Gleditsia thorn *(zao jiao ci)* discharges pus and moves the blood. Astragalus *(huang qi)* supports the spleen. Cinnamon bark *(rou gui)* warms the kidneys. Bupleurum *(chai hu)* and cimicifuga *(sheng ma)* raise yang qi.

## Ingredients

Salviae Miltiorrhizae Radix (Chinese Salvia Root / **Dan Shen**) 10%
Astragali Radix (Astragalus / **Huang Qi**) 9%
Sargentodoxae Caulis (Sargentodoxa Caulis / **Hong Teng**) 8%
Cyperi Rhizoma (Cyperus, Nut-Grass / **Xiang Fu**) 8%
Patriniae Herba (Patrinia, Snow Thistle / **Bai Jiang Cao**) 8%
Angelicae Sinensis Radix (Dong Quai, Tang Kuei / **Dang Gui**) 8%
Myrrha (Myrrh / **Mo Yao**) 8%
Sparganii Rhizoma (Sparganium, Bur-Reed Rhizome / **San Leng**) 8%
Curcumae Rhizoma (Zedoary Rhizome / **E Zhu**) 8%
Prunellae Spica (Prunella, Heal All, Self-Heal Spike / **Xia Ku Cao**) 6%
Gleditsiae Spina (Gleditsia Thorn / **Zao Jiao Ci**) 6%
Chuanxiong Rhizoma (Ligusticum Wallichii Rhizome / **Chuan Xiong**) 4%
Cinnamomi Cortex (Cassia Bark, Cinnamon Bark / **Rou Gui**) 3%
Bupleuri Radix (Bupleurum Root / **Chai Hu**) 3%
Cimicifugae Rhizoma (Chinese Cimicifuga / **Sheng Ma**) 3%

## Chinese Medical Actions

Moves blood, transforms stasis, disperses nodules, regulates qi, clears heat-toxin, eliminates dampness, alleviates pain, supports the spleen and kidneys.

## Indications

Abdominal pain
Amenorrhea
Constipation
Endometriosis
Endometritis
Fibromyalgia w/ blood stasis
Infertility, w/ blood stasis
Menopausal symptoms
Menstrual pain
Menstruation, irregular
Ovarian cysts
Pelvic Inflammatory Disease
Prostatitis, chronic, w/ blood stasis
Sexual dysfunction, male, w/ blood stasis and damp-heat
Uterine bleeding, dysfunctional

**Tongue:** Purple or dark red, with dark or purple spots.
**Pulse:** Deep, choppy, or wiry.

## Contraindications

DO NOT USE DURING PREGNANCY. Do not use in cases with heavy menstrual bleeding or any active hemorrhagic disorder.

# STOMACH-HARMONIZING FORMULA

**Stomach Harmonizing Formula** *(Jia Jian Bao He Wan)*. This modification of Harmony-Preserving Pills *(Bao He Wan)* is intended to treat acute upset of the digestive tract with belching, acid reflux, a full feeling in the stomach, bloating, nausea, a foul taste in the mouth, abdominal cramping, diarrhea, or constipation. Whether from overeating, poor food combining, weak digestion, or other factors such as emotional upset, an acute upset is often characterized by stagnation of qi and food and counterflow of stomach qi. Hawthorn fruit *(shan zha)*, leaven *(shen qu)*, and radish seed *(lai fu zi)* disperse food accumulation. Tangerine peel *(chen pi)*, melia *(chuan lian zi)*, pinellia *(zhi ban xia)*, and ginger *(sheng jiang)* rectify qi flow and direct qi downward. White peony *(bai shao)* and poria *(fu ling)* harmonize the spleen and liver. Coptis *(huang lian)* and forsythia *(lian qiao)* clear heat that arises from digestive stagnation. This formula can relieve the discomfort of overeating and the stagnation of damp-heat associated with hangover from drinking too much alcohol.

## Ingredients

Crataegi Fructus (Chinese Hawthorn Fruit / **Shan Zha**) 18%
Paeoniae Radix, alba (Chinese White Peony / **Bai Shao**) 12%
Massa Fermentata (Fermented Leaven / **Shen Qu**) 12%
Forsythiae Fructus (Forsythia Fruit / **Lian Qiao**) 12%
Pinelliae Rhizoma Preparatum (Pinellia, ginger-cured / **Zhi Ban Xia**) 10%
Poria (Poria, Hoelen, Tuckahoe / **Fu Ling**) 10%
Citri Reticulatae Pericarpium (Tangerine Peel / **Chen Pi**) 7%
Toosendan Fructus (Melia Fruit, Chinaberry / **Chuan Lian Zi**) 5%
Zingiberis Rhizoma Recens (Fresh Ginger / **Sheng Jiang**) 5%
Raphani Semen (Radish Seed / **Lai Fu Zi**) 5%
Coptidis Rhizoma (Coptis / **Huang Lian**) 4%

## Chinese Medical Actions

Disperses accumulation and stagnation of food, clears heat, directs qi downward, rectifies qi flow, harmonizes the stomach and intestines.

| Indications | |
|---|---|
| Abdominal cramping | Constipation |
| Abdominal distension, acute | Diarrhea |
| Acid reflux, acute | Flatulence |
| Appetite reduced | Food stagnation |
| Bad breath | Hangover |
| Belching of sour, foul-tasting fluid | Nausea or vomiting |

**Tongue:** Thick, with yellow coating. **Pulse:** Slippery, possibly rapid.

**Note:** For short-term use only. Once food stagnation is relieved, a formula to supplement the spleen such as **Six Gentlemen Formula** is usually appropriate. If this pattern recurs frequently, the root disharmony must be addressed by other formulas such as **Earth Harmonizing Formula**, **Bupleurum & Tang Kuei Formula**, or **Free & Easy Wanderer Plus**.

# TANG KUEI & PEONY FORMULA

**Tang Kuei & Peony Formula** (*Dang Gui Shao Yao San)* is a classical formula for supplementing the blood. It is an excellent tonic for pregnancy and post-partum. It is a balanced, mild formula that can be used long-term as a women's tonic in cases where there is liver blood deficiency and spleen deficiency with stagnation from dampness.

## Ingredients

Paeoniae Radix, alba (Chinese White Peony / **Bai Shao**) 25%
Poria (Poria, Hoelen, Tuckahoe / **Fu Ling**) 16.6%
Atractylodis Macrocephalae Rhizoma (White Atractylodes Rhizome / **Bai Zhu**) 16.6%
Alismatis Rhizoma (Asian Water Plantain / **Ze Xie**) 16.6%
Angelicae Sinensis Radix (Dong Quai, Tang Kuei / **Dang Gui**) 12.6%
Chuanxiong Rhizoma (Ligusticum Wallichii Rhizome / **Chuan Xiong**) 12.6%

## Chinese Medical Actions

Builds and nourishes blood, increases vitality, strengthens the spleen, spreads liver qi, resolves dampness.

## Indications

Abdominal pain
Back weakness and numbness
Back pain (lower)
Edema
Hemorrhoids
Hypotension
Leg weakness
Menstrual pain
Menstruation, irregular
Miscarriage, habitual or threatened
Nephritis, chronic
Pelvic Inflammatory Disease
Post-partum weakness
Pregnancy, weakness during
Premenstrual syndrome
Toxemia of pregnancy
Urination, difficult

**Tongue:** Pale, may be normal.
**Pulse:** Slightly slippery, may be wiry.

# TANG KUEI & SALVIA FORMULA

**Tang Kuei & Salvia Formula** *(Jia Wei Si Wu Tang)* is an augmentation of the classical formula known as "Four-Substance Decoction" *(Si Wu Tang)* or "Tang Kuei Four," used for building blood. Four-Substance Decoction is the primary formula used for addressing chronic blood deficiency. Polygonum *(he shou wu)* has been added to nourish the blood and strengthen the liver. Salvia *(dan shen)* has been included to augment the formula's ability to invigorate or move the blood, thereby addressing the blood stasis often found in chronic blood deficiency.

## Ingredients

Rehmanniae Radix Preparata (Cured Rehmannia Root / **Shu Di Huang**) 25.9%
Paeoniae Radix, alba (Chinese White Peony / **Bai Shao**) 18.5%
Polygoni Multiflori Radix Preparata (Polygonum Root, Fo Ti / **Zhi He Shou Wu**) 18.5%
Angelicae Sinensis Radix (Dong Quai, Tang Kuei / **Dang Gui**) 14.8%
Salviae Miltiorrhizae Radix (Chinese Salvia Root / **Dan Shen**) 14.8%
Chuanxiong Rhizoma (Ligusticum Wallichii Rhizome / **Chuan Xiong**) 7.5%

## Chinese Medical Actions

Supplements and moves blood, nourishes the liver.

## Indications

Abdominal masses, fixed
Abdominal pain
Amenorrhea
Anemia
Complexion, lusterless
Constipation
Dizziness
Dry skin
Fatigue
Hair, dry and brittle
Hives
Itching
Lactation, insufficient
Menstrual pain
Menstruation, irregular
Nails, brittle
Ovulation, bleeding during
Palpitation
Post-menstrual fatigue
Post-partum fatigue
Umbilical pain
Uterine bleeding, dysfunctional
Vision, blurred or spots in
Weakness, generalized

**Tongue**: Pale.
**Pulse:** Thin, wiry and/or choppy.

## Contraindications

Not for severe cases of blood deficiency with severe weakness, labored breathing, and diarrhea. In cases with deficiency of spleen yang with loose stools, add an appropriate formula to strengthen the spleen, such as **Six Gentlemen Formula**, **Sea of Qi Formula** or **Ginseng & Astragalus Formula.**

# TANG KUEI & TRIBULUS FORMULA

**Tang Kuei & Tribulus Formula** *(Dang Gui Yin Zi)* is from the *Teachings of Zhu Dan-Xi* and is ideal for skin disorders such as eczema, hives, dermatitis, and psoriasis arising from blood deficiency. Angelica *(dang gui)* and ligusticum *(chuan xiong)* nourish and invigorate the blood. Rehmannia *(sheng di)* cools the blood and moistens dryness. Polygonum *(zhi he shou wu)* and white peony *(bai shao)* nourish the blood, especially liver blood. Tribulus *(bai ji li)*, schizonepeta *(jing jie)*, and siler (*fang feng*) dispel wind and relieve itching. Spirodela *(fu ping)* has been added to vent rashes as well as stop itching. Astragalus *(huang qi)* tonifies the spleen and *wei* (protective) qi. Licorice *(gan cao)* supports the qi, as well as slightly clearing heat and eliminating toxins. This formula is especially good for the elderly or physically weak persons and is suitable for long-term use.

## Ingredients

Tribuli Fructus (Tribulus, Puncture-Vine Fruit, Caltrop Fruit / **Bai Ji Li**) 15%
Rehmanniae Radix (Rehmannia Root, unprocessed / **Sheng Di Huang**) 11%
Paeoniae Radix, alba (Chinese White Peony / **Bai Shao**) 11%
Polygoni Multiflori Radix Preparata (Polygonum Root, Fo Ti / **Zhi He Shou Wu**) 10%
Schizonepetae Herba (Schizonepeta / **Jing Jie**) 10%
Saposhnikoviae Radix (Siler / **Fang Feng**) 10%
Angelicae Sinensis Radix (Dong Quai, Tang Kuei / **Dang Gui**) 8%
Paeoniae Radix, rubra (Chinese Red Peony / **Chi Shao**) 7%
Astragali Radix (Astragalus / **Huang Qi**) 5%
Chuanxiong Rhizoma (Ligusticum Wallichii Rhizome / **Chuan Xiong**) 5%
Glycyrrhizae Radix (Chinese Licorice Root / **Gan Cao**) 4%
Spirodelae Herba (Spirodela / **Fu Ping**) 4%

## Chinese Medical Actions

Nourishes blood, moistens blood dryness, dispels wind, relieves itching.

## Indications

| | |
|---|---|
| Dermatitis | Skin dry and itchy due to blood deficiency and blood dryness |
| Eczema | Skin rash, red with itching |
| Hives | |
| Psoriasis | |

**Tongue:** Pale, with a dry coating, may have red tip.
**Pulse:** Thin, weak, and deep.

## Contraindications

DO NOT USE DURING PREGNANCY. In some cases it may be necessary initially to combine this formula with another formula to treat the root symptoms. For instance, if there is a red, itching rash due to liver qi stagnation with heat, combine with the **Free & Easy Wanderer Plus**. As the symptoms improve, combine with a more constitutional formula such as the **Bupleurum & Tang Kuei Formula**.

# TIEH TA FORMULA

**Tieh Ta Formula** *(Die Da Wan)* is based on traditional formulas used in the martial arts for traumatic injury. It moves the qi and blood, reduces pain and swelling, and aids in the rapid resolution of many types of injury. It is an excellent formula to keep in the household medicine chest.

## Ingredients

Notoginseng Radix (Tienqi Ginseng, Pseudoginseng Root / **San Qi, Tian Qi**) 14.35%
Angelicae Sinensis Radix (Dong Quai, Tang Kuei / **Dang Gui**) 14.35%
Curcumae Radix (Turmeric, Curcuma Tuber / **Yu Jin**) 9.5%
Amomi Fructus Rotundus (Chinese Amomum / **Bai Dou Kou**) 9.5%
Rhei Radix et Rhizoma (Chinese Rhubarb / **Da Huang**) 9.5%
Carthami Flos (Safflower, Carthamus Flower / **Hong Hua**) 7.1%
Achyranthis Bidentatae Radix (Achyranthes / **Huai Niu Xi**) 7.1%
Dipsaci Radix (Japanese Teasel Root, Dipsacus / **Xu Duan**) 7.1%
Drynariae Rhizoma (Drynaria Rhizome / **Gu Sui Bu**) 7.1%
Cyperi Rhizoma (Cyperus, Nut-Grass / **Xiang Fu**) 4.8%
Olibanum (Frankincense / **Ru Xiang**) 4.8%
Myrrha (Myrrh / **Mo Yao**) 4.8%

## Chinese Medical Actions

Moves blood, transforms blood stasis, reduces swelling, alleviates pain.

## Indications

| | |
|---|---|
| Bruises | Pain and distension from injury |
| Fractures or broken bones | Post-operative pain |
| Joint dislocations | Sports injury |
| Ligaments, torn | Sprains |
| Muscle strains | Traumatic injury |

## Contraindications

DO NOT USE DURING PREGNANCY OR WHILE NURSING.

# TRAUMA 1 FORMULA

**Trauma 1 Formula** *(Die Da 1 Hao Fang)* is for the first stage of traumatic injury. Immediately after a trauma, the site of the injury experiences swelling, heat, and pain. Modern medicine calls this inflammation and sees it as the body's reaction to trauma. The treatment principle for this stage of trauma is to clear heat from inflammation, reduce swelling so that healing is not hindered, relieve pain, and quicken blood movement so that stasis is minimized. This formula uses herbs such as honeysuckle *(jin yin hua)* to clear heat and resolve toxin, and forsythia *(lian qiao)* to disperse accumulation and swelling combined with agents to move blood and relieve pain. This is Chinese medicine's approach to helping the body get rid of damaged tissue and rebuild the tissue injured by trauma.

## Ingredients

Persicae Semen (Peach Kernel, Persica Seed / **Tao Ren**) 12%
Forsythiae Fructus (Forsythia Fruit / **Lian Qiao**) 12%
Lonicerae Flos (Japanese Honeysuckle Flower / **Jin Yin Hua**) 12%
Carthami Flos (Safflower, Carthamus Flower / **Hong Hua**) 10%
Olibanum (Frankincense / **Ru Xiang**) 9%
Myrrha (Myrrh / **Mo Yao**) 9%
Scutellariae Radix (Chinese Scullcap, Scutellaria, Scute / **Huang Qin**) 8%
Angelicae Sinensis Radix (Dong Quai, Tang Kuei / **Dang Gui**) 8%
Bupleuri Radix (Bupleurum Root / **Chai Hu**) 8%
Rhei Radix et Rhizoma (Chinese Rhubarb / **Da Huang**) 5%
Angelicae Dahuricae Radix (Purple Angelica / **Bai Zhi**) 4%
Glycyrrhizae Radix (Chinese Licorice Root / **Gan Cao**) 3%

## Chinese Medical Actions

Clears heat, resolves toxin, relieves pain, moves blood, dispels stasis.

## Indications

Bruises
Cartilage damage
Fractures or broken bones
Jammed fingers or toes
Ligaments or tendons, torn
Sprains
Traumatic injury (first stage) with heat, swelling, and pain

## Contraindications

DO NOT USE DURING PREGNANCY OR WHILE NURSING.

**Note:** The first stage of trauma can last from several hours to a week or so depending on the severity of the injury. As long as redness, heat, and swelling exist, one can assume that the injury is still in the first stage of recovery.

# TRAUMA 2 FORMULA

**Trauma 2 Formula** *(Die Da 2 Hao Fang)* is intended to treat the second stage of trauma. After the inflammation and swelling associated with first-stage trauma have receded, the area of the trauma experiences stasis of the blood that left the vessels at the time of the initial trauma. This, combined with congestion of fluids and qi at the site, causes stiffness and pain and sets the stage for the invasion of wind and dampness. The formula aims to dispel blood stasis, relieve pain, dispel wind and dampness, and clear any heat remaining from the body's inflammatory response to the trauma. It can be used for any second stage trauma when bleeding is not a factor.

## Ingredients

Angelicae Sinensis Radix (Dong Quai, Tang Kuei / **Dang Gui**) 9%
Olibanum (Frankincense / **Ru Xiang**) 9%
Myrrha (Myrrh / **Mo Yao**) 9%
Cyathulae Radix (Cyathula Root / **Chuan Niu Xi**) 9%
Saposhnikoviae Radix (Siler / **Fang Feng**) 9%
Spatholobi Caulis (Spatholobus / **Ji Xue Teng**) 9%
Paeoniae Radix, rubra (Chinese Red Peony / **Chi Shao**) 9%
Poria (Poria, Hoelen, Tuckahoe / **Fu Ling**) 8%
Carthami Flos (Safflower, Carthamus Flower / **Hong Hua**) 7%
Sappan Lignum (Sappanwood / **Su Mu**) 6%
Notoginseng Radix (Tienqi Ginseng, Pseudoginseng Root / **San Qi, Tian Qi**) 5%
Angelicae Dahuricae Radix (Purple Angelica / **Bai Zhi**) 4%
Rhei Radix et Rhizoma (Chinese Rhubarb / **Da Huang**) 4%
Glycyrrhizae Radix (Chinese Licorice Root / **Gan Cao**) 3%

## Chinese Medical Actions

Moves blood, dispels stasis, relieves pain, dispels wind and dampness, clears heat.

## Indications

| | |
|---|---|
| Bruises | Ligaments or tendons, torn |
| Cartilage damage | Sprains |
| Fractures or broken bones | Traumatic injury (second stage) w/ stiffness and pain |
| Jammed fingers or toes | |

## Contraindications

DO NOT USE DURING PREGNANCY OR WHILE NURSING.

**Note:** Second-stage trauma can start from two days to ten days after the injury and could last from several days to several weeks. The timeframe depends on the extent of the injury and the healing capacity of the patient.

# TRUE YIN FORMULA

**True Yin Formula** *(Zuo Gui Jia Er Zhi Wan)* is a combination of two classical Chinese formulas: Restore the Left Kidney Decoction *(Zuo Gui Wan)* and the Two Ultimate Pill *(Er Zhi Wan)*. The left kidney is considered by some texts to be the root of the true or source yin. Yin energy allows us the ability to be calm, quiet, receptive and stable. This formula is excellent for treating deficiency of yin, which arises from the demands and stresses of modern life or from excessive sexual activity. It directly supplements the yin of the liver and kidneys, the reservoir of yin for the entire body. **True Yin Formula** is commonly combined with formulas that could damage yin, as a yin protector.

## Ingredients

Rehmanniae Radix Preparata (Cured Rehmannia Root / **Shu Di Huang**) 20.2%
Ligustri Lucidi Fructus (Ligustrum, Privet Fruit / **Nu Zhen Zi**) 12.7%
Ecliptae Herba (Eclipta / **Han Lian Cao**) 12.7%
Dioscoreae Rhizoma (Chinese Yam / **Shan Yao**) 10.1%
Lycii Fructus (Lycium Fruit, Chinese Wolfberry / **Gou Qi Zi**) 10.1%
Poria (Poria, Hoelen, Tuckahoe / **Fu Ling**) 10.1%
Corni Fructus (Asiatic Dogwood Fruit, Cornelian Cherry / **Shan Zhu Yu**) 10.1%
Schisandrae Fructus (Schisandra Fruit / **Wu Wei Zi**) 8.9%
Glycyrrhizae Radix Preparata (Chinese Licorice Root, honey-fried / **Zhi Gan Cao**) 5.1%

## Chinese Medical Actions

Nourishes the yin, benefits and supplements the liver and kidneys.

## Indications

Back weakness and soreness
Dizziness
Dream-disturbed sleep
Dry mouth
Hair, premature graying
Hair loss
Hearing loss
Insomnia
Knees, weak
Legs, weak
Memory, poor
Night sweats
Spontaneous emissions
Thirst
Throat, dry
Vision, blurred or spots in

**Tongue:** Peeled, shiny.
**Pulse:** Thin, rapid.

## Contraindications

This formula is for cases of yin deficiency without signs of fire. In cases with fire, use **Rehmannia & Scrophularia Formula** instead. With spleen or stomach deficiency, supplement with an appropriate formula.

# TWO IMMORTALS FORMULA

**Two Immortals Formula** *(Jia Jian Er Xian Tang)* is a modification of a traditional formula *(Er Xian Tang)* developed to treat problems common in menopause. These problems are associated with a deficiency of the *ren* and *chong* vessels and a decline of the energy of the kidney, with a flaring up of fire. This produces such symptoms as hypertension, hot flashes, sweating, fatigue, insomnia and emotional imbalances.

## Ingredients

Salviae Miltiorrhizae Radix (Chinese Salvia Root / **Dan Shen**) 11.7%
Polygoni Multiflori Radix Preparata (Polygonum Root, Fo Ti / **Zhi He Shou Wu**) 11.7%
Epimedii Herba (Epimedium / **Yin Yang Huo**) 9.4%
Moutan Cortex (Tree Peony Root Bark / **Mu Dan Pi**) 9.4%
Angelicae Sinensis Radix (Dong Quai, Tang Kuei / **Dang Gui**) 9.4%
Morindae Officinalis Radix (Morinda / **Ba Ji Tian**) 9.4%
Cistanches Herba (Broomrape, Cistanches / **Rou Cong Rong**) 9.4%
Cuscutae Semen (Chinese Dodder Seed, Chinese Cuscuta / **Tu Si Zi**) 7.75%
Poria (Poria, Hoelen, Tuckahoe / **Fu Ling**) 7.75%
Curculiginis Rhizoma (Curculigo Rhizome / **Xian Mao**) 4.7%
Anemarrhenae Rhizoma (Anemarrhena Rhizome / **Zhi Mu**) 4.7%
Phellodendri Cortex (Phellodendron Bark / **Huang Bai**) 4.7%

## Chinese Medical Actions

Replenishes kidney yin and yang, regulates the *ren* and *chong* vessels, harmonizes the blood, drains fire.

## Indications

Anxiety
Amenorrhea
Depression
Dizziness
Fatigue
Hot flashes
Hypertension, menopausal
Infertility
Insomnia
Irritability
Melancholy, excessive
Night sweats
Palpitation
Psoriasis, improves in pregnancy, worse after childbirth
Urinary tract infection, chronic
Urination, frequent

**Tongue:** Pale, with thin coating; may be swollen, with teeth marks.
**Pulse:** Thready, rapid.

# VIOLA CLEAR FIRE FORMULA

**Viola Clear Fire Formula** *(Di Ding Qing Huo Pian)*. The herbs in this formula, according to modern pharmacological and clinical research, have inhibitory effects against many viruses, bacteria, and fungi. In the years that this formula was tested clinically, it was found effective against a variety of infections, especially respiratory infections. It is safe for long-term use in the management or elimination of deep-seated or stubborn viruses such as Epstein-Barr, HIV, and herpes.

## Ingredients

Hedyotis Diffusae Herba (Hedyotis, Oldenlandia / **Bai Hua She She Cao**) 18%
Houttuyniae Herba (Houttuynia / **Yu Xing Cao**) 16%
Violae Herba (Viola, Tokyo Violet / **Zi Hua Di Ding**) 12%
Isatidis Folium (Isatis Leaf, Indigo Woad Leaf / **Da Qing Ye**) 8%
Isatidis seu Baphicacanthis Radix (Isatis Root / **Ban Lan Gen**) 8%
Andrographitis Herba (Andrographis / **Chuan Xin Lian**) 8%
Lonicerae Flos (Japanese Honeysuckle Flower / **Jin Yin Hua**) 7%
Prunellae Spica (Prunella, Heal All, Self-Heal Spike / **Xia Ku Cao**) 6%
Forsythiae Fructus (Forsythia Fruit / **Lian Qiao**) 6%
Citri Reticulatae Pericarpium (Tangerine Peel / **Chen Pi**) 4%
Glycyrrhizae Radix (Chinese Licorice Root / **Gan Cao**) 4%
Coptidis Rhizoma (Coptis / **Huang Lian**) 3%

## Chinese Medical Actions

Clears and quells fire, clears heat-toxin, cools the blood.

## Indications

AIDS/HIV heat-toxin
Bronchitis
Chicken pox
Cough
Diarrhea from damp-heat
Fever
Genital sores
Herpes, any type
Kidney infection
Laryngitis
Lymph nodes, enlarged
Mononucleosis
Pneumonia
Respiratory infection
Sinus infection
Strep throat
Throat, sore
Tonsillitis
Urinary tract infection

**Tongue:** Red.
**Pulse:** Rapid.

## Contraindications

Do not use in the absence of heat.

**Dosage:** Can range according to the symptoms and the intensity. Patients on higher doses should be monitored and should decrease dose as symptoms abate.

**Note:** Can be used safely over a long period of time. Can be combined with an appropriate tonic formula, ideally, **Astragalus & Ligustrum Formula**.

**Viola Clear Fire Formula,** in combination with **Minor Bupleurum Formula,** have been found to be effective in the treatment of mononucleosis.

# VITAL TREASURE FORMULA

**Vital Treasure Formula** *(Zhen Bao Fang)* is designed to support the yang aspects of male function. It is especially appropriate as men age and the yang qi naturally declines. Since the kidney is the source of all yang, the primary herbs in this formula are herbs that supplement the yang of the kidney: epimedium *(yin yang huo)*, cuscuta *(tu si zi)*, morinda *(ba ji tian)* and psoralea *(bu gu zhi)*. Ginseng *(ren shen)* is used to supplement the central qi. Ophiopogon *(mai men dong)* and broussonetia *(chu shi zi)* are yin-supplementing herbs that help to prevent over-heating from yang supplementation. White peony *(bai shao)* is used to supplement the blood and curcuma *(yu jin)* invigorates and cools liver blood. Rhodiola *(hong jing tian)* invigorates blood and has been shown to increase arterial oxygen. Plantago *(che qian zi)* guides excess heat out of the body though the urinary bladder. These herbs make this an excellent yang support for men while also supporting qi and yin and preventing the excessive build-up of fire.

## Ingredients

Epimedii Herba (Epimedium / **Yin Yang Huo**) 12%
Cuscutae Semen (Chinese Dodder Seed, Chinese Cuscuta / **Tu Si Zi**) 12%
Morindae Officinalis Radix (Morinda / **Ba Ji Tian**) 12%
Psoraleae Fructus (Psoralea Fruit / **Bu Gu Zhi**) 10%
Rhodiola Herba (Rhodiola / **Hong Jing Tian**) 10%
Ophiopogonis Radix (Ophiopogon Tuber / **Mai Men Dong**) 8%
Paeoniae Radix, alba (Chinese White Peony / **Bai Shao**) 8%
Ginseng Radix (Asian Ginseng Root / **Ren Shen**) 8%
Broussonetiae Fructus (Broussonetia Fruit / **Chu Shi Zi**) 8%
Curcumae Radix (Turmeric, Curcuma Tuber / **Yu Jin**) 8%
Plantaginis Semen (Asian Plantain Seed, Plantago Seed / **Che Qian Zi**) 4%

## Chinese Medical Actions

Supplements kidney yang, supplements qi and yin, invigorates and supplements liver blood.

## Indications

Circulation, poor
Cold limbs
Fatigue
Hypothyroidism
Hypotension
Impotence
Premature ejaculation
Sexual dysfunction, male
Weakness, in lower back and knees

## Contraindications

Do not take this formula when signs of heat are present (red tongue and rapid pulse). WOMEN SHOULD NOT TAKE THIS FORMULA DURING PREGNANCY.

# WOMEN'S PRECIOUS FORMULA

**Women's Precious Formula** *(Ba Zhen Tang)* is a modification of Motherwort Eight Precious Pills—leonurus (motherwort), plus a combination of Four Gentlemen (a qi-supplementing formula) with the Soup of Four Things (a blood-supplementing formula). Four additional herbs, useful for life in modern times, have been added: polygonum *(zhi he shou wu)* and mori *(sang shen)* to nourish essence; tangerine peel *(chen pi)* to move the qi and prevent the qi stagnation that can occur from taking tonic formulas; and fresh ginger *(sheng jiang)* to nourish the spleen and stomach and aid digestion. This formula can be used by both men and women for qi and blood deficiency. It is an effective aid in post-partum recovery.

## Ingredients

Codonopsis Pilosae Radix (Codonopsis / **Dang Shen**) 11.3%
Rehmanniae Radix Preparata (Cured Rehmannia Root / **Shu Di Huang**) 11.3%
Atractylodis Macrocephalae Rhizoma (White Atractylodes Rhizome / **Bai Zhu**) 9%
Poria (Poria, Hoelen, Tuckahoe / **Fu Ling**) 9%
Angelicae Sinensis Radix (Dong Quai, Tang Kuei / **Dang Gui**) 9%
Paeoniae Radix, alba (Chinese White Peony / **Bai Shao**) 9%
Polygoni Multiflori Radix Preparata (Polygonum Root, Fo Ti / **Zhi He Shou Wu**) 9%
Chuanxiong Rhizoma (Ligusticum Wallichii Rhizome / **Chuan Xiong**) 6%
Mori Fructus (White Mulberry Fruit / **Sang Shen**) 6%
Leonuri Herba (Chinese Motherwort / **Yi Mu Cao**) 5.3%
Citri Reticulatae Pericarpium (Tangerine Peel / **Chen Pi**) 5.3%
Zingiberis Rhizoma Recens (Fresh Ginger / **Sheng Jiang**) 5.3%
Glycyrrhizae Radix (Chinese Licorice Root / **Gan Cao**) 4.5%

## Chinese Medical Actions

Builds and nourishes qi and blood, supplements yin and essence, moves blood and qi, drains damp, strengthens stomach and spleen.

## Indications

Abdominal distension
Appetite disorders
Back soreness, lower
Breast distension
Complexion, pale
Dizziness
Fatigue
Labor, difficult
Lactation, insufficient
Menarche, late
Menstrual pain
Menstruation, irregular or scanty
Miscarriage, habitual
Palpitation
Post-partum recovery
Premenstrual abdominal pain
Skin rash or dryness w/ blood *xu*
Uterine bleeding, dysfunctional
Vaginal discharge
Weakness

**Tongue:** Pale with white coating. **Pulse:** Thin, weak.

## Contraindications

DO NOT USE DURING PREGNANCY. (Use **Tang Kuei & Peony Formula** instead.) Modify to smaller doses if diarrhea or stomach upset occur. Do not use in cases with heat from yin deficiency.

# WU HUA FORMULA

**Wu Hua Formula** *(Wu Hua Tang)* is a Chinese formula used to treat dysentery, diarrhea, gastrointestinal inflammation, intestinal parasites, and skin disorders from heat in the blood. It is an excellent formula to take while traveling in places where dysentery or gastrointestinal disorders are prevalent.

## Ingredients

Lonicerae Flos (Japanese Honeysuckle Flower / **Jin Yin Hua**) 40%
Hibisci Flos (Hibiscus Flower / **Mu Jin Hua**) 20%
Celosiae Cristatae Flos (Cockscomb Flower / **Ji Guan Hua**) 20%
Magnoliae Officinalis Flos (Magnolia Flower / **Hou Po Hua**) 10%
Puerariae Flos (Pueraria Flower / **Ge Hua**) 10%

## Chinese Medical Actions

Removes damp-heat, clears heat-toxin, cools blood, promotes urination.

## Indications

- Appendicitis
- Blood in the stool
- Boils
- Diarrhea
- Dysentery
- Eczema
- Furuncle
- Gastrointestinal inflammation
- Hemorrhoids
- Hives
- Intestinal abscess
- Parasites, intestinal
- Rectal bleeding with heat-toxin
- Skin rash

**Tongue:** Red, or with red spots.
**Pulse:** Rapid, big.

## Contraindications

Do not take in cases of deficiency cold.

# XANTHIUM & MAGNOLIA FORMULA

**Xanthium & Magnolia Formula** *(Jia Wei Xin Yi San)* is a modified combination of *Cang Er Zi San* and *Xin Yi San* to treat severe nasal congestion with constant or copious, clear nasal discharge or post-nasal drip. Tetrapanax *(tong cao)* has been added to assist in guiding fluids downward. Red Peony *(chi shao)* has been added to invigorate blood and reduce swelling. These two herbs also moderate the warmth of the other herbs in the formula. Ideally, **Xanthium & Magnolia Formula** should be used for a short duration due to the acrid and warm nature of the formula. It is important that the underlying constitutional issues be addressed, as these symptoms could be due to chronic deficiency of the kidney, lung, or spleen.

## Ingredients

Angelicae Dahuricae Radix (Purple Angelica / **Bai Zhi**) 30%.
Xanthii Fructus (Xanthium Fruit, Siberian Cocklebur / **Cang Er Zi**) 12%
Magnoliae Flos (Magnolia Flower / **Xin Yi Hua**) 12%
Paeoniae Radix, rubra (Chinese Red Peony / **Chi Shao**) 10%
Ligustici Rhizoma (Chinese Lovage, Ligusticum / **Gao Ben**) 8%
Chuanxiong Rhizoma (Ligusticum Wallichii Rhizome / **Chuan Xiong**) 8%
Tetrapanacis Medulla (Tetrapanax, Rice Paper Plant Pith / **Tong Cao**) 6%
Puerariae Radix (Kudzu Root, Pueraria / **Ge Gen**) 6%
Glycyrrhizae Radix (Chinese Licorice Root / **Gan Cao**) 4%
Camelliae Folium (Green Tea Leaf / **Lu Cha**) 4%

## Chinese Medical Actions

Dispels wind, dries dampness, and frees the nasal passages.

## Indications

- Allergies
- Earaches
- Headache, from wind-cold
- Post-nasal drip
- Rhinitis, acute or chronic
- Sinus congestion and pain
- Sinus discharge, clear and profuse or persistent
- Sinus inflammation, acute or chronic
- Smell, loss of

**Tongue:** Normal, or may have a thick, white coating.
**Pulse:** May be floating or slippery.

## Contraindications

DO NOT USE DURING PREGNANCY.

# XANTHIUM NASAL FORMULA

**Xanthium Nasal Formula** *(Jia Wei Cang Er Pian)* is a modification of Xanthium Combination *(Cang Er Zi San)* for treating heat and phlegm in the upper burner and head, with congestion of the sinuses and nasal passages. This type of condition is generally acute and can be the result of either an exterior invasion or an internal disharmony. The formula centers on clearing heat and transforming dampness. Scutellaria *(huang qin)* clears heat in the upper burner, red peony *(chi shao)* cools blood and also moves blood in the nasal passages. Pueraria *(ge gen)* clears heat and guides the formula to the upper body. Xanthium *(cang er zi),* angelica *(bai zhi),* and magnolia *(xin yi hua)* dry dampness, dispel turbidity, and open the nasal passages. Mint *(bo he)* helps with this latter function and also clears heat pathogens that linger in the exterior. Ilicis *(ku ding cha)* clears heat, resolves toxin, and leads the herbs to the head.

## Ingredients

Scutellariae Radix (Chinese Scullcap, Scutellaria, Scute / **Huang Qin**) 20%
Paeoniae Radix, rubra (Chinese Red Peony / **Chi Shao**) 15%
Xanthii Fructus (Xanthium Fruit, Siberian Cocklebur / **Cang Er Zi**) 13%
Angelicae Dahuricae Radix (Purple Angelica / **Bai Zhi**) 13%
Magnoliae Flos (Magnolia Flower / **Xin Yi Hua**) 13%
Menthae Haplocalysis Herba (Chinese Mint / **Bo He**) 10%
Ilicis Folium (Ilicis Leaf **/ Ku Ding Cha**) 10%
Puerariae Radix (Kudzu Root, Pueraria / **Ge Gen**) 6%

## Chinese Medical Actions

Clears heat, resolves toxin, moves and cools blood, transforms phlegm, dries dampness and frees the nasal passages.

## Indications

Allergies
Feeling of pressure in head
Headache or sinus pain
Sinus congestion
Sinus discharge, yellow or green
Sinus infection, acute

**Tongue:** Yellow coating.
**Pulse:** Rapid.

## Contraindications

This formula is too drying for those with pronounced yin deficiency. It is also not appropriate for long-term use to treat chronic conditions, although it may be applied to acute infections related to long-term sinus disorders.

# YIN CHIAO FORMULA

**Yin Chiao Formula** *(Yin Qiao San)* also known as "Honeysuckle and Forsythia" is a popular Chinese formula used for treating invasion by wind-heat. It is very effective when taken at the onset of common cold or flu and in cases where the patient has a sore throat, fever, or signs of external heat.

## Ingredients

Lonicerae Flos (Japanese Honeysuckle Flower / **Jin Yin Hua**) 15.6%
Forsythiae Fructus (Forsythia Fruit / **Lian Qiao**) 15.6%
Phragmitis Rhizoma (Phragmites, Common Reed Rhizome / **Lu Gen**) 15.6%
Arctii Fructus (Arctium, Burdock Fruit / **Niu Bang Zi**) 12.4%
Schizonepetae Herba (Schizonepeta / **Jing Jie**) 9.3%
Platycodi Radix (Platycodon Root, Balloon Flower Root / **Jie Geng**) 6.3%
Menthae Haplocalysis Herba (Chinese Mint / **Bo He**) 6.3%
Sojae Semen Preparatum (Prepared Soybean / **Dan Dou Chi**) 6.3%
Lophatheri Herba (Lophatherum / **Dan Zhu Ye**) 6.3%
Glycyrrhizae Radix (Chinese Licorice Root / **Gan Cao**) 6.3%

## Chinese Medical Actions

Expels wind-heat from the exterior, clears heat, relieves toxicity.

## Indications

Body aches
Chicken pox
Common cold
Conjunctivitis
Cough
Fever, with or without chills
Gastritis, acute
Headache from wind-heat
Hives
Influenza
Itching from wind-heat
Lymph nodes, enlarged
Measles
Neck stiffness
Respiratory infections, upper
Shoulders, sore
Sinus congestion
Throat, sore

**Tongue:** White or yellow coating, may have red tip.
**Pulse:** Rapid, floating.

**Note:** This formula is most effective when taken during the early stages of the symptoms. The dose can be increased to every 3 hours during the first day of the symptoms, and then taken every 4-5 hours as needed. Some imported versions of this formula contain sugar, caffeine, and western drugs.

# YIN VALEY FORMULA

**Yin Valley Formula** *(Yin Gu Fang)* treats a variety of gynecological conditions presenting with yin deficiency, dryness, and heat, including cervical dysplasia, vaginal irritation or discharge, and abnormal uterine bleeding. Ophiopogon *(mai men dong)*, lycium *(gou qi zi)*, and polygonatum *(yu zhu)* moisten and nourish the liver and kidney yin. Eclipta *(han lian cao)* cools, nourishes yin, and stops bleeding. Pseudostellaria *(tai zi shen)* strengthens the spleen and generates fluids. Solanum *(long kui)*, phellodendron *(huang bai)*, lonicera *(jin yin hua)*, sargentodoxa *(hong teng)*, and oldenlandia *(bai hua she she cao)* clear heat and toxin, and are effective in treating the human pappilomavirus (HPV) infection that is often associated with cervical cancer. Solanum *(long kui)* and oldenlandia *(bai hua she she cao)* are anti-neoplastic herbs, as is zedoary *(e zhu)*, which is also used to invigorate and enliven where dryness and congestion has led to poor blood circulation and unhealthy tissues.

## Ingredients

Solani Nigri Herba (Black Solanum / **Long Kui**) 12%
Pseudostellariae Radix (Pseudostellaria Root / **Tai Zi Shen**) 11%
Hedyotis Diffusae Herba (Hedyotis, Oldenlandia / **Bai Hua She She Cao**) 11%
Ophiopogonis Radix (Ophiopogon Tuber / **Mai Men Dong**) 10%
Lonicerae Flos (Japanese Honeysuckle Flower / **Jin Yin Hua**) 10%
Polygonati Odorati Rhizoma (Aromatic Solomon's Seal / **Yu Zhu**) 9%
Phellodendri Cortex (Phellodendron Bark / **Huang Bai**) 9%
Lycii Fructus (Lycium Fruit, Chinese Wolfberry / **Gou Qi Zi**) 9%
Ecliptae Herba (Eclipta / **Han Lian Cao**) 8%
Sargentodoxae Caulis (Sargentodoxa Caulis / **Hong Teng**) 6%
Curcumae Rhizoma (Zedoary Rhizome / **E Zhu**) 5%

## Chinese Medical Actions

Nourishes liver and kidney yin, clears heat and toxin in the lower burner, cools heat in the blood, invigorates blood stasis.

## Indications

Back pain, lower
Bleeding, post-coital
Cervical dysplasia
Cervicitis
Genital itching and swelling
HPV
Menstrual bleeding (bright red or brown in color)
Menstrual cycle shortened w/ scanty bleeding
Night sweats
Ovulation, light bleeding during
Restlessness
Seminal emissions
Sexual intercourse, pain with
Vaginal discharge (scanty, yellow, brownish, or blood streaked)
Vaginal dryness or irritation
Vaginitis

**Tongue:** Dry, cracked, or reddish tongue body.
**Pulse:** Thin or thready, rapid, weak in kidney position.

## Contraindications

DO NOT USE DURING PREGNANCY. Not to be used when there are cold signs or yang deficiency. In cases with damp-heat, use **Immortal Valley Formula** instead.

**Note:**

In the treatment of cervical dysplasia, this formula should be taken along with **Rehmannia & Scrofularia Formula** when there is kidney yin deficiency with empty heat signs, or with **True Yin Formula** for yin deficiency without empty heat. In cases where there is concern for the development of cervical cancer, **Five Mushroom Formula** may be added for further immune support.

# YUAN SUPPORT FORMULA

**Yuan Support Formula** *(Jia Wei Jian Gu Tang)* includes codonopsis *(dang shen)*, white atractylodes *(bai zhu)*, poria *(fu ling)*, and Chinese yam *(shan yao)* to supplement and invigorate spleen qi, as well as cuscuta *(tu si zi)*, dipsacus *(xu duan)*, and eucommia (du zhong) to support the yang. When supporting the menstrual cycle by phases, it is appropriate to support the qi and yang in the luteal phase, as these substances are dominant in the second half of the cycle. *Dang gui*, white peony *(bai shao)*, and lycium *(gou qi zi)* nourish the blood to provide a strong foundation for the yang. Bupleurum *(chai hu)* moves stagnant liver qi and polygonum vine *(ye jiao teng)* nourishes and calms the heart spirit. This formula is useful for infertility with deficient qi and yang, as well as for lumbar weakness with concurrent qi and blood deficiency.

## Ingredients

Polygoni Multiflori Caulis (Fo-ti Stem, Polygonum Vine / **Ye Jiao Teng**) 10%
Dioscoreae Rhizoma (Chinese Yam / **Shan Yao**) 10%
Cuscutae Semen (Chinese Dodder Seed, Chinese Cuscuta / **Tu Si Zi**) 10%
Angelicae Sinensis Radix (Dong Quai, Tang Kuei / **Dang Gui**) 9%
Dipsaci Radix (Japanese Teasel Root, Dipsacus / **Xu Duan**) 9%
Paeoniae Radix, alba (Chinese White Peony / **Bai Shao**) 9%
Codonopsis Pilosae Radix (Codonopsis / **Dang Shen**) 8%
Atractylodis Macrocephalae Rhizoma (White Atractylodes Rhizome / **Bai Zhu**) 8%
Poria (Poria, Hoelen, Tuckahoe / **Fu Ling**) 8%
Eucommiae Cortex (Eucommia Bark / **Du Zhong**) 7%
Lycii Fructus (Lycium Fruit, Chinese Wolfberry / **Gou Qi Zi**) 6%
Bupleuri Radix (Bupleurum Root / **Chai Hu**) 6%

## Chinese Medical Actions

Supplements spleen qi and kidney yang, nourishes blood, moves liver qi stagnation, nourishes and calms spirit.

## Indications

Abdomen, lower, cold
Anemia
Back weakness, lower
Basal body temperature, drops in luteal phase
Cold, whole body
Endometrium, too thin
Fatigue
Hypotension
Infertility, w/ deficient qi and yang
Libido, low
Low back, pain and weakness
Luteal phase insufficiency
Miscarriage, early recurrent
Post-partum weakness
Progesterone, low
Spotting, prior to menses
Weight gain, easy

**Tongue:** Pale, may be swollen or with teeth marks.
**Pulse:** Empty, weak, especially in spleen and kidney positions.

**Note:** Use with **Bupleurum & Tang Kuei Formula** as needed for significant premenstrual liver qi stagnation.

# ZHONG GAN LING FORMULA

**Zhong Gan Ling Formula** *(Zhong Gan Ling Pian)* is a Chinese patent formula for severe common cold or flu, with fever from wind-heat. Isatis *(da qing ye)* and oldenlandia *(bai hua she she cao)* have been added to augment the formula's ability to clear heat-toxin.

## Ingredients

Ilicis Pubescentis Radix (Pubescent Holly Root, Ilex / **Mao Dong Qing**) 19.6%
Puerariae Radix (Kudzu Root, Pueraria / **Ge Gen**) 19.6%
Isatidis Folium (Isatis Leaf, Indigo Woad Leaf / **Da Qing Ye**) 14.6%
Verbenae Herba (Verbena / **Ma Bian Cao**) 13%
Hedyotis Diffusae Herba (Hedyotis, Oldenlandia / **Bai Hua She She Cao**) 13%
Isatidis seu Baphicacanthis Radix (Isatis Root / **Ban Lan Gen**) 10.1%
Artemisiae Annuae Herba (Artemisia, Sweet Wormwood / **Qing Hao**) 5%
Gypsum Fibrosum (Gypsum / **Shi Gao**) 2.9%
Notopterygii Rhizoma seu Radix (Notopterygium / **Qiang Huo**) 2.2%

## Chinese Medical Actions

Dispels wind-heat, clears heat-toxin, promotes sweating, reduces inflammation.

## Indications

Body aches
Bronchitis
Common cold
Cough
Fever
Headache
Influenza
Lymph nodes, enlarged
Neck and shoulders, sore
Throat, sore
Strep throat

**Tongue:** Red, or red tip.
**Pulse:** Rapid, forceful, and superficial.

## Contraindications

Do not use in cases where patient is cold or experiencing strong chills.

**Dosage:** Can range according to the symptoms and the intensity. Can be taken up to every two hours, in the acute phase of infection.

# ZIZYPHUS FORMULA

**Zizyphus Formula** *(Suan Zao Ren Tang)* is a classical formula for irritability and insomnia caused by deficiency heat from deficient liver and heart blood and yin. Schisandra *(wu wei zi)* was added for night sweats and to further calm the spirit.

## Ingredients

Ziziphi Spinosa Semen (Sour Date Seed, Jujube Seed / **Suan Zao Ren**) 39.3%
Poriae Sclerotium Pararadicis (Poria Spirit / **Fu Shen**) 17.6%
Schisandrae Fructus (Schisandra Fruit / **Wu Wei Zi**) 17.6%
Anemarrhenae Rhizoma (Anemarrhena Rhizome / **Zhi Mu**) 11.8%
Chuanxiong Rhizoma (Ligusticum Wallichii Rhizome / **Chuan Xiong**) 7.8%.
Glycyrrhizae Radix (Chinese Licorice Root / **Gan Cao**) 5.9%

## Chinese Medical Actions

Nourishes the blood, calms the spirit, clears heat, soothes irritability.

## Indications

Dizziness
Dream-disturbed sleep
Dry mouth
Fright
Hot flashes
Insomnia
Irritability
Night sweats
Palpitation
Restlessness
Sleep, disturbed or restless
Throat, dry
Vision, blurred

**Tongue:** Dry, pale, with red tip.
**Pulse:** Thin or wiry, rapid.

## Contraindications

With kidney yin deficiency with heat use **Heavenly Emperor's Formula** instead. When no signs of heat are present use **Peaceful Spirit Formula**.

# *APPENDICES*

## ENGLISH / PIN YIN (TRADITIONAL NAMES)

| English | Pin Yin |
|---|---|
| Amber Stone-Transforming Formula | *Hu Po Hua Shi Pian* |
| Andrographis Formula | *Chuan Xin Lian Kang Yan Pian* |
| Astragalus Formula | *Huang Qi Jian Zhong Tang* |
| Astragalus & Ligustrum Formula | *Huang Qi Dong Qing Pian* |
| Blood Palace Formula | *Xue Fu Zhu Yu Tang* |
| Bone & Sinew Formula | *Zheng Gu Xu Jin Fang* |
| Bupleurum & Cinnamon Formula | *Chai Hu Gui Zhi Tang* |
| Bupleurum & Tang Kuei Formula | *Xiao Yao San* |
| Bupleurum D Formula | *Chai Hu Jia Long Gu Mu Li Tang* |
| Chase Wind, Penetrate Bone Formula | *Zhui Feng Tou Gu Wan* |
| Children's Ear Formula | *Hai Er Fang* |
| Chong Release Formula | *Jia Wei Tao Hong Si Wu Tong* |
| Cinnamon & Poria Formula | *Gui Zhi Fu Ling Wan* |
| Cinnamon D Formula | *Gui Zhi Jia Long Gu Mu Li Tang* |
| Cinnamon Twig Formula | *Gui Zhi Tang* |
| Citrus & Pinellia Formula | *Er Chen Tang* |
| Clematis & Stephania Formula | *Shu Jing Huo Xue Tang* |
| Coptis Relieve Toxicity Formula | *Huang Lian Jie Du Pian* |
| Corydalis Formula | *Shao Yao Gan Cao Jia Yan Hu Tang* |
| Curcuma Longa Formula | *Jiang Huang Wan* |
| Du Huo & Loranthus Formula | *Du Huo Ji Sheng Tang* |
| Earth-Harmonizing Formula | *He Tu Pian* |
| Ease Digestion Formula | *Jia Wei Kang Ning Wan* |
| Eight Immortals Formula | *Ba Xian Chang Shou Wan* |
| Eleuthero Tablets | *Wu Jia Shen Pian* |
| Essential Yang Formula | *Jia Jian Jin Gui Shen Qi Wan* |
| Five Mushroom Formula | *Wu Gu Fang* |
| Four Marvel Formula | *Si Miao Wan* |
| Free & Easy Wanderer Plus | *Jia Wei Xiao Yao San* |
| Fritillaria & Pinellia Formula | *Chuan Bei Ban Xia Tang* |
| Gan Mao Ling Formula | *Gan Mao Ling Pian* |
| Gastrodia & Uncaria Formula | *Tian Ma Gou Teng Yin* |
| General Tonic Formula | *Shi Quan Da Bu Wan* |
| Gentiana Drain Fire Formula | *Long Dan Xie Gan Tang* |
| Ginkgo Formula | *Yin Guo Ye Wan* |
| Ginseng & Astragalus Formula | *Bu Zhong Yi Qi Tang* |
| Ginseng & Longan Formula | *Gui Pi Tang* |
| Ginseng Endurance Formula | *Ren Shen Pian* |
| Ginseng Nourishing Formula | *Ren Shen Yang Ying Wan* |
| Hawthorn & Fennel Formula | *Shan Zha Xiao Hui Xiang Fang* |
| Head Relief Formula | *Tou Tong Pian* |
| He Shou Wu Tablets | *Shou Wu Pian* |
| Heavenly Emperor's Formula | *Tian Wang Bu Xin Dan* |

| | |
|---|---|
| Immortal Valley Formula | *Xian Gu Fang* |
| Intestinal Fungus Formula | *Chang Mei Jun Fang* |
| Jade Screen & Xanthium Formula | *Yu Ping Feng Jia Cang Er San* |
| Jade Source Formula | *Jia Jian Yu Quan Wan* |
| Jade Windscreen Formula | *Yu Ping Feng San* |
| Ji Xue Formula | *Huang Qi Ji Xue Wan* |
| Jing Qi Formula | *Jing Qi Pian* |
| Juan Bi Formula | *Juan Bi Tang* |
| Lily Preserve Metal Formula | *Bai He Gu Jin Tang* |
| Ling Zhi Lung Formula | *Ling Zhi Fei Pian* |
| Linking Formula | *Yi Guan Jian* |
| Liver C Formula | *Gan C Pian* |
| Luo Bu Ma Formula | *Luo Bu Ma Pian* |
| Lysimachia GB Formula | *Xiao Chai Hu Jia Jin Qian Cao Fang* |
| Margarita Complexion Formula | *Zhen Zhu Yu Rong Fang* |
| Ming Mu Formula | *Ming Mu Di Huang Wan* |
| Minor Bupleurum Formula | *Xiao Chai Hu Tang* |
| Mobilize Essence Formula | *Fu Ren Bu Yin Pian* |
| Mulberry & Lycium Formula | *Xie Bai San* |
| Nourish Essence Formula | *Zi Jing Di Huang Wan* |
| Nourish Ren & Chong Formula | *Jia Wei Gui Shao Di Huang Wan* |
| Oregano Oil Formula | *Jia Wei Tu Yin Chen You Jiao Nang* |
| Peaceful Spirit Formula | *Yang Xin Ning Shen Wan* |
| Persica & Cistanches Formula | *Tao Ren Cong Rong Wan* |
| Phlegm-Transforming Formula | *Xia Ku Hua Tan Pian* |
| Pinellia & Magnolia Bark Formula | *Ban Xia Hou Po Tang* |
| Polyporus & Dianthus Formula | *Zhu Ling Qu Mai Tang* |
| Poria & Bamboo Formula | *Wen Dan Tang* |
| Poria Fifteen Formula | *Shi Wu Wei Fu Ling Pian* |
| Poria Five Formula | *Wu Ling San* |
| Prostate Formula | *Qiang Lie Xian Fang* |
| Pulsatilla Intestinal Formula | *Bai Tou Weng Li Chang Fang* |
| Rabdosia Prostate Formula | *Dong Ling Cao Fang* |
| Rehmannia & Scrophularia Formula | *Zhi Bai Di Huang Wan* |
| Rehmannia Cool Blood Formula | *Tu Fu Ling Sheng Di Huang Wan* |
| Rehmannia Six Formula | *Liu Wei Di Huang Wan* |
| Resolve the Middle Formula | *Jia Wei Ping Wei Fang* |
| Restful Sleep Formula | *An Xin Pian* |
| Restorative Formula | *Yang Xue Zhuang Jin Jian Bu Wan* |
| Restore the Lung Formula | *Bu Fei Tang* |
| Salvia Ten Formula | *Dan Shen Jia Si Jun Zi Pian* |
| San Qi Formula | *San Qi Pian* |
| San Qi Tablets | *San Qi Wan* |

| | |
|---|---|
| Sea of Qi Formula | *Qi Hai Yao Fang* |
| Seven Treasures Formula | *Jin Hua Mei Ran Wan* |
| Sheng Mai Formula | *Sheng Mai San* |
| Shu Gan Formula | *Shu Gan Wan* |
| Siler & Platycodon Formula | *Fang Feng Tong Sheng San* |
| Six Gentlemen Formula | *Liu Jun Zi Tang* |
| Stasis-Transforming Formula | *Dan Shen Hua Yu Pian* |
| Stomach-Harmonizing Formula | *Jia Jian Bao He Wan* |
| Tang Kuei & Peony Formula | *Dang Gui Shao Yao San* |
| Tang Kuei & Salvia Formula | *Jia Wei Si Wu Tang* |
| Tang Kuei & Tribulus Formula | *Dang Gui Yin Zi* |
| Tieh Ta Formula | *Die Da Wan* |
| Trauma 1 Formula | *Die Da 1 Hao Fang* |
| Trauma 2 Formula | *Die Da 2 Hao Fang* |
| True Yin Formula | *Zuo Gui Jia Er Zhi Wan* |
| Two Immortals Formula | *Jia Jian Er Xian Tang* |
| Viola Clear Fire Formula | *Di Ding Qing Huo Pian* |
| Vital Treasure Formula | *Zhen Bao Fang* |
| Women's Precious Formula | *Ba Zhen Tang* |
| Wu Hua Formula | *Wu Hua Tang* |
| Xanthium & Magnolia Formula | *Jia Wei Xin Yi San* |
| Xanthium Nasal Formula | *Jia Wei Cang Er Pian* |
| Yin Chiao Formula | *Yin Qiao San* |
| Yin Valley Formula | *Yin Gu Fang* |
| Yuan Support Formula | *Jia Wei Jian Gu Tang* |
| Zhong Gan Ling Formula | *Zhong Gan Ling Pian* |
| Zizyphus Formula | *Suan Zao Ren Tang* |

## *PIN YIN (TRADITIONAL NAMES) / ENGLISH*

| | |
|---|---|
| *An Xin Pian* | Restful Sleep Formula |
| *Ba Xian Chang Shou Wan* | Eight Immortals Formula |
| *Ba Zhen Tang* | Women's Precious Formula |
| *Bai He Gu Jin Tang* | Lily Preserve Metal Formula |
| *Bai Tou Weng Li Chang Fang* | Pulsatilla Intestinal Formula |
| *Ban Xia Hou Po Tang* | Pinellia & Magnolia Bark Formula |
| *Bu Fei Tang* | Restore the Lung Formula |
| *Bu Zhong Yi Qi Tang* | Ginseng & Astragalus Formula |
| *Chai Hu Gui Zhi Tang* | Bupleurum & Cinnamon Formula |
| *Chai Hu Jia Long Gu Mu Li Tang* | Bupleurum D Formula |
| *Chang Mei Jun Fang* | Intestinal Fungus Formula |
| *Chuan Bei Ban Xia Tang* | Fritillaria & Pinellia Formula |
| *Chuan Xin Lian Kang Yan Pian* | Andrographis Formula |
| *Dan Shen Hua Yu Pian* | Stasis-Transforming Formula |
| *Dan Shen Jia Si Jun Zi Pian* | Salvia Ten Formula |
| *Dang Gui Shao Yao San* | Tang Kuei & Peony Formula |
| *Dang Gui Yin Zi* | Tang Kuei & Tribulus Formula |
| *Di Ding Qing Huo Pian* | Viola Clear Fire Formula |
| *Die Da 1 Hao Fang* | Trauma 1 Formula |
| *Die Da 2 Hao Fang* | Trauma 2 Formula |
| *Die Da Wan* | Tieh Ta Formula |
| *Dong Ling Cao Fang* | Rabdosia Prostate Formula |
| *Du Huo Ji Sheng Tang* | Du Huo & Loranthus Formula |
| *Er Chen Tang* | Citrus & Pinellia Formula |
| *Fang Feng Tong Sheng San* | Siler & Platycodon Formula |
| *Fu Ren Bu Yin Pian* | Mobilize Essence Formula |
| *Gan C Pian* | Liver C Formula |
| *Gan Mao Ling Pian* | Gan Mao Ling Formula |
| *Gui Pi Tang* | Ginseng & Longan Formula |
| *Gui Zhi Fu Ling Wan* | Cinnamon & Poria Formula |
| *Gui Zhi Jia Long Gu Mu Li Tang* | Cinnamon D Formula |
| *Gui Zhi Tang* | Cinnamon Twig Formula |
| *Hai Er Fang* | Children's Ear Formula |
| *He Tu Pian* | Earth-Harmonizing Formula |
| *Hu Po Hua Shi Pian* | Amber Stone-Transforming Formula |
| *Huang Lian Jie Du Pian* | Coptis Relieve Toxicity Formula |
| *Huang Qi Dong Qing Pian* | Astragalus & Ligustrum Formula |
| *Huang Qi Ji Xue Wan* | Ji Xue Formula |
| *Huang Qi Jian Zhong Tang* | Astragalus Formula |
| *Jia Jian Bao He Wan* | Stomach-Harmonizing Formula |
| *Jia Jian Er Xian Tang* | Two Immortals Formula |
| *Jia Jian Jin Gui Shen Qi Wan* | Essential Yang Formula |
| *Jia Jian Yu Quan Wan* | Jade Source Formula |
| *Jia Wei Cang Er Pian* | Xanthium Nasal Formula |

| | |
|---|---|
| *Jia Wei Jian Gu Tang* | Yuan Support Formula |
| *Jia Wei Ping Wei Fang* | Resolve the Middle Formula |
| *Jia Wei Gui Shao Di Huang Wan* | Nourish Ren & Chong Formula |
| *Jia Wei Kang Ning Wan* | Ease Digestion Formula |
| *Jia Wei Si Wu Tang* | Tang Kuei & Salvia Formula |
| *Jia Wei Tao Hong Si Wu Tong* | Chong Release Formula |
| *Jia Wei Tu Yin ChenYou Jiao Nang* | Oregano Oil Formula |
| *Jia Wei Xiao Yao San* | Free & Easy Wanderer Plus |
| *Jia Wei Xin Yi San* | Xanthium & Magnolia Formula |
| *Jiang Huang Wan* | Curcuma Longa Formula |
| *Jin Hua Mei Ran Wan* | Seven Treasures Formula |
| *Jing Qi Pian* | Jing Qi Formula |
| *Juan Bi Tang* | Juan Bi Formula |
| *Ling Zhi Fei Pian* | Ling Zhi Lung Formula |
| *Liu Jun Zi Tang* | Six Gentlemen Formula |
| *Liu Wei Di Huang Wan* | Rehmannia Six Formula |
| *Long Dan Xie Gan Tang* | Gentiana Drain Fire Formula |
| *Luo Bu Ma Pian* | Luo Bu Ma Formula |
| *Ming Mu Di Huang Wan* | Ming Mu Formula |
| *Qi Hai Yao Fang* | Sea of Qi Formula |
| *Qiang Lie Xian Fang* | Prostate Formula |
| *Ren Shen Pian* | Ginseng Endurance Formula |
| *Ren Shen Yang Ying Wan* | Ginseng Nourishing Formula |
| *San Qi Pian* | San Qi Formula |
| *San Qi Wan* | San Qi Tablets |
| *Shan Zha Xiao Hui Xiang Fang* | Hawthorn & Fennel Formula |
| *Shao Yao Gan Cao Jia Yan Hu Tang* | Corydalis Formula |
| *Sheng Mai San* | Sheng Mai Formula |
| *Shi Quan Da Bu Wan* | General Tonic Formula |
| *Shi Wu Wei Fu Ling Pian* | Poria Fifteen Formula |
| *Shou Wu Pian* | He Shou Wu Tablets |
| *Shu Gan Wan* | Shu Gan Formula |
| *Shu Jing Huo Xue Tang* | Clematis & Stephania Formula |
| *Si Mao Wan* | Four Marvel Formula |
| *Suan Zao Ren Tang* | Zizyphus Formula |
| *Tao Ren Cong Rong Wan* | Persica & Cistanches Formula |
| *Tian Ma Gou Teng Yin* | Gastrodia & Uncaria Formula |
| *Tian Wang Bu Xin Dan* | Heavenly Emperor's Formula |
| *Tou Tong Pian* | Head Relief Formula |
| *Tu Fu Ling Sheng Di Huang Wan* | Rehmannia Cool Blood Formula |
| *Wen Dan Tang* | Poria & Bamboo Formula |
| *Wu Gu Fang* | Five Mushroom Formula |
| *Wu Hua Tang* | Wu Hua Formula |
| *Wu Jia Shen Pian* | Eleuthero Tablets |
| *Wu Ling San* | Poria Five Formula |
| *Xia Ku Hua Tan Pian* | Phlegm-Transforming Formula |

| | |
|---|---|
| *Xian Gu Fang* | Immortal Valley Formula |
| *Xiao Chai Hu Jia Jin Qian Cao Fang* | Lysimachia GB Formula |
| *Xiao Chai Hu Tang* | Minor Bupleurum Formula |
| *Xiao Yao San* | Bupleurum & Tang Kuei Formula |
| *Xie Bai San* | Mulberry & Lycium Formula |
| *Xue Fu Zhu Yu Tang* | Blood Palace Formula |
| *Yang Xin Ning Shen Wan* | Peaceful Spirit Formula |
| *Yang Xue Zhuang Jin Jian Bu Wan* | Restorative Formula |
| *Yi Guan Jian* | Linking Formula |
| *Yin Gu Fang* | Yin Valley Formula |
| *Yin Guo Ye Wan* | Ginkgo Formula) |
| *Yin Qiao San* | Yin Chiao Formula |
| *Yu Ping Feng Jia Cang Er San* | Jade Screen & Xanthium Formula |
| *Yu Ping Feng San* | Jade Windscreen Formula |
| *Zhen Bao Fang* | Vital Treasure Formula |
| *Zhen Zhu Yu Rong Fang* | Margarita Complexion Formula |
| *Zheng Gu Xu Jin Fang* | Bone & Sinew Formula |
| *Zhi Bai Di Huang Wan* | Rehmannia & Scrophularia Formula |
| *Zhong Gan Ling Pian* | Zhong Gan Ling Formula |
| *Zhu Ling Qu Mai Tang* | Polyporus & Dianthus Formula |
| *Zhui Feng Tou Gu Wan* | Chase Wind, Penetrate Bone Formula |
| *Zi Jing Di Huang Wan* | Nourish Essence Formula |
| *Zuo Gui Jia Er Zhi Wan* | True Yin Formula |

# *CHINESE ENERGETIC INDEX*

This index lists formulas by their most appropriate energetic category.

## FORMULAS THAT RELEASE THE EXTERIOR

**Formulas that Release Exterior Wind-Cold**

CINNAMON TWIG FORMULA *(GUI ZHI TANG)*
XANTHIUM & MAGNOLIA FORMULA *(JIA WEI XIN YI SAN)*

**Formulas that Release Exterior Wind-Heat**

GAN MAO LING FORMULA *(GAN MAO LING PIAN)*
SILER & PLATYCODON FORMULA *(FANG FENG TONG SHENG SAN)*
YIN CHIAO FORMULA *(YIN QIAO SAN)*
ZHONG GAN LING FORMULA *(ZHONG GAN LING PIAN)*

**Formulas that Release Exterior Disorders with Head and Neck Symptoms**

HEAD RELIEF FORMULA *(TOU TONG PIAN)*
JADE SCREEN & XANTHIUM FORMULA *(YU PING FENG JIA CANG ER SAN)*
XANTHIUM NASAL FORMULA *(JIA WEI CANG ER PIAN)*

## FORMULAS THAT CLEAR HEAT

**Formulas that Clear Heat from the Nutritive Level and Cool the Blood**

REHMANNIA COOL BLOOD FORMULA *(TU FU LING SHENG DI HUANG WAN)*

**Formulas that Clear Heat and Relieve Toxicity**

ANDROGRAPHIS FORMULA *(CHUAN XIN LIAN KANG YAN PIAN)*
CHILDREN'S EAR FORMULA *(HAI ER FANG)*
COPTIS RELIEVE TOXICITY FORMULA *(HUANG LIAN JIE DU PIAN)*
CURCUMA LONGA FORMULA *(JIANG HUANG WAN)*
MARGARITA COMPLEXION FORMULA *(ZHEN ZHU YU RONG FANG)*
RABDOSIA PROSTATE FORMULA *(DONG LING CAO FANG)*
SILER & PLATYCODON FORMULA *(FANG FENG TONG SHENG SAN)*
VIOLA CLEAR FIRE FORMULA *(DI DING QING HUO PIAN)*
WU HUA FORMULA *(WU HUA TANG)*
XANTHIUM NASAL FORMULA *(JIA WEI CANG ER PIAN)*
YIN VALLEY FORMULA *(YIN GU FANG)*

**Formulas that Clear Heat from the Organs**

GENTIANA DRAIN FIRE FORMULA *(LONG DAN XIE GAN TANG)*
INTESTINAL FUNGUS FORMULA *(CHANG MEI JUN FANG)*
LIVER C FORMULA *(GAN C PIAN)*
LUO BU MA FORMULA *(LUO BU MA JIANG YA WAN)*
MULBERRY & LYCIUM FORMULA *(XIE BAI SAN)*
PULSATILLA INTESTINAL FORMULA *(BAI TOU WENG LI CHANG FANG)*

**Formulas that Clear Heat from Deficiency**

LINKING FORMULA *(YI GUAN JIAN)*
REHMANNIA & SCROPHULARIA FORMULA *(ZHI BAI DI HUANG WAN)*

## FORMULAS THAT DRAIN DOWNWARD

**Formulas that Drive out Excess Water and Unblock the Bowels**

HAWTHORN & FENNEL FORMULA *(SHAN ZHA XIAO HUI XIANG FANG)*
PORIA FIFTEEN FORMULA *(SHI WU WEI FU LING PIAN)*

**Formulas that Moisten the Intestines and Unblock the Bowels**

PERSICA & CISTANCHES FORMULA *(TAO REN CONG RONG WAN)*

## FORMULAS THAT HARMONIZE

**Formulas that Harmonize Lesser Yang-Stage Disorders**

BUPLEURUM & CINNAMON FORMULA *(CHAI HU GUI ZHI TANG)*
MINOR BUPLEURUM FORMULA *(XIAO CHAI HU TANG)*

**Formulas that Regulate and Harmonize the Liver and Spleen**

BUPLEURUM & TANG KUEI FORMULA *(XIAO YAO SAN)*
EARTH-HARMONIZING FORMULA *(HE TU PIAN)*
FREE & EASY WANDERER PLUS *(JIA WEI XIAO YAO SAN)*
IMMORTAL VALLEY FORMULA *(XIAN GU FANG)*

**Formulas that Regulate and Harmonize the Liver and Stomach**

EARTH-HARMONIZING FORMULA *(HE TU PIAN)*
SHU GAN FORMULA *(SHU GAN WAN)*

## FORMULAS THAT TREAT DRYNESS

HE SHOU WU TABLETS (*SHOU WU PIAN*)

**Formulas that Enrich the Yin and Moisten Dryness**

EIGHT IMMORTALS FORMULA *(BA XIAN CHANG SHOU WAN)*
LILY PRESERVE METAL FORMULA *(BAI HE GU JIN TANG)*

**Formulas that Enrich the Yin, Generate Fluids, and Clear Heat**

JADE SOURCE FORMULA *(JIA JIAN QUAN WAN)*

## FORMULAS THAT EXPEL DAMPNESS

**Formulas that Promote Urination and Leach out Dampness**

HAWTHORN & FENNEL FORMULA *(SHAN ZHA XIAO HUI XIANG FANG)*
POLYPORUS & DIANTHUS FORMULA *(ZHU LING QU MAI TANG)*
PORIA FIFTEEN FORMULA *(SHI WU WEI FU LING PIAN)*
PORIA FIVE FORMULA *(WU LING SAN)*

**Formulas that Transform Damp Turbidity**

RESOLVE THE MIDDLE FORMULA *(JIA WEI PING WEI FANG)*

**Formulas that Clear Damp-Heat**

FOUR MARVEL FORMULA *(SI MIAO WAN)*
IMMORTAL VALLEY FORMULA *(XIAN GU FANG)*
RABDOSIA PROSTATE FORMULA *(DONG LING CAO FANG)*
WU HUA FORMULA (WU HUA TANG)

**Formulas that Clear Damp-Heat and Expel Stones**

AMBER STONE-TRANSFORMING FORMULA *(HU PO HUA SHI PIAN)*
LYSIMACHIA GB FORMULA *(XIAO CHAI HU JIA JIN QIAN CAO FANG)*

**Formulas that Dispel Wind-Dampness**

BONE & SINEW FORMULA *(ZHENG GU XU JIN FANG)*
CHASE WIND, PENETRATE BONE FORMULA *(ZHUI FENG TOU GU WAN)*

Du Huo & Loranthus Formula *(Du Huo Ji Sheng Tang)*
Ease Digestion Formula *(Kang Ning Wan)*
Eleuthero Tablets *(Wu Jia Shen Pian)*
Juan Bi Formula *(Juan Bi Tang)*

## FORMULAS THAT WARM INTERIOR COLD

### Formulas that Warm the Middle and Dispel Cold

Astragalus Formula *(Huang Qi Jian Zhong Tang)*
Sea of Qi Formula *(Qi Hai Yao Fang)*

## FORMULAS THAT SUPPLEMENT

### Formulas that Supplement the Qi

Eleuthero Tablets *(Wu Jia Shen Pian)*
Five Mushroom Formula *(Wu Gu Fang)*
Ginseng & Astragalus Formula *(Bu Zhong Yi Qi Tang)*
Ginseng Endurance Formula *(Ren Shen Pian)*
Restore the Lung Formula *(Bu Fei Tang)*
Sea Of Qi Formula *(Qi Hai Yao Fang)*
Sheng Mai Formula *(Sheng Mai San)*
Six Gentlemen Formula *(Liu Jun Zi Tang)*

### Formulas that Supplement the Blood

He Shou Wu Tablets *(Shou Wu Pian)*
Ji Xue Formula *(Huang Qi Ji Xue Wan)*
Seven Treasures Formula *(Jin Hua Mei Ran Wan)*
Tang Kuei & Peony Formula *(Dang Gui Shao Yao San)*
Tang Kuei & Salvia Formula *(Jia Wei Si Wu Tang)*
Tang Kuei & Tribulus Formula *(Dang Gui Yin Zi)*

### Formulas that Supplement the Blood and Yin

Nourish Ren & Chong Formula *(Jia Wei Gui Shao Di Huang Wan)*

### Formulas that Supplement the Qi and Blood

Astragalus & Ligustrum Formula *(Huang Qi Dong Qing Pian)*
General Tonic Formula *(Shi Quan Da Bu Wan)*
Ginseng & Longan Formula *(Gui Pi Tang)*
Ginseng Nourishing Formula *(Ren Shen Yang Ying Wan)*
Restorative Formula *(Yang Xue Zhuang Jin Jian Bu Wan)*
Women's Precious Formula *(Ba Zhen Tang)*

### Formulas that Nourish Qi and Yin

Jing Qi Formula *(Jing Qi Pian)*
Sheng Mai Formula *(Sheng Mai San)*

### Formulas that Nourish and Supplement the Yin

Eight Immortals Formula *(Ba Xian Chang Shou Wan)*
Lily Preserve Metal Formula *(Bai He Gu Jin Tang)*
Linking Formula *(Yi Guan Jian)*
Ming Mu Formula *(Ming Mu Di Huang Wan)*
Rehmannia & Scrophularia Formula *(Zhi Bai Di Huang Wan)*
Rehmannia Six Formula *(Liu Wei Di Huang Wan)*
Seven Treasures Formula *(Jin Hua Mei Ran Wan)*
True Yin Formula *(Zuo Gui Jia Er Zhi Wan)*
Yin Valley Formula *(Yin Gu Fang)*

### Formulas that Nourish Yin and Yang

Mobilize Essence Formula *(Fu Ren Bu Yin Pian)*
Nourish Essence Formula *(Zi Jing Di Huang Wan)*

### Formulas that Warm and Supplement the Yang

Essential Yang Formula *(Jia Jian Jin Gui Shen Qi Wan)*
Sea of Qi Formula *(Qi Hai Yao Fang)*
Two Immortals Formula *(Jia Jian Er Xian Tang)*
Vital Treasure Formula *(Zhen Bao Fang)*
Yuan Support Formula *(Jia Wei Jian Gu Tang)*

## FORMULAS THAT REGULATE THE QI

### Formulas that Promote the Movement of Qi

Pinellia & Magnolia Bark Formula *(Ban Xia Hou Po Tang)*

### Formulas that Direct Rebellious Qi Downward

Ling Zhi Lung Formula *(Ling Zhi Fei Pian)*
Restore the Lung Formula *(Bu Fei Tang)*
Shu Gan Formula *(Shu Gan Wan)*
Stomach-Harmonizing Formula *(Jia Jian Bao He Wan)*

## FORMULAS THAT INVIGORATE THE BLOOD

### Formulas that Transform Blood Stasis

Blood Palace Formula *(Xue Fu Zhu Yu Tang)*
Clematis & Stephania Formula *(Shu Jing Huo Xue Tang)*
Mobilize Essence Formula *(Fu Ren Bu Yin Pian)*
San Qi Formula *(San Qi Pian)*
San Qi Tablets *(San Qi Wan)*
Stasis-Transforming Formula *(Dan Shen Hua Yu Pian)*

### Formulas that Warm the Menses and Dispel Blood Stasis

Chong Release Formula *(Jia Wei Tao Hong Si Wu Tong)*
Cinnamon & Poria Formula *(Gui Zhi Fu Ling Wan)*

### Formulas that Invigorate the Blood for Treatment of Traumatic Injury

Corydalis Formula *(Shao Yao Gan Cao Jia Yan Hu Tang)*
Tieh Ta Formula *(Die Da Wan)*
Trauma 1 Formula *(Die Da 1 Hao Fang)*
Trauma 2 Formula *(Die Da 2 Hao Fang)*

## FORMULAS THAT STOP BLEEDING

San Qi Formula *(San Qi Pian)*
San Qi Tablets *(San Qi Wan)*

## FORMULAS THAT STABILIZE AND BIND

### Formulas that Stabilize the Exterior and the Lungs

Jade Screen & Xanthium Formula *(Yu Ping Feng Jia Cang Er San)*
Jade Windscreen Formula *(Yu Ping Feng San)*

### Formulas that Stabilize the Kidneys

Cinnamon D Formula *(Gui Zhi Jia Long Gu Mu Li Tang)*
Prostate Formula *(Qiang Lie Xian Fang)*

## FORMULAS THAT CALM THE SPIRIT

**Formulas that Nourish the Heart and Calm the Spirit**

GINKGO FORMULA *(YIN GUO YE WAN)*
HEAVENLY EMPEROR'S FORMULA *(TIAN WANG BU XIN DAN)*
PEACEFUL SPIRIT FORMULA *(YANG XIN NING SHEN WAN)*
RESTFUL SLEEP FORMULA *(AN XIN PIAN)*
YUAN SUPPORT FORMULA *(JIA WEI JIAN GU TANG)*
ZIZYPHUS FORMULA *(SUAN ZAO REN TANG)*

**Formulas that Sedate and Calm the Spirit**

BUPLEURUM D FORMULA *(CHAI HU JIA LONG GU MU LI TANG)*
SALVIA TEN FORMULA *(DAN SHEN JIA SI JUN ZI PIAN)*

## FORMULAS THAT EXPEL WIND

**Formulas that Extinguish Internal Wind**

GASTRODIA & UNCARIA FORMULA *(TIAN MA GOU TENG YIN)*
LUO BU MA FORMULA *(LUO BU MA JIANG YA WAN)*

## FORMULAS THAT TREAT PHLEGM

**Formulas that Dry Dampness and Expel Phlegm**

CITRUS & PINELLIA FORMULA *(ER CHEN TANG)*

**Formulas that Clear Heat and Transform Phlegm**

FRITILLARIA & PINELLIA FORMULA *(CHUAN BEI BAN XIA TANG)*
PORIA & BAMBOO FORMULA *(WEN DAN TANG)*

**Formulas that Moisten Dryness and Transform Phlegm**

LILY PRESERVE METAL FORMULA *(BAI HE GU JIN TANG)*

**Formulas that Transform Phlegm and Dissipate Nodules**

PHLEGM-TRANSFORMING FORMULA *(XIA KU HUA TAN PIAN)*

## FORMULAS THAT REDUCE FOOD STAGNATION

EASE DIGESTION FORMULA *(KANG NING WAN)*
HAWTHORN & FENNEL FORMULA *(SHAN ZHA XIAO HUI XIANG FANG)*
PORIA FIFTEEN FORMULA *(SHI WU WEI FU LING PIAN)*
RESOLVE THE MIDDLE FORMULA *(JIA WEI PING WEI FANG)*
STOMACH-HARMONIZING FORMULA *(JIA JIAN BAO HE WAN)*

## FORMULAS THAT EXPEL PARASITES

OREGANO OIL FORMULA *(JIA WEI TU YIN CHEN YOU JIAO NANG)*
WU HUA FORMULA (WU HUA TANG)

# *ZANG-FU INDEX*

## LUNG

**Clears Heat and Transforms Phlegm**

XANTHIUM NASAL FORMULA *(JIA WEI CANG ER PIAN)*

**Redirects Lung Qi**

LING ZHI LUNG FORMULA *(LING ZHI FEI PIAN)*
RESTORE THE LUNG FORMULA *(BU FEI TANG)*

**Release Heat from Lung**

CHILDREN'S EAR FORMULA *(HAI ER FANG)*
GAN MAO LING *(GAN MAO LING PIAN)*
MULBERRY & LYCIUM FORMULA *(XIE BAI SAN)*
RESTORE THE LUNG FORMULA *(BU FEI TANG)*
VIOLA CLEAR FIRE FORMULA *(DI DING QING HUO PIAN)*
YIN CHIAO FORMULA *(YIN QIAO SAN)*
ZHONG GAN LING FORMULA *(ZHONG GAN LING PIAN)*

**Supplements Lung Yin**

EIGHT IMMORTALS FORMULA *(BA XIAN CHANG SHOU WAN)*
LILY PRESERVE METAL FORMULA *(BAI HE GU JIN TANG)*
SHENG MAI FORMULA *(SHENG MAI SAN)*

**Supplements Lung Qi**

GINSENG & ASTRAGALUS FORMULA *(BU ZHONG YI QI TANG)*
SHENG MAI FORMULA *(SHENG MAI SAN)*
SIX GENTLEMEN FORMULA *(LIU JUN ZI TANG)*

**Supplements Lung Qi and Stabilizes the Exterior**

JADE SCREEN & XANTHIUM FORMULA *(YU PING FENG JIA CANG ER SAN)*
JADE WINDSCREEN FORMULA *(YU PING FENG SAN)*

**Transforms Phlegm-Heat**

FRITILLARIA & PINELLIA FORMULA *(CHUAN BEI BAN XIA TANG)*

**Transforms Phlegm-Damp**

CITRUS & PINELLIA FORMULA *(ER CHEN TANG)*

## LARGE INTESTINE

**Clears Damp Heat from Large Intestine**

ANDROGRAPHIS FORMULA *(CHUAN XIN LIAN KANG YAN PIAN)*
COPTIS RELIEVE TOXICITY FORMULA *(HUANG LIAN JIE DU PIAN)*
INTESTINAL FUNGUS FORMULA *(CHANG MEI JUN FANG)*
OREGANO OIL FORMULA *(JIA WEI TU YIN CHEN YOU JIAO NANG)*
PULSATILLA INTESTINAL FORMULA *(BAI TOU WENG LI CHANG FANG)*
WU HUA FORMULA *(WU HUA TANG)*

**Moistens and Unblocks the Large Intestine**

PERSICA & CISTANCHES FORMULA *(TAO REN CONG RONG WAN)*

**Moves Stagnant Qi in the Large Intestine**

HAWTHORN & FENNEL FORMULA *(SHAN ZHA XIAO HUI XIANG FANG)*
PORIA FIFTEEN FORMULA *(SHI WU WEI FU LING PIAN)*

## STOMACH

### Clears Fire from the Stomach

Andrographis Formula (*Chuan Xin Lian Kang Yan Pian)*
Coptis Relieve Toxicity Formula *(Huang Lian Jie Du Pian)*
Wu Hua Formula *(Wu Hua Tang)*

### Harmonizes the Stomach and Liver

Earth-Harmonizing Formula *(He Tu Pian)*
Shu Gan Formula *(Shu Gan Wan)*

### Moves Stagnant Qi of the Stomach

Ease Digestion Formula *(Kang Ning Wan)*
Poria & Bamboo Formula *(Wen Dan Tang)*
Resolve the Middle Formula *(Jia Wei Ping Wei Fang)*
Stomach-Harmonizing Formula *(Jia Jian Bao He Wan)*

### Supplements Stomach Yin

Eight Immortals Formula *(Ba Xian Chang Shou Wan)*
Sheng Mai Formula *(Sheng Mai San)*

## SPLEEN

### Dispels Spleen Dampness

Citrus & Pinellia Formula *(Er Chen Tang)*
Hawthorn & Fennel Formula *(Shan Zha Xiao Hui Xiang Fang)*
Phlegm-Transforming Formula *(Xia Ku Hua Tan Pian)*
Poria Fifteen Formula *(Shi Wu Wei Fu Ling Pian)*
Resolve the Middle Formula *(Jia Wei Ping Wei Fang)*

### Supplements Spleen Qi

Astragalus & Ligustrum Formula *(Huang Qi Dong Qing Pian)*
Bupleurum & Tang Kuei Formula *(Xiao Yao San)*
General Tonic Formula *(Shi Quan Da Bu Wan)*
Ginseng & Astragalus Formula *(Bu Zhong Yi Qi Tang)*
Ginseng & Longan Formula *(Gui Pi Tang)*
Ginseng Endurance Formula *(Ren Shen Pian)*
Ginseng Nourishing Formula *(Ren Shen Yang Ying Wan)*
Jade Source Formula *(Jia Jian Yu Quan Wan)*
Ji Xue Formula *(Huang Qi Ji Xue Wan)*
Peaceful Spirit Formula *(Yang Xin Ning Shen Wan)*
Salvia Ten Formula *(Dan Shen Jia Si Jun Zi Pian)*
Six Gentlemen Formula *(Liu Jun Zi Tang)*
Women's Precious Formula *(Ba Zhen Tang)*

### Supplements and Warms Spleen Qi

Astragalus Formula *(Huang Qi Jian Zhong Tang)*

### Supplements Spleen Yang

Ginseng & Astragalus Formula *(Bu Zhong Yi Qi Tang)*
Prostate Formula *(Qiang Lie Xian Fang)*
Sea of Qi Formula *(Qi Hai Yao Fang)*

## HEART

**Clears Heat from the Heart**

BUPLEURUM D FORMULA *(CHAI HU JIA LONG GU MU LI TANG)*

**Harmonizes Heart and Kidneys**

CINNAMON D FORMULA *(GUI ZHI JIA LONG GU MU LI TANG)*
HEAVENLY EMPEROR'S FORMULA *(TIAN WANG BU XIN DAN)*

**Moves Heart Blood**

BLOOD PALACE FORMULA *(XUE FU ZHU YU TANG)*

**Moves Heart Blood and Supplements Heart Blood**

TANG KUEI & SALVIA FORMULA *(JIA WEI SI WU TANG)*

**Supplements Heart Blood**

GINKGO FORMULA *(YIN GUO YE WANG)*
GINSENG & LONGAN FORMULA *(GUI PI TANG)*
ZIZYPHUS FORMULA *(SUAN ZAO REN TANG)*

**Supplements Heart Qi and Blood**

GINSENG & LONGAN FORMULA *(GUI PI TANG)*
GINSENG NOURISHING FORMULA *(REN SHEN YANG YING WAN)*
PEACEFUL SPIRIT FORMULA *(YANG XIN NING SHEN WAN)*
RESTFUL SLEEP FORMULA *(AN XIN PIAN)*

**Supplements Heart Yin**

HEAVENLY EMPEROR'S FORMULA *(TIAN WANG BU XIN DAN)*
ZIZYPHUS FORMULA *(SUAN ZAO REN TANG)*

## SMALL INTESTINE

**For Pain along the Channel**

CHASE WIND, PENETRATE BONE FORMULA *(ZHUI FENG TOU GU WAN)*
CURCUMA LONGA FORMULA *(JIANG HUANG WAN)*
JUAN BI FORMULA *(JUAN BI TANG)*

**For Functional Weakness of Small Intestine, See Spleen**

## URINARY BLADDER

**Dispels Dampness**

PORIA FIVE FORMULA *(WU LING SAN)*

**Drains Damp-Heat**

ANDROGRAPHIS FORMULA *(CHUAN XIN LIAN KANG YAN PIAN)*
POLYPORUS & DIANTHUS FORMULA *(ZHU LING QU MAI TANG)*
RABDOSIA PROSTATE FORMULA *(DONG LING CAO FANG)*

**Expels Stones and Drains Damp-Heat**

AMBER STONE-TRANSFORMING FORMULA *(HU PO HUA SHI PIAN)*

**For Functional Weakness of Urinary Bladder, See Kidney**

## KIDNEY

**Harmonizes Kidneys and Heart**

CINNAMON D FORMULA *(GUI ZHI JIA LONG GU MU LI TANG)*
HEAVENLY EMPEROR'S FORMULA *(TIAN WANG BU XIN DAN)*

**Supplements Kidney Yang**

Bone & Sinew Formula *(Zheng Gu Xu Jin Fang)*
Essential Yang Formula *(Jia Jian Jin Gui Shen Qi Wan)*
Prostate Formula *(Qiang Lie Xian Fang)*
Sea Of Qi Formula *(Qi Hai Yao Fang)*
Two Immortals Formula *(Jia Jian Er Xian Tang)*
Vital Treasure Formula *(Zhen Bao Fang)*
Yuan Support Formula *(Jia Wei Jian Gu Tang)*

**Supplements Kidney Yin**

Eight Immortals Formula *(Ba Xian Chang Shou Wan)*
He Shou Wu Tablets (*Shou Wu Pian*)
Jing Qi Formula *(Jing Qi Pian)*
Ming Mu Formula *(Ming Mu Di Huang Wan)*
Nourish Ren & Chong Formula *(Jia Wei Gui Shao Di Huang Wan)*
Rehmannia & Scrophularia Formula *(Zhi Bai Di Huang Wan)*
Rehmannia Six Formula *(Liu Wei Di Huang Wan)*
Seven Treasures Formula *(Jin Hua Mei Ran Wan)*
True Yin Formula *(Zuo Gui Jia Er Zhi Wan)*

**Supplements Kidney Yin and Yang**

Eleuthero Tablets *(Wu Jia Shen Pian)*
Essential Yang Formula *(Jia Jian Jin Gui Shen Qi Wan)*
Nourish Essence Formula *(Zi Jing Di Huang Wan)*
Two Immortals Formula *(Jia Jian Er Xian Tang)*

**Expels Stones**

Amber Stone-Transforming Formula *(Hu Po Hua Shi Pian)*

## LIVER

**Calms the Liver and Extinguishes Internal Wind**

Gastrodia & Uncaria Formula *(Tian Ma Gou Teng Yin)*
Luo Bu Ma Formula *(Luo Bu Ma Jiang Ya Wan)*
Tang Kuei & Tribulus Formula *(Dang Gui Yin Zi)*

**Drains Fire from the Liver**

Gentiana Drain Fire Formula *(Long Dan Xie Gan Tang)*
Liver C Formula *(Gan C Pian)*
Luo Bu Ma Formula *(Luo Bu Ma Jiang Ya Wan)*
Margarita Complexion Formula *(Zhen Zhu Yu Rong Fang)*
Yin Valley Formula *(Yin Gu Fang)*

**Moves Stagnant Liver Blood**

Chong Release Formula *(Jia Wei Tao Hong Si Wu Tong)*
Cinnamon & Poria Formula *(Gui Zhi Fu Ling Wan)*
Stasis-Transforming Formula *(Dan Shen Hua Yu Pian)*
Tang Kuei & Salvia Formula *(Jia Wei Si Wu Tang)*

**Moves Stagnant Liver Qi**

Bupleurum & Tang Kuei Formula *(Xiao Yao San)*
Free & Easy Wanderer Plus *(Jia Wei Xiao Yao San)*
Immortal Valley Formula *(Xian Gu Fang)*

Pinellia & Magnolia Bark Formula *(Ban Xia Hou Po Tang)*
Yuan Support Formula *(Jia Wei Jian Gu Tang)*

**Soothes the Liver and Regulates the Stomach**

Earth-Harmonizing Formula *(He Tu Pian)*
Shu Gan Formula *(Shu Gan Wan)*

**Spreads Liver Qi**

Linking Formula *(Yi Guan Jian)*
Tang Kuei & Peony Formula *(Dang Gui Shao Yao San)*

**Supplements Liver Blood**

Chong Release Formula *(Jia Wei Tao Hong Si Wu Tong)*
He Shou Wu Tablets *(Shou Wu Pian)*
Seven Treasures Formula *(Jin Hua Mei Ran Wan)*
Ji Xue Formula *(Huang Qi Ji Xue Wan)*
Tang Kuei & Salvia Formula *(Jia Wei Si Wu Tang)*
Tang Kuei & Tribulus Formula *(Dang Gui Yin Zi)*
Women's Precious Formula *(Ba Zhen Tang)*
Zizyphus Formula *(Suan Zao Ren Tang)*

**Supplements Liver Yin**

He Shou Wu Tablets *(Shou Wu Pian)*
Linking Formula *(Yi Guan Jian)*
Ming Mu Formula *(Ming Mu Di Huang Wan)*
True Yin Formula *(Zuo Gui Jia Er Zhi Wan)*
Yin Valley Formula *(Yin Gu Fang)*
Zizyphus Formula *(Suan Zao Ren Tang)*

## GALLBLADDER

**Drains Fire from the Gallbladder**

Gentiana Drain Fire Formula *(Long Dan Xie Gan Tang)*
Poria & Bamboo Formula *(Wen Dan Tang)*

**Harmonizes and Releases Shao Yang Stage Disorders**

Bupleurum & Cinnamon Formula *(Chai Hu Gui Zhi Tang)*
Minor Bupleurum Formula *(Xiao Chai Hu Tang)*
Lysimachia GB Formula *(Xiao Chai Hu Jia Jin Qian Cao Fang)*

**Expels Stones**

Lysimachia GB Formula *(Xiao Chai Hu Jia Jin Qian Cao Fang)*

# SYMPTOM INDEX

Stasis-Transforming Formula (chronic, with qi and blood stagnation, and damp-heat)
Stomach-Harmonizing Formula (cramping, acute, with food stagnation and heat)
Tang Kuei & Peony Formula (with liver blood and spleen qi deficiency and dampness)
Tang Kuei & Salvia Formula (with blood deficiency and stagnation)
Women's Precious Formula (with qi and blood deficiency)

**ABSCESSES**

Coptis Relieve Toxicity Formula (with more severe heat)
Viola Clear Fire Formula (with heat-toxin)

**ACID REGURGITATION OR REFLUX**

Coptis Relieve Toxicity Formula (with fire)
Earth-Harmonizing Formula (with liver/stomach disharmony, food stagnation, and heat)
Ease Digestion Formula (from wind, damp, stomach phlegm, or food stagnation)
Free & Easy Wanderer Plus (with liver/spleen disharmony)
Pinellia & Magnolia Bark Formula (with constrained qi and phlegm)
Resolve the Middle Formula (with damp turbidity and stagnation in the middle burner)
Six Gentlemen Formula (with spleen and stomach qi deficiency and phlegm or dampness)
Shu Gan Formula (with liver qi stagnation)
Stomach-Harmonizing Formula (acute, foul-tasting or sour)

**ACNE**

Coptis Relieve Toxicity Formula (with liver heat, heat in the blood, or damp-heat)
Margarita Complexion Formula (adolescent or adult, with heat in the blood or stomach heat)

**AFTERNOON FEVER (See FEVER)**

**AIDS/HIV**

Astragalus & Ligustrum Formula (for deficiency)
Ji Xue Formula (with qi and blood deficiency and stagnation, heat-toxin, and dampness)
Viola Clear Fire Formula (with heat-toxin)

**ALLERGIES (See also FOOD ALLERGIES)**

Astragalus Formula (chronic, with cold in the middle burner)
Bupleurum & Tang Kuei Formula (chronic, with liver/spleen disharmony)
Cinnamon Twig Formula (with disharmony between ying and wei)
Jade Screen & Xanthium Formula (general, or with wind-heat)
Jade Windscreen Formula (with weak wei qi)
Xanthium Nasal Formula (acute sinus congestion, with heat, dampness, or phlegm)
Xanthium & Magnolia Formula (acute, nasal congestion or post-nasal drip, with cold)

**ALTITUDE SICKNESS**

Eleuthero Tablets
Ginseng & Astragalus Formula (with deficient qi of the middle burner)
Ginseng Endurance Formula (with qi, blood, and yang deficiency)
Ji Xue Formula (with qi and blood deficiency and stagnation)

**AMENORRHEA (See MENSTRUATION, SCANTY OR ABSENT)**

**AMNESIA**

Ginkgo Formula (with liver fire or wind, and heart and liver blood deficiency)
Ginseng Nourishing Formula (with qi and blood deficiency, and emotional symptoms)

**ANGINA (See CHEST PAIN)**

**ANEMIA (See BLOOD DEFICIENCY PATTERNS)**

**ANGER OUTBURSTS (See IRRITABILITY)**

**ANXIETY AND NERVOUSNESS**

Bupleurum D Formula (with liver qi stagnation, phlegm and disturbed shen)
Cinnamon D Formula (with heart/kidney disharmony)
Free & Easy Wanderer Plus (with constrained liver qi or liver/spleen disharmony)
Ginseng & Longan Formula (with spleen qi, heart qi, and blood deficiency)
Ginseng Nourishing Formula (with qi and blood deficiency, and unstable shen)
Heavenly Emperor's Formula (with heart yin deficiency)
Jing Qi Formula (with kidney, liver yin, and spleen qi deficiency, and constrained liver qi)
Peaceful Spirit Formula (with spleen qi and heart qi and blood deficiency)
Poria & Bamboo Formula (with stomach-gallbladder disharmony, phlegm-heat and stagnation)
Salvia Ten Formula (with depression)
Two Immortals Formula (with kidney yin and yang deficiency, and flaring-up of fire)

**APPENDICITIS**

Pulsatilla Intestinal Formula (with intestinal inflammation from heat-toxin)
Wu Hua Formula (with damp-heat)

**APPETITE, INCREASED**

Coptis Relieve Toxicity Formula (with stomach fire)
Jade Source Formula (with yin deficiency fire and deficient fluids)

**APPETITE, POOR, REDUCED, OR LOSS OF**

Astragalus Formula (with cold and deficiency in the middle burner)
Bupleurum & Tang Kuei Formula (with liver/spleen disharmony)
Eleuthero Tablets (with spleen and kidney deficiency, and stagnation)
Earth-Harmonizing Formula (with liver/stomach disharmony, food stagnation, and heat)
Free & Easy Wanderer Plus (with liver/spleen disharmony and heat)
General Tonic Formula (with qi and blood deficiency, and internal cold)
Ginseng & Astragalus Formula (with deficient qi of the middle burner)
Ginseng & Longan Formula (with spleen qi, heart qi, and blood deficiency)
Ginseng Endurance Formula (with qi, blood, and yang deficiency)
Ginseng Nourishing Formula (with qi, blood, and yang deficiency)
Ji Xue Formula (with qi and blood deficiency and stagnation, heat-toxin, and dampness)
Jing Qi Formula (with kidney, liver yin, and spleen qi deficiency, and constrained liver qi)
Minor Bupleurum Formula (with shao yang stage disorders)
Poria & Bamboo Formula (with stomach-gallbladder disharmony, phlegm-heat and stagnation)

Resolve the Middle Formula (with damp turbidity and stagnation in the middle burner)
Salvia Ten Formula (from depression with spleen qi deficiency)
Sea of Qi Formula (with spleen yang and kidney yang deficiency)
Shu Gan Formula (with liver qi stagnation)
Six Gentlemen Formula (with spleen and stomach qi deficiency and phlegm or dampness)
Stomach-Harmonizing Formula (with food stagnation and heat)
Women's Precious Formula (with qi and blood deficiency)

**ARMS AND LEGS (See LIMBS)**

**ARTHRITIS OR JOINT PAIN**

Bupleurum & Cinnamon Formula (with crackling sensation or shao yang disorders)
Chase Wind, Penetrate Bone Formula (with wind-cold, wind-damp, qi and blood stagnation)
Clematis & Stephania Formula (with wind-damp and qi and blood stagnation)
Curcuma Longa Formula (with qi and blood stagnation, and heat)
Du Huo & Loranthus Formula (lower body with kidney and liver deficiency)
Eleuthero Tablets (with spleen and kidney deficiency, and stagnation)
Essential Yang Formula (with kidney yang deficiency)
Four Marvel Formula (with dampness and heat in the lower burner)
Juan Bi Formula (upper body, with wind-damp, cold and blood stasis)
Rehmannia & Scrophularia Formula (with kidney yin deficiency heat)
Restorative Formula (with qi, blood, yin and yang deficiency, wind, and dampness)

**ASTHMA**

Eight Immortals Formula (with lung, kidney, and stomach yin deficiency)
Essential Yang Formula (chronic, with kidney yang deficiency)
Fritillaria & Pinellia Formula (with phlegm-heat)
Lily Preserve Metal Formula (chronic, with lung yin deficiency)
Ling Zhi Lung Formula (for kidneys not grasping lung qi, with phlegm)
Minor Bupleurum Formula (liver/spleen disharmony with phlegm)
Mulberry & Lycium Formula (with lung heat or fire)
Pinellia & Magnolia Bark Formula (with constrained qi and phlegm)

**ATHELETE'S FOOT**

Oregano Oil Formula (topically)

**ATHELETIC PERFORMANCE**

Ginseng Endurance Formula (with qi, blood, and yang deficiency)

**ATROPHY**

Four Marvel Formula (with dampness and heat in the lower burner)
Du Huo & Loranthus Formula (lower limbs, with kidney and liver deficiency)
Ji Xue Formula (with qi and blood deficiency and poor circulation)

**B**

**BACK PAIN OR STIFFNESS**

Amber Stone-Transforming Formula (lower, from bladder or kidney stones)
Chase Wind, Penetrate Bone Formula (with wind-cold and wind-damp, qi and blood stagnation)
Cinnamon & Poria Formula (lower, with blood stasis)
Clematis & Stephania Formula (lower, with wind-damp and qi and blood stagnation)

Corydalis Formula (muscle spasms)
Du Huo & Loranthus Formula (lower, with kidney and liver deficiency)
Eleuthero Tablets (with spleen and kidney deficiency, and stagnation)
Essential Yang Formula (chronic, with kidney yang deficiency)
Prostate Formula (with prostate symptoms)
Rehmannia & Scrophularia Formula (with kidney yin deficiency heat)
Rehmannia Six Formula (with kidney and liver yin deficiency)
Seven Treasures Formula (lower, with deficient jing and kidney and liver yin, and deficient blood)
Tang Kuei & Peony Formula (with gynecological symptoms, liver blood deficiency and dampness)
True Yin Formula (with kidney and liver yin deficiency)
Women's Precious Formula (with gynecological symptoms, qi and blood deficiency)
Yin Valley Formula (with yin deficiency dryness and heat)

**BACK SPASMS**

Astragalus Formula (with cold and deficiency in the middle burner)
Corydalis Formula (for pain from)

**BACK WEAKNESS**

Du Huo & Loranthus Formula (lower, with kidney and liver deficiency)
Eleuthero Tablets (with stress, kidney and spleen deficiency, and stagnation)
Essential Yang Formula (with kidney yang deficiency)
General Tonic Formula (with qi and blood deficiency, and internal cold)
He Shou Wu Tablets (with deficient blood, and kidney/liver yin deficiency)
Nourish Essence Formula (with kidney yin and yang deficiency, liver yin deficiency)
Rehmannia Six Formula (with kidney and liver yin deficiency)
Seven Treasures Formula (lower, with deficient jing and kidney and liver yin, and deficient blood)
Tang Kuei & Peony Formula (with liver blood deficiency, spleen deficiency and dampness)
True Yin Formula (with kidney and liver yin deficiency)
Vital Treasure Formula (with kidney yang deficiency, qi and yin deficiency)
Yuan Support Formula (with spleen qi, kidney yang, and blood deficiency)

**BACTERIAL INFECTION**

Andrographis Formula (with heat-toxin)
Coptis Relieve Toxicity Formula (with more severe heat)
Oregano Oil Formula (anti-microbial)
Polyporus & Dianthus Formula (urinary)
Viola Clear Fire Formula (respiratory)
Wu Hua Formula (gastrointestinal, with damp-heat)

**BAD BREATH**

Coptis Relieve Toxicity Formula (acute, with liver heat, heat in the blood, or damp-heat)
Earth-Harmonizing Formula (chronic, with liver/stomach disharmony, food stagnation, and heat)
Stomach-Harmonizing Formula (acute, with food stagnation and stomach heat)

**BASAL TEMPERATURE LOW**

Yuan Support Formula (with spleen qi, kidney yang, and blood deficiency)

**BELCHING**

- Earth-Harmonizing Formula (with liver/stomach disharmony, food stagnation, and heat)
- Ease Digestion Formula (from wind, damp, stomach phlegm or food stagnation)
- Resolve the Middle Formula (with damp turbidity and stagnation in the middle burner)
- Six Gentlemen Formula (with spleen and stomach qi deficiency and phlegm or dampness)
- Shu Gan Formula (with liver qi stagnation)
- Stomach-Harmonizing Formula (of sour, foul-tasting liquid, acute)

**BI SYNDROME (See ARTHRITIS)**

**BITTER, SOUR, OR BAD TASTE IN MOUTH**

- Earth-Harmonizing Formula (with liver/stomach disharmony, food stagnation, and heat)
- Gentiana Drain Fire Formula (with liver and/or gallbladder fire)
- Linking Formula (with yin deficiency, qi stagnation, and fire)
- Minor Bupleurum Formula (with shao yang stage disorders, liver/spleen disharmony)
- Poria & Bamboo Formula (with stomach-gallbladder disharmony, phlegm-heat and stagnation)
- Shu Gan Formula (with liver qi stagnation)
- Siler & Platycodon Formula (for wind-heat with heat in the interior)

**BLADDER STONES**

- Amber Stone-Transforming Formula (acute or chronic)

**BLEEDING**

- Coptis Relieve Toxicity Formula (from excess heat)
- San Qi Formula (internal or external)
- San Qi Tablets (internal or external)
- Yin Valley Formula (with yin deficiency dryness and heat in the blood)

**BLOATING (See ABDOMINAL DISTENSION)**

**BLOOD DEFICIENCY PATTERNS**

- General Tonic Formula (with qi and blood deficiency and internal cold)
- Ginseng & Longan Formula (with spleen qi, heart qi, and blood deficiency)
- Ginseng Nourishing Formula (with qi, blood, and yang deficiency)
- He Shou Wu Tablets (with deficiency of liver and kidney yin)
- Ji Xue Formula (with qi and blood deficiency and stagnation, heat-toxin, and dampness)
- Nourish Essence Formula (with kidney yin and yang deficiency, liver yin deficiency)
- Nourish Ren & Chong Formula (with deficient blood and yin, and heat and stagnation in liver and heart)
- Seven Treasures Formula (with deficient jing and kidney and liver yin, and deficient blood)
- Tang Kuei & Peony Formula (with spleen deficiency and dampness)
- Tang Kuei & Salvia Formula (with blood stasis)
- Tang Kuei & Tribulus Formula (with blood deficiency and dryness)
- Women's Precious Formula (with qi and blood deficiency)
- Yuan Support Formula (with spleen qi, kidney yang, and blood deficiency)

**BLOOD IN STOOLS**

Coptis Relieve Toxicity Formula (with liver heat, heat in the blood, or damp-heat)
Rehmannia Cool Blood Formula (with heat in the blood)
San Qi Formula (controls bleeding)
San Qi Tablets (controls bleeding)
Wu Hua Formula (with dysentery from damp-heat)

**BLOOD IN URINE**

Amber Stone-Transforming Formula (from bladder or kidney stones)
Coptis Relieve Toxicity Formula (with liver heat, heat in the blood, or damp-heat)
Polyporus & Dianthus Formula (with damp-heat)
Rehmannia Cool Blood Formula (with heat in the blood)
San Qi Formula (controls bleeding)
San Qi Tablets (controls bleeding)

**BLOOD STAGNATION**

Blood Palace Formula (upper body)
Chong Release Formula (with blood deficiency)
Cinnamon & Poria Formula (lower body)
Clematis & Stephania Formula (with wind-dampness and qi and blood stagnation)
Curcuma Longa Formula (with inflammation, qi and blood stagnation and heat)
Ji Xue Formula (with qi and blood deficiency and stagnation, heat-toxin, and dampness)
Mobilize Essence Formula (with yin and yang deficiency)
Salvia Ten Formula (with depression and spleen qi deficiency)
San Qi Tablet (controls bleeding)
Stasis-Transforming Formula (with qi and blood stagnation, and damp-heat)
Tang Kuei & Salvia Formula (with blood deficiency)
Tieh Ta Formula (from traumatic injury)
Trauma 1 Formula (stage 1 traumatic injury)
Trauma 2 Formula (stage 1 traumatic injury)

**BLURRED VISION (See VISION, BLURRED)**

**BODY ACHES (See ACHES, GENERAL BODY)**

**BOILS**

Andrographis Formula (with heat-toxin)
Coptis Relieve Toxicity Formula (with liver heat, heat in the blood, or damp-heat)
Margarita Complexion Formula (with heat in the blood, or stomach heat)
Rehmannia Cool Blood Formula (with heat in the blood)
Siler & Platycodon Formula (for wind-heat with heat in the interior)
Wu Hua Formula (with damp-heat)

**BONE BREAKS (See Fractures)**

**BONE DEGENERATION OR WEAKNESS**

Bone & Sinew Formula (second and third stage trauma)
Chase Wind, Penetrate Bone Formula (with kidney yin and yang deficiency and painful obstruction)
Du Huo & Loranthus Formula (lower body, with kidney and liver deficiency)
Eleuthero Tablets (with kidney and spleen deficiency and stagnation)
Essential Yang Formula (with kidney yang deficiency)

**BOUNDARY ISSUES, PSYCHOLOGICAL**

Bupleurum & Cinnamon Formula (with liver/spleen disharmony; use low dose)

Cinnamon D Formula (with heart/kidney disharmony; use low dose)

Cinnamon Twig Formula (regulates wei qi and ying qi; use low dose)

**BREAST DISTENSION, PAIN OR TENDERNESS**

Bupleurum & Tang Kuei Formula (with constrained liver qi, and liver blood and yin deficiency)

Free & Easy Wanderer Plus (same as above, but with heat)

Women's Precious Formula (with qi and blood deficiency and stagnation)

**BREAST LUMPS, FIBROCYSTIC**

Blood Palace Formula (with blood stasis in upper body)

Bupleurum & Tang Kuei Formula (with constrained liver qi)

Free & Easy Wanderer Plus (with constrained liver qi, and heat)

Phlegm-Transforming Formula (with phlegm accumulation, deficiency, and qi or blood stagnation)

**BREATHING DIFFICULTY (See ASTHMA)**

**BREATHING LABORED UPON EXERTION**

Ginseng Endurance Formula (with qi deficiency)

Ling Zhi Lung Formula (for kidneys not grasping lung qi, with phlegm)

**BREATHING SHALLOW (See SHORTNESS OF BREATH)**

**BRONCHITIS**

Andrographis Formula (acute, with heat-toxin)

Citrus & Pinellia Formula (chronic, with phlegm-damp, and clear or white sputum)

Fritillaria & Pinellia Formula (with lung heat or phlegm-heat, and yellow or green sputum)

Ginseng & Astragalus Formula (chronic, with deficient middle qi)

Jade Windscreen Formula (mild, in children with no fever)

Lily Preserve Metal Formula (chronic, with lung yin deficiency)

Ling Zhi Lung Formula (with wheezing, phlegm, and no fever)

Minor Bupleurum Formula (acute shao yang stage, or chronic)

Mulberry & Lycium Formula (with constrained heat in the lung)

Pinellia & Magnolia Bark Formula (with constrained qi and phlegm)

Poria & Bamboo Formula (with stomach-gallbladder disharmony, phlegm-heat and stagnation)

Phlegm-Transforming Formula (chronic, with phlegm accumulation, deficiency, and qi or blood stagnation)

Restore the Lung Formula (chronic, with lung qi deficiency)

Siler & Platycodon Formula (for wind-heat with heat in the interior)

Viola Clear Fire Formula (with heat-toxin)

Zhong Gan Ling Formula (with wind-heat)

**BRONCHIAL ASTHMA (See ASTHMA)**

**BRUISES**

Ginseng & Longan Formula (chronic, or bruises easily)

San Qi Tablets

Tieh Ta Formula (late first or early second stage trauma, with little or no heat)

Trauma 1 Formula (first stage trauma, with swelling, heat, and pain)

Trauma 2 Formula (second stage trauma, with stasis, stiffness, and pain)

**BURSITIS**

Juan Bi Formula (upper body, with wind-damp, cold and blood stasis)

## C

**CANDIDA INFECTION (See YEAST)**

**CARBUNCLE**

Andrographis Formula (with heat-toxin)
Coptis Relieve Toxicity Formula (with heat in the liver, heart, or blood)
He Shou Wu Tablets (with deficient blood, and kidney/liver yin deficiency)
Rehmannia Cool Blood Formula (with heat in the blood)

**CARTILAGE DAMAGE**

Bone & Sinew Formula (second and third stage trauma)
Trauma 1 Formula (first stage trauma, with swelling, heat, and pain)
Trauma 2 Formula (second stage trauma, with stasis, stiffness, and pain)

**CATARACTS**

Essential Yang Formula (with kidney yang deficiency)
Ming Mu Formula (liver and kidney deficiency, with liver heat or internal wind)

**CERVICAL DYSPLASIA OR CERVICITIS**

Immortal Valley Formula (with dampness, heat, and blood stasis)
Yin Valley Formula (with yin deficiency dryness and heat)

**CERVICAL MUCUS, DRY OR SCANTY**

Nourish Ren & Chong Formula (with deficient blood and yin, and heat and stagnation in liver and heart)

**CERVICITIS**

Immortal Valley Formula (with dampness, heat, and blood stasis)
Yin Valley Formula (with yin deficiency dryness and heat)

**CHEMOTHERAPY, RECOVERY FROM, OR SIDE EFFECTS OF**

Astragalus & Ligustrum Formula (with deficiency of normal qi)
Eleuthero Tablets (with kidney and spleen deficiency, and stagnation)
Five Mushroom Formula (general tonic for lung, kidney, liver, spleen, and immune system)
Ji Xue Formula (with qi and blood deficiency and stagnation, heat-toxin, and dampness)
Jing Qi Formula (with kidney, liver yin, and spleen qi deficiency, and constrained liver qi)
Poria & Bamboo Formula (with stomach-gallbladder disharmony, phlegm-heat and stagnation)

**CHEST PAIN**

Blood Palace Formula (with blood stasis in upper body)
San Qi Tablets (with blood stasis)
Sheng Mai Formula (with lung yin and qi deficiency)

**CHEST, FULLNESS OF, OR STIFLING SENSATION IN**

Blood Palace Formula (with blood stasis in upper body)
Bupleurum D Formula (with liver qi stagnation, phlegm and disturbed shen)
Citrus & Pinellia Formula (with phlegm-damp)
Fritillaria & Pinellia Formula (with lung heat or phlegm-heat)
Minor Bupleurum Formula (with shao yang stage disorders)
Mulberry & Lycium Formula (with constrained heat in the lung)
Pinellia & Magnolia Bark Formula (with constrained qi and phlegm)
Poria & Bamboo Formula (with stomach-gallbladder disharmony, phlegm-heat and stagnation)

Six Gentlemen Formula (with spleen and stomach qi deficiency and phlegm or dampness)
Sheng Mai Formula (with lung qi or yin deficiency or with injury to yin from summer heat)

**CHICKEN POX**

Andrographis Formula (with heat-toxin)
Coptis Relieve Toxicity Formula (with high fever)
Rehmannia Cool Blood Formula (with intense itching)
Viola Clear Fire Formula (with heat-toxin)
Yin Chiao Formula (to vent rash)

**CHILDREN, POOR HEALTH IN**

Astragalus Formula (with cold and deficiency in the middle burner)
Jade Windscreen Formula (chronic colds)
Minor Bupleurum Formula (chronic ear infections)
Rehmannia Six Formula (slow development)

**CHILLS**

Bupleurum & Cinnamon Formula (with concurrent tai yang and shao yang patterns)
Cinnamon Twig Formula (with fever unrelieved by sweating, from wind-cold)
Minor Bupleurum Formula (alternating with fever, shao yang stage)

**CHOLECYSITIS (See GALLBLADDER INFLAMMATION)**

**CHOLESTEROL ELEVATED**

Hawthorn & Fennel Formula (with obesity and chronic food stagnation)
He Shou Wu Tablets (with deficient blood, and kidney/liver yin deficiency)
Luo Bu Ma Formula (with liver heat or fire and dampness or phlegm)
Poria Fifteen Formula (with obesity and chronic food stagnation)
San Qi Tablets

**CHRONIC FATIGUE SYNDROME**

Astragalus & Ligustrum Formula (for deficiency)
Ji Xue Formula (with qi and blood deficiency and stagnation, heat-toxin and dampness)
Minor Bupleurum Formula (with latent pathogenic factor)
Viola Clear Fire Formula (with active pathogenic factor)

**CIRRHOSIS OF THE LIVER**

Free & Easy Wanderer Plus (with liver/spleen disharmony and heat)
Liver C Formula (early stage)

**COLD, AVERSION OR SENSITIVITY TO**

General Tonic Formula (with qi and blood deficiency, and internal cold)
Ginseng & Astragalus Formula (with spleen and stomach qi deficiency)
Sea of Qi Formula (with spleen yang and kidney yang deficiency)
Yuan Support Formula (with spleen qi, kidney yang, and blood deficiency)

**COLD LIMBS OR EXTREMITIES**

Astragalus Formula (with cold and deficiency in the middle burner)
Cinnamon Twig Formula (from wind-cold)
Cinnamon D Formula (with heart/kidney disharmony)
Du Huo & Loranthus Formula (lower body, with kidney and liver deficiency)
Essential Yang Formula (with kidney yang deficiency)
General Tonic Formula (with qi and blood deficiency, and internal cold)
Sea of Qi Formula (with spleen yang and kidney yang deficiency)
Vital Treasure Formula (with kidney yang deficiency, qi and yin deficiency)
Yuan Support Formula (with spleen qi, kidney yang, and blood deficiency)

**COMMON COLD**

Andrographis Formula (with heat-toxin)
Bupleurum & Cinnamon Formula (with concurrent tai yang and shao yang patterns, with chest constriction)
Cinnamon Twig Formula (from wind-cold)
Gan Mao Ling Formula (from wind-heat)
Jade Windscreen Formula (recurrent, or in weak patients)
Minor Bupleurum Formula (with lingering fever, or goes into chest, shao yang stage)
Siler & Platycodon Formula (for wind-heat with heat in the interior)
Yin Chiao Formula (early stages, wind-heat)
Zhong Gan Ling Formula (from wind-heat)

**COMPLEXION, LUSTERLESS, PALE, OR SALLOW**

Astragalus Formula (with cold in the middle burner)
Essential Yang Formula (with kidney yang deficiency)
General Tonic Formula (with qi and blood deficiency, and internal cold)
Ginseng & Astragalus Formula (with spleen qi and yang deficiency)
Jade Windscreen Formula (with weak wei qi)
Ji Xue Formula (with qi and blood deficiency and stagnation, heat-toxin and dampness)
Restful Sleep Formula (with insomnia, deficient qi and heart blood, and heat)
Sea of Qi Formula (with spleen yang and kidney yang deficiency)
Tang Kuei & Salvia Formula (with blood deficiency and stagnation)
Women's Precious Formula (with qi and blood deficiency)

**CONCENTRATION, POOR**

Eleuthero Tablets
Ginkgo Formula (with liver fire or wind, and heart and liver blood deficiency)
Ginseng & Longan Formula (with spleen qi, heart qi, and blood deficiency)
Heavenly Emperor's Formula (with heart and kidney yin deficiency)
Ji Xue Formula (with qi and blood deficiency and stagnation, heat-toxin and dampness)

**CONCUSSION (See POST-CONCUSSION SYNDROME**)

**CONJUNCTIVITIS**

Coptis Relieve Toxicity Formula (acute, with heat, or damp-heat)
Gentiana Drain Fire Formula (acute, with damp-heat in liver or liver fire)
Heavenly Emperor's Formula (chronic, with heart and kidney yin deficiency fire)
Siler & Platycodon Formula (for wind-heat with heat in the interior)
Yin Chiao Formula (with wind-heat)

**CONSTIPATION**

Bupleurum & Tang Kuei Formula (with liver/spleen disharmony)
Bupleurum D Formula (with liver qi stagnation, phlegm and irritability)
Earth-Harmonizing Formula (with liver/stomach disharmony, food stagnation, and heat)
Ease Digestion Formula (from wind, damp, stomach phlegm or food stagnation)
Eight Immortals Formula (from dryness with lung, kidney, and stomach yin deficiency)
Essential Yang Formula (with kidney yang deficiency)
Free & Easy Wanderer Plus (with liver/spleen disharmony and heat)

Ginseng & Astragalus Formula (with spleen and stomach qi deficiency)
Hawthorn & Fennel Formula (with obesity and chronic food stagnation)
He Shou Wu Tablets (with deficient blood, and kidney/liver yin deficiency)
Minor Bupleurum Formula (with shao yang stage disorders)
Nourish Essence Formula (with kidney yin and yang deficiency, liver yin deficiency)
Persica & Cistanches Formula (with dry, hard or difficult to pass stool)
Poria Fifteen Formula (with obesity and chronic food stagnation)
Resolve the Middle Formula (with damp turbidity and stagnation in the middle burner)
Restful Sleep Formula (dry stool, with insomnia, deficient qi and heart blood, and heat)
Siler & Platycodon Formula (for wind-heat with heat in the interior)
Stasis-Transforming Formula (with qi and blood stagnation, and damp-heat)
Stomach-Harmonizing Formula (acute, with food stagnation and heat)
Tang Kuei & Salvia Formula (from blood deficiency and stagnation)

**CONSTITUTION, DELICATE**

Astragalus Formula (in children)
Bupleurum & Cinnamon Formula (harmonizes nutritive and protective qi)
Ginseng & Astragalus Formula (with spleen and stomach qi deficiency)
Ginseng & Longan Formula (with spleen qi, heart qi, and blood deficiency)
Ginseng Endurance Formula (with qi, blood, and yang deficiency)
Ginseng Nourishing Formula (with qi, blood, and yang deficiency)
Jade Windscreen Formula (recurrent colds or flu)
Rehmannia Six Formula (with kidney and liver yin deficiency)

**CONVULSIONS**

Bupleurum D Formula (with liver qi stagnation and phlegm)
Gastrodia & Uncaria Formula (with liver yang rising and liver wind)

**CORONARY ARTERY DISEASE**

Blood Palace Formula (with blood stasis in upper body)
San Qi Tablet (with blood stasis)

**COUGH**

Citrus & Pinellia Formula (with sticky, clear or white sputum)
Eight Immortals Formula (chronic, with lung, kidney, and stomach yin deficiency)
Five Mushroom Formula (chronic, general tonic for lung, kidney, liver, spleen, and immune system)
Fritillaria & Pinellia Formula (thick, sticky, yellow or green sputum from lung-heat or phlegm-heat)
General Tonic Formula (chronic, with qi and blood deficiency, and internal cold)
Lily Preserve Metal Formula (dry, blood streaked or sticky sputum from lung yin deficiency)
Ling Zhi Lung Formula (with wheezing and phlegm)
Minor Bupleurum Formula (with shao yang stage disorders)
Mulberry & Lycium Formula (with lung heat or fire)
Pinellia & Magnolia Bark Formula (with constrained qi and profuse sputum)
Poria Five Formula (with fluid retention)
Restore the Lung Formula (with lung qi deficiency)

Sea of Qi Formula (with white sputum, spleen and kidney yang deficiency)
Sheng Mai Formula (chronic, with difficult to expectorate sputum and lung qi or yin deficiency)
Siler & Platycodon Formula (for wind-heat with heat in the interior)
Six Gentlemen Formula (with copious thin, white sputum, spleen and stomach qi deficiency)
Viola Clear Fire Formula (respiratory infection, heat-toxin)
Yin Chiao Formula (from initial stage wind-heat)
Zhong Gan Ling Formula (from severe wind-heat)

**COUGHING UP BLOOD**
Coptis Relieve Toxicity Formula (with heat)
Eight Immortals Formula (with lung, kidney, and stomach yin deficiency)
Mulberry & Lycium Formula (with lung heat or fire)
San Qi Formula (controls bleeding)

**CROHN'S DISEASE**
Pulsatilla Intestinal Formula (with intestinal inflammation from heat-toxin)
San Qi Formula (acute attacks)
San Qi Tablets (acute attacks)

**CYSTITIS (See URINARY TRACT INFECTION)**
**CYSTS, GANGLIONIC (See GANGLIONIC CYSTS)**
**CYSTS, OVARIAN (See OVARIAN CYSTS)**

## D

**DEBILITY (See WEAKNESS)**
**DELIRIUM**
Bupleurum D Formula (with liver qi stagnation, phlegm, and disturbed shen)
Coptis Relieve Toxicity Formula (with fire or heat)
Rehmannia Cool Blood Formula (with heat in the blood)

**DEPRESSION**
Blood Palace Formula (with blood stasis in upper body, and a sensation of warmth in chest)
Bupleurum & Tang Kuei Formula (with constrained liver qi)
Free & Easy Wanderer Plus (with constrained liver qi and heat)
Ji Xue Formula (with qi and blood deficiency and stagnation, heat-toxin and dampness)
Poria & Bamboo Formula (with stomach-gallbladder disharmony, phlegm-heat and stagnation)
Salvia Ten Formula (with spleen qi deficiency)
Two Immortals Formula (with kidney yin and yang deficiency and flaring-up of fire)

**DIABETES**
Eight Immortals Formula (with lung, kidney, and stomach yin deficiency)
Essential Yang Formula (with kidney yang deficiency)
Jade Source Formula (with yin deficiency fire and deficient fluids)
Rehmannia & Scrophularia Formula (with kidney yin deficiency heat)
Rehmannia Six Formula (with kidney and liver yin deficiency)

**DIARRHEA OR LOOSE STOOLS**
Andrographis Formula (acute, with heat-toxin)
Cinnamon D Formula (with heart/kidney disharmony)
Coptis Relieve Toxicity Formula (with blood in stools from heat)

Earth-Harmonizing Formula (with liver/stomach disharmony, food stagnation, and heat)
Ease Digestion Formula (from wind, damp, stomach phlegm or food stagnation)
Ginseng & Astragalus Formula (chronic, with spleen and stomach qi deficiency)
Ginseng Nourishing Formula (chronic, with qi, blood, and yang deficiency)
Intestinal Fungus Formula (with heat-toxin and dampness)
Minor Bupleurum Formula (with shao yang stage disorders)
Poria Five Formula (acute, with vomiting and heaviness or edema)
Pulsatilla Intestinal Formula (with intestinal inflammation from heat-toxin)
Resolve the Middle Formula (with damp turbidity and stagnation in the middle burner)
Sea of Qi Formula (chronic, with spleen yang and kidney yang deficiency)
Six Gentlemen Formula (with spleen and stomach qi deficiency and phlegm or dampness)
Stomach-Harmonizing Formula (acute, with heat and food stagnation)
Viola Clear Fire Formula (from damp-heat)
Wu Hua Formula (with damp-heat or heat-toxin)

**DIGESTIVE DISCOMFORT, CHRONIC**

Earth-Harmonizing Formula (with liver/stomach disharmony, food stagnation, and heat)
Linking Formula (with yin deficiency, qi stagnation, and fire)

**DIGESTION, WEAK**

Astragalus Formula (with cold in the middle burner, especially in children)
General Tonic Formula (with qi and blood deficiency, and internal cold)
Ginseng & Astragalus Formula (with spleen and stomach qi deficiency)
Ginseng Nourishing Formula (with qi, blood, and yang deficiency)
Hawthorn & Fennel Formula (with food stagnation)
Ji Xue Formula (with qi and blood deficiency and stagnation, heat-toxin and dampness)
Jing Qi Formula (with kidney, liver yin, and spleen qi deficiency, and constrained liver qi)
Poria Fifteen Formula (with food stagnation)
Salvia Ten Formula (with depression)
Sea of Qi Formula (with kidney and spleen yang deficiency)
Shu Gan Formula (with liver qi stagnation)
Six Gentlemen Formula (with spleen and stomach qi deficiency and phlegm or dampness)

**DIZZINESS**

Bupleurum & Tang Kuei Formula (with constrained liver qi, liver blood deficiency)
Cinnamon D Formula (with heart/kidney disharmony)
Citrus & Pinellia Formula (with phlegm-damp)
Coptis Relieve Toxicity Formula (with fire or heat-toxin)
Eight Immortals Formula (with lung, kidney, and stomach yin deficiency)
Free & Easy Wanderer Plus (with constrained liver qi, liver blood deficiency and heat)
Gastrodia & Uncaria Formula (with liver yang rising and liver wind)
General Tonic Formula (with qi and blood deficiency, and internal cold)
Gentiana Drain Fire Formula (with liver fire, damp-heat)

Ginkgo Formula (with poor mental functioning)
Ginseng & Astragalus Formula (with spleen and stomach qi deficiency)
He Shou Wu Tablets (with deficient blood, and kidney/liver yin deficiency)
Ji Xue Formula (with qi and blood deficiency and stagnation, heat-toxin and dampness)
Jing Qi Formula (with kidney, liver yin, and spleen qi deficiency, and constrained liver qi)
Luo Bu Ma Formula (with liver heat or fire and dampness or phlegm)
Minor Bupleurum Formula (with shao yang stage disorders)
Nourish Essence Formula (with kidney yin and yang deficiency, liver yin deficiency)
Nourish Ren & Chong Formula (with deficient blood and yin and heat and stagnation in liver and heart)
Peaceful Spirit Formula (with spleen qi and heart qi and blood deficiency)
Poria & Bamboo Formula (with stomach-gallbladder disharmony, phlegm-heat and stagnation)
Poria Five Formula (with retention of fluids)
Rehmannia & Scrophularia Formula (with kidney yin deficiency heat)
Rehmannia Six Formula (with kidney and liver yin deficiency)
Sea of Qi Formula (with spleen yang and kidney yang deficiency)
Sheng Mai Formula (with lung qi or yin deficiency, or with injury to yin from summer heat)
Six Gentlemen Formula (due to stomach phlegm accumulation)
Tang Kuei & Salvia Formula (with blood deficiency and stagnation)
True Yin Formula (with kidney and liver yin deficiency)
Two Immortals Formula (with kidney yin and yang deficiency, and flaring up of fire)
Women's Precious Formula (with qi and blood deficiency)

**DREAM-DISTURBED SLEEP**

Bupleurum D Formula (with liver qi stagnation, phlegm, and disturbed shen)
Cinnamon D Formula (with heart/kidney disharmony)
Gastrodia & Uncaria Formula (with liver yang rising and liver wind)
Ginkgo Formula (with poor mental functioning, liver fire or wind, and heart and liver blood deficiency)
Ginseng & Longan Formula (with spleen qi, heart qi, and blood deficiency)
Heavenly Emperor's Formula (with heart and kidney yin deficiency fire)
Peaceful Spirit Formula (with spleen qi and heart qi and blood deficiency)
True Yin Formula (with kidney and liver yin deficiency)

**DRUG WITHDRAWAL**

Bupleurum D Formula (with liver qi stagnation, phlegm, and disturbed shen)

**DRY HEAVES**

Blood Palace Formula (with blood stasis in upper body)
Cinnamon Twig Formula (from wind-cold, or disharmony of ying and wei)

**DRYNESS**

Coptis Relieve Toxicity Formula (mouth and throat, with fire)
Eight Immortals Formula (skin, mouth or throat, with lung, kidney, and stomach yin deficiency)
He Shou Wu Tablets (with deficient blood, and kidney/liver yin deficiency)
Heavenly Emperor's Formula (with yin and blood)
Jade Source Formula (of mouth and tongue, with yin deficiency fire and deficient fluids)

Lily Preserve Metal Formula (lips, mouth, nose, with lung yin deficiency)
Linking Formula (with yin deficiency, qi stagnation, and fire)
Mulberry & Lycium Formula (mouth, with lung heat or fire)
Nourish Essence Formula (mouth, with kidney yin and yang deficiency, liver yin deficiency)
Rehmannia & Scrophularia Formula (throat, with kidney yin deficiency heat)
Rehmannia Cool Blood Formula (with heat in the blood)
Rehmannia Six Formula (with kidney and liver yin deficiency)
Sheng Mai Formula (with lung yin deficiency)
Tang Kuei & Salvia Formula (hair, skin and nails, from blood deficiency)
Tang Kuei & Tribulus Formula (with blood deficiency and dryness)
True Yin Formula (of mouth and throat, with kidney and liver yin deficiency)
Women's Precious Formula (hair, skin and nails, with blood and qi deficiency)
Zizyphus Formula (mouth and throat, with liver and heart blood and yin deficiency, and heat)

**DYSENTERY**

Andrographis Formula (bacterial with heat-toxin)
Oregano Oil Formula (anti-microbial, clears heat-toxin)
Wu Hua Formula (with damp-heat or heat-toxin)

**DYSMENORRHEA (See MENSTRUAL PAIN)**

## E

**EARACHES, OR INFECTIONS**

Andrographis Formula (with heat-toxin)
Astragalus Formula (chronic)
Children's Ear Formula (acute)
Gan Mao Ling Formula (from wind-heat)
Gentiana Drain Fire Formula (with liver/gallbladder fire)
Minor Bupleurum Formula (with shao yang stage disorders)
Xanthium & Magnolia Formula (with nasal congestion)

**EAR DRUM INFLAMED OR BULGING**

Children's Ear Formula
Gentiana Drain Fire Formula (with damp-heat, liver fire)

**ECZEMA**

Cinnamon Twig Formula (from wind-cold, or disharmony of ying and wei)
Coptis Relieve Toxicity Formula (with heat or fire)
Du Huo & Loranthus Formula (in children)
Four Marvel Formula (lower body, with damp-heat)
Gentiana Drain Fire Formula (with damp-heat, liver fire)
He Shou Wu Tablets (with deficient blood, and kidney/liver yin deficiency)
Margarita Complexion Formula (with heat in the blood or stomach heat)
Rehmannia Cool Blood Formula (with heat in the blood)
Tang Kuei & Tribulus Formula (with blood deficiency and dryness)
Wu Hua Formula (with damp-heat, heat in the blood, or heat-toxin)

**EDEMA**

Clematis & Stephania Formula (with wind-damp, and qi and blood stagnation)
Essential Yang Formula (with kidney yang deficiency)
Four Marvel Formula (lower body, with damp-heat)

Hawthorn & Fennel Formula (with obesity)
Luo Bu Ma Formula (with liver heat or fire and dampness or phlegm)
Poria Fifteen Formula (with obesity)
Poria Five Formula (from tai yang disorders, spleen deficiency, or congestion of fluids in the lower burner)
Sea of Qi Formula (with spleen yang and kidney yang deficiency)
Tang Kuei & Peony Formula (with liver blood and spleen deficiency and dampness)

**EMOTIONAL INSTABILITY**

Astragalus Formula (lack of sense of self, with cold in the middle burner)
Blood Palace Formula (outbursts or extreme mood swings, with blood stagnation in upper body)
Bupleurum & Cinnamon Formula (with liver/spleen disharmony)
Bupleurum & Tang Kuei Formula (with constrained liver qi, liver blood deficiency)
Bupleurum D Formula (with liver qi stagnation, phlegm, and disturbed shen)
Cinnamon D Formula (with heart/kidney disharmony)
Coptis Relieve Toxicity Formula (with liver heat or fire)
Free & Easy Wanderer Plus (with constrained liver qi, liver blood deficiency and heat)
Gastrodia & Uncaria Formula (with liver yang rising and wind)
Ginseng Nourishing Formula (with qi and blood deficiency)
Heavenly Emperor's Formula (with heart and kidney yin deficiency fire)

**ENDOMETRIOSIS**

Chong Release Formula (with blood deficiency and stagnation)
Cinnamon & Poria Formula (with blood stasis)
Phlegm-Transforming Formula (with phlegm accumulation, deficiency, and qi or blood stagnation)
Stasis-Transforming Formula (with qi and blood stagnation, and damp-heat)

**ENDOMETRITIS**

Stasis-Transforming Formula (with qi and blood stagnation, and damp-heat)

**ENDOMETRIUM TOO THIN**

Yuan Support Formula (with spleen qi, kidney yang, and blood deficiency)

**ENERGY LOW (See FATIGUE)**

**EPIGASTRIC PAIN (See STOMACH ACHE)**

**EPISTAXIS (See NOSEBLEED)**

**EPSTEIN-BARR VIRUS (EBV)**

Astragalus & Ligustrum Formula (for deficiency)
Minor Bupleurum Formula (with latent pathogenic factor)
Viola Clear Fire Formula (with active pathogenic factor)

**ERECTILE DYSFUNCTION (See SEXUAL DYSFUNCTION, MALE)**

**ESOPHAGEAL CONSTRICTION, NEUROTIC**

Pinellia & Magnolia Bark Formula (with constrained qi and phlegm)

**EXHAUSTION (See FATIGUE)**

**EYES DRY, RED, ITCHY, PAINFUL, OR SENSITIVE TO LIGHT**

Curcuma Longa Formula (with inflammation, qi and blood stagnation and heat)
Free & Easy Wanderer Plus (with constrained liver qi, liver blood deficiency, and heat)

Gan Mao Ling Formula (red, from wind-heat)
Gastrodia & Uncaria Formula (with liver yang rising and liver wind)
Gentiana Drain Fire Formula (with more severe heat and fullness)
Jade Screen & Xanthium Formula (with allergy symptoms)
Luo Bu Ma Formula (with liver heat or fire and dampness or phlegm)
Ming Mu Formula (with kidney deficiency and liver blood deficiency)
Siler & Platycodon Formula (for wind-heat with heat in the interior)
Yin Chiao Formula (with wind-heat)

## F

**FACIAL SWELLING**

Jade Screen & Xanthium Formula (with allergy symptoms)
Poria Five Formula (with water metabolism dysfunction)

**FATIGUE**

Astragalus & Ligustrum Formula (with deficiency of normal qi)
Astragalus Formula (with cold and deficiency in the middle burner)
Bupleurum & Tang Kuei Formula (with constrained liver qi, liver blood and yin deficiency)
Eleuthero Tablets (with stress, kidney and spleen deficiency, and stagnation)
Essential Yang Formula (with kidney yang deficiency)
General Tonic Formula (with qi and blood deficiency, and internal cold)
Ginseng & Astragalus Formula (with spleen and stomach qi deficiency, and sunken yang)
Ginseng Endurance Formula (with qi, blood, and yang deficiency)
Ginseng Nourishing Formula (with qi and blood deficiency, and emotional symptoms)
Ji Xue Formula (with qi and blood deficiency and stagnation, heat-toxin and dampness)
Jing Qi Formula (with kidney, liver yin, and spleen qi deficiency, and slight liver qi constraint)
Liver C Formula (with chronic hepatitis)
Nourish Essence Formula (with kidney yin and yang deficiency, liver yin deficiency)
Nourish Ren & Chong Formula (with deficient blood and yin, and heat and stagnation in liver and heart)
Pulsatilla Intestinal Formula (with intestinal inflammation from heat- toxin)
Rehmannia Six Formula (with kidney and liver yin deficiency)
Resolve the Middle Formula (with damp turbidity and stagnation in the middle burner)
Restful Sleep Formula (from insomnia, with deficient qi and heart blood, and heat)
Restore the Lung Formula (with lung qi deficiency)
Salvia Ten Formula (with depression and spleen qi deficiency)
Sea of Qi Formula (with spleen yang and kidney yang deficiency)
Sheng Mai Formula (with lung qi or yin deficiency or with injury to yin from summer heat)
Six Gentlemen Formula (with spleen and stomach qi deficiency and phlegm or dampness)
Tang Kuei & Salvia Formula (with blood deficiency and stagnation)

Two Immortals Formula (with kidney yin and yang deficiency, and flaring-up of fire)
Vital Treasure Formula (with kidney yang deficiency, qi and yin deficiency)
Women's Precious Formula (with qi and blood deficiency)
Yuan Support Formula (with spleen qi, kidney yang, and blood deficiency)

**FEVER**

Andrographis Formula (with heat-toxin)
Astragalus Formula (low grade or occasional)
Blood Palace Formula (afternoon, with blood stasis in upper body)
Children's Ear Formula (in children prone to ear infections)
Cinnamon Twig Formula (unrelieved by sweating, from wind-cold)
Coptis Relieve Toxicity Formula (high fever)
Eight Immortals Formula (tidal, with lung, kidney, and stomach yin deficiency)
Gan Mao Ling Formula (from wind-heat invasion)
Ginseng & Astragalus Formula (chronic, intermittent, worse with exertion)
Ginseng & Longan Formula (chronic, from deficiency, with spleen qi and heart qi and blood deficiency)
Ji Xue Formula (low-grade, with qi and blood deficiency and stagnation, heat-toxin and dampness)
Minor Bupleurum Formula (with alternating chills, shao yang stage, or lingering)
Mulberry & Lycium Formula (with lung heat or fire)
Polyporus & Dianthus Formula (with urinary tract infections)
Poria Five Formula (tai yang stage, with water accumulation)
Rehmannia & Scrophularia Formula (low grade, afternoon or tidal, with kidney yin deficiency)
Rehmannia Six Formula (with kidney and liver yin deficiency)
Siler & Platycodon Formula (for wind-heat with heat in the interior)
Viola Clear Fire Formula (with heat-toxin)
Yin Chiao Formula (with wind-heat)
Zhong Gan Ling Formula (from severe wind-heat)

**FIBROIDS, UTERINE (See UTERINE FIBROIDS)**

**FIBROMYALGIA (See also PAIN)**

Blood Palace Formula (with blood stasis in upper body)
Ji Xue Formula (with qi and blood deficiency and stagnation, heat-toxin, and dampness)
Restorative Formula (with qi, blood, yin and yang deficiency, wind, and dampness)
Stasis-Transforming Formula (with qi and blood stasis, and damp-heat)

**FLATULENCE**

Bupleurum & Cinnamon Formula (with liver/spleen disharmony)
Ease Digestion Formula (from wind-damp, stomach phlegm, or food stagnation)
Ginseng & Astragalus Formula (with spleen and stomach qi deficiency)
Intestinal Fungus Formula (with heat-toxin and dampness)
Resolve the Middle Formula (with damp turbidity and stagnation in the middle burner)
Sea of Qi Formula (with spleen yang and kidney yang deficiency)
Shu Gan Formula (with liver qi stagnation)
Stomach-Harmonizing Formula (with and food stagnation)

**FLU (See INFLUENZA)**

**FOOD ALLERGIES**

- Bupleurum & Tang Kuei Formula (with constrained liver qi, liver blood and yin deficiency)
- Ease Digestion Formula (acute, with wind and dampness, stomach phlegm, or food stagnation)
- Pulsatilla Intestinal Formula (with intestinal inflammation from heat-toxin)

**FOOD POISONING**

- Coptis Relieve Toxicity Formula (with liver heat or fire)
- Ease Digestion Formula (with wind, dampness, or stomach phlegm)
- Intestinal Fungus Formula (with heat-toxin and dampness)
- Oregano Oil Formula (anti-microbial)
- Wu Hua Formula (with damp-heat)

**FOOD STAGNATION**

- Citrus & Pinellia Formula (with disharmony of stomach or spleen from phlegm-damp)
- Earth-Harmonizing Formula (chronic, with liver/stomach disharmony and heat)
- Ease Digestion Formula (acute, with wind, dampness, or stomach phlegm)
- Hawthorn & Fennel Formula (chronic)
- Poria Fifteen Formula (chronic)
- Resolve the Middle Formula (with damp turbidity and stagnation in the middle burner)
- Stomach-Harmonizing Formula (acute with heat)

**FORGETFULNESS (See MEMORY, POOR)**

**FRACTURES**

- Bone & Sinew Formula (second and third stage)
- Curcuma Longa Formula (with inflammation and pain)
- Tieh Ta Formula (late first/early second stage with little or no heat)
- Trauma 1 Formula (first stage trauma, with swelling, heat, and pain)
- Trauma 2 Formula (second stage trauma, with stasis, stiffness, and pain)

**FRIGHT**

- Astragalus Formula (in children, with cold and deficiency in middle burner)
- Bupleurum D Formula (with liver qi stagnation, phlegm, and disturbed shen)
- Ginseng & Longan Formula (with spleen qi, heart qi, and blood deficiency)
- Poria & Bamboo Formula (with stomach-gallbladder disharmony, phlegm-heat and stagnation)
- Zizyphus Formula (with liver and heart blood and yin deficiency, disturbed sleep)

## G

**GALLBLADDER INFLAMMATION**

- Gentiana Drain Fire Formula (with liver and gallbladder fire, and/or damp-heat)
- Lysimachia GB Formula (with damp-heat and constrained qi in the liver and gallbladder and pain)
- Minor Bupleurum Formula (with shao yang stage disorders)
- Poria & Bamboo Formula (with stomach-gallbladder disharmony, phlegm-heat and stagnation)

**GALLBLADDER SPASMS**

Corydalis Formula (for pain)

Lysimachia GB Formula (with damp-heat and constrained qi in the liver and gallbladder, and pain)

Minor Bupleurum Formula (with shao yang stage disorders)

**GALLSTONES**

Bupleurum & Cinnamon Formula (with liver/spleen disharmony in weaker patients)

Gentiana Drain Fire Formula (with damp-heat or fire in gallbladder)

Lysimachia GB Formula (with damp-heat and constrained qi in the liver and gallbladder and pain)

Minor Bupleurum Formula (with shao yang stage disorders)

**GANGLIONIC CYSTS**

Phlegm-Transforming Formula (with phlegm accumulation, deficiency, and qi or blood stagnation)

**GAS (See BELCHING, BLOATING, OR FLATULENCE)**

**GASTRITIS (See also STOMACH ACHE)**

Coptis Relieve Toxicity Formula (with liver heat or fire)

Curcuma Longa Formula (with inflammation, qi and blood stagnation and heat)

Linking Formula (with yin deficiency, qi stagnation, and fire)

Poria & Bamboo Formula (with stomach-gallbladder disharmony, phlegm-heat and stagnation)

Resolve the Middle Formula (with damp turbidity and stagnation in the middle burner)

**GASTROENTERITIS (STOMACH FLU)**

Adrographis Formula (with heat-toxin)

Ease Digestion Formula (from wind, damp, stomach phlegm or food stagnation)

Intestinal Fungus Formula (with heat-toxin and dampness)

Poria Five Formula (tai yang stage, with water accumulation)

Wu Hua Formula (with damp-heat)

**GASTROINTESTINAL INFLAMMATION**

Curcuma Longa Formula (with inflammation, qi and blood stagnation and heat)

Pulsatilla Intestinal Formula (with intestinal inflammation from heat-toxin)

Wu Hua Formula (with damp-heat or heat-toxin)

**GIARDIA**

Intestinal Fungus Formula (with heat-toxin and dampness)

Oregano Oil Formula (with damp-heat, and heat-toxin, anti-microbial)

**GLAUCOMA**

Essential Yang Formula (with kidney yang deficiency)

Ming Mu Formula (liver/kidney deficiency with liver heat or internal wind)

**GLANDS, SWOLLEN (See LYMPH NODES, ENLARGED)**

**GENITAL ITCHING AND SWELLING**

Four Marvel Formula (from damp-heat)

Gentiana Drain Fire Formula (damp-heat in the liver/gallbladder)

Immortal Valley Formula (with dampness, heat, and blood stasis in lower abdomen)

Yin Valley Formula (with yin deficiency dryness and heat)

**GENITAL PAIN, MALE**

Four Marvel Formula (from damp-heat)
Gentiana Drain Fire Formula (damp-heat in the liver/gallbladder)
Rabdosia Prostate Formula (with heat or damp-heat and prostate symptoms)

**GENITALS, COLDNESS IN**

Cinnamon D Formula (with heart/kidney disharmony)

**GENITAL SORES**

Four Marvel Formula (with dampness and heat in the lower burner)
Gentiana Drain Fire Formula (damp-heat in the liver/gallbladder)
Immortal Valley Formula (with dampness, heat, and blood stasis in lower abdomen)
Viola Clear Fire Formula (with heat-toxin)

**GOITER**

Phlegm-Transforming Formula (with phlegm accumulation, deficiency, and qi or blood stagnation)

**GOUT**

Clematis & Stephania Formula (with wind-damp, and qi and blood stagnation)
Curcuma Longa Formula (anti-inflammatory, qi and blood stagnation and heat)
Four Marvel Formula (with dampness and heat in the lower burner)
Juan Bi Formula (upper body, with wind-damp, cold and blood stasis)

**GUMS BLEEDING**

San Qi Formula (controls bleeding)
San Qi Tablets (controls bleeding)

**GUM INFECTIONS**

Andrographis Formula (with heat-toxin)
Coptis Relieve Toxicity Formula (with liver heat or fire)

## H

**HAIR, DRY OR BRITTLE (See DRYNESS)**

**HAIR LOSS**

Cinnamon D Formula (with heart/kidney disharmony)
Ginseng Nourishing Formula (from injury to blood)
Ji Xue Formula (from chemotherapy, with qi and blood deficiency and stagnation, heat-toxin and dampness)
Seven Treasures Formula (with deficient jing and kidney and liver yin, and deficient blood)
True Yin Formula (with kidney and liver yin deficiency)

**HAIR, PREMATURE GRAYING**

He Shou Wu Tablets (with deficient blood, and kidney/liver yin deficiency)
Nourish Essence Formula (with kidney yin and yang deficiency, liver yin deficiency)
Seven Treasures Formula (with deficient jing and kidney and liver yin, and deficient blood)
True Yin Formula (with kidney and liver yin deficiency)

**HANGOVER**

Citrus & Pinellia Formula (with phlegm-damp)
Coptis Relieve Toxicity Formula (with liver heat or fire)
Ease Digestion Formula (with digestive upset and dampness or phlegm)

Gentiana Drain Fire Formula (damp-heat in the liver/gallbladder)
Head Relief Formula (from wind or muscle tension)
Resolve the Middle Formula (with damp turbidity and stagnation in the middle burner)
Stomach-Harmonizing Formula (with digestive upset and heat)

**HAY FEVER (See ALLERGIES)**

**HEADACHE**

Blood Palace Formula (fixed, piercing pain, with blood stasis in upper body)
Bupleurum & Tang Kuei Formula (with constrained liver qi, liver blood and yin deficiency)
Bupleurum D Formula (with liver qi stagnation, phlegm, and disturbed shen)
Cinnamon Twig Formula (with wind-cold invasion)
Corydalis Formula (for pain or muscle tension)
Free & Easy Wanderer Plus (with constrained liver qi, liver blood deficiency, and heat)
Gan Mao Ling Formula (from wind-heat)
Gastrodia & Uncaria Formula (with liver yang rising and wind)
Gentiana Drain Fire Formula (with liver/gallbladder fire)
Ginseng & Astragalus Formula (with spleen and stomach qi deficiency)
Head Relief Formula (from wind-cold, muscle tension, or trauma)
He Shou Wu Tablets (with blood deficiency)
Jade Screen & Xanthium Formula (from allergies)
Luo Bu Ma Formula (with liver heat or fire and dampness or phlegm)
Minor Bupleurum Formula (with shao yang stage disorders)
Mobilize Essence Formula (mid-menstrual cycle)
Nourish Ren & Chong Formula (with deficient blood and yin, and heat and stagnation in liver and heart)
Poria Five Formula (tai yang stage, with water accumulation)
Tang Kuei & Salvia Formula (with blood deficiency and stagnation)
Xanthium & Magnolia Formula (with nasal congestion or post-nasal drip)
Xanthium Nasal Formula (acute sinus congestion, with heat, dampness, or phlegm)
Yin Chiao Formula (from wind-heat)
Zhong Gan Ling Formula (from wind-heat)
Zizyphus Formula (one sided, with liver and heart blood and yin deficiency, and heat)

**HEARING LOSS**

Gentiana Drain Fire Formula (acute, from fever with liver fire)
Nourish Essence Formula (with kidney yin and yang deficiency, liver yin deficiency)
Rehmannia Six Formula (with kidney and liver yin deficiency)
True Yin Formula (with kidney and liver yin deficiency)

**HEARTBURN**

Coptis Relieve Toxicity Formula (with liver heat or fire)
Minor Bupleurum Formula (with shao yang stage disorders)
Stomach-Harmonizing Formula (from overeating)

**HEART DISEASE**

Blood Palace Formula (with blood stasis)
Curcuma Longa Formula (with inflammation, qi and blood stagnation and heat)

Ginseng & Longan Formula (with spleen qi, heart qi, and blood deficiency)
San Qi Tablets (with blood stasis)
Sheng Mai Formula (with lung qi or yin deficiency, or with injury to yin from summer heat)

**HEART PALPITATION (See PALPITATION)**

**HEAT, AVERSION TO**

Rehmannia Cool Blood Formula (with heat in the blood)

**HEAT EXHAUSTION**

Sheng Mai Formula

**HEAT RASH (See SKIN RASH)**

**HEAT SENSATION IN HEAD**

Bupleurum D Formula (with liver qi stagnation, phlegm, and disturbed shen)
Gastrodia & Uncaria Formula (with liver yang rising and liver wind)

**HEAVINESS, GENERALIZED BODY**

Poria Fifteen Formula (chronic, with obesity)
Poria Five Formula (with spleen deficiency and water accumulation)
Resolve the Middle Formula (with damp turbidity and stagnation in the middle burner)

**HEMATURIA (See BLOOD, IN URINE)**

**HEMOPTYSIS (See COUGHING UP BLOOD)**

**HEMORRHOIDS**

Astragalus Formula (with cold and deficiency in the middle burner)
Ginseng & Astragalus Formula (with spleen and stomach qi deficiency, and sunken yang)
San Qi Formula (controls bleeding)
San Qi Tablets (controls bleeding)
Tang Kuei & Peony Formula (with liver blood and spleen deficiency, and dampness)
Wu Hua Formula (with damp-heat)

**HEPATITIS**

Andrographis Formula (acute, with heat-toxin)
Bupleurum & Cinnamon Formula (acute, type A, with liver/spleen disharmony or shao yang stage disorders)
Five Mushroom Formula (general tonic for lung, kidney, liver, spleen, and immune system)
Free & Easy Wanderer Plus (chronic, Type B or C)
Gentiana Drain Fire Formula (acute, with liver fire, damp-heat)
Linking Formula (with yin deficiency, qi stagnation, and fire)
Liver C Formula (chronic)
Lysimachia GB Formula (acute, with damp-heat and constrained qi in the liver and gallbladder)
Minor Bupleurum Formula (chronic, Type A or B)
Poria & Bamboo Formula (with stomach-gallbladder disharmony, phlegm-heat and stagnation)
Shu Gan Formula (acute, with liver qi stagnation and phlegm)

**HEPATOMEGALY**

Liver C Formula

**HERNIA**

Ginseng & Astragalus Formula

**HERPES SIMPLEX**

Andrographis Formula (for Herpes Simplex 1)
Coptis Relieve Toxicity Formula (for Herpes Simplex 1)
Gentiana Drain Fire Formula (for Herpes Simplex 2)
Immortal Valley Formula (for Herpes Simplex 2)
Viola Clear Fire Formula (for either 1 or 2)

**HERPES ZOSTER (SHINGLES)**

Andrographis Formula (with heat-toxin)
Corydalis Formula (for pain from)
Gentiana Drain Fire Formula (with liver fire, damp-heat)
Minor Bupleurum Formula (with shao yang stage disorders)
Viola Clear Fire Formula (with heat-toxin)

**HICCOUGH**

Blood Palace Formula (chronic, with blood stasis in upper body)
Poria & Bamboo Formula (with stomach-gallbladder disharmony, phlegm-heat and stagnation)
Shu Gan Formula (with liver qi stagnation and phlegm)

**HIVES**

Cinnamon Twig Formula (with wind-cold invasion)
Heavenly Emperor's Formula (with heart and kidney yin deficiency fire)
Margarita Complexion Formula (with heat in the blood or stomach heat)
Rehmannia Cool Blood Formula (with heat in the blood)
Siler & Platycodon Formula (for wind-heat with heat in the interior)
Tang Kuei & Salvia Formula (with blood deficiency)
Tang Kuei & Tribulus Formula (with blood deficiency and dryness)
Wu Hua Formula (with damp-heat)
Yin Chiao Formula (from wind-heat invasion)

**HOARSENESS**

Eight Immortals Formula (with lung, kidney, and stomach yin deficiency)
Viola Clear Fire Formula (with heat-toxin)

**HOT FLASHES**

Bupleurum & Tang Kuei Formula (with constrained liver qi, liver blood and yin deficiency)
Bupleurum D Formula (with liver qi stagnation, phlegm, and disturbed shen)
Free & Easy Wanderer Plus (with constrained liver qi, liver blood and yin deficiency, and heat)
Heavenly Emperor's Formula (with heart and kidney yin deficiency fire)
Rehmannia & Scrophularia Formula (with kidney yin deficiency and fire)
Sea of Qi Formula (with spleen yang and kidney yang deficiency)
Two Immortals Formula (with deficiency of ren and chong channels, and kidney deficiency)
Women's Precious Formula (with qi and blood deficiency)
Zizyphus Formula (with liver and heart blood and yin deficiency, and heat)

**HUMAN PAPILLOMAVIRUS (HPV) INFECTION**

Immortal Valley Formula (with dampness, heat, and blood stasis in lower abdomen)
Yin Valley Formula (with yin deficiency dryness and heat)

**HYPERGLYCEMIA**

Hawthorn & Fennel Formula (with dampness and stagnation)
Five Mushroom Formula (regulates blood glucose)

**HYPERLIPIDEMIA** **(See CHOLESTEROL, ELEVATED)**

**HYPERTENSION**

Blood Palace Formula (with blood stasis in upper body)
Bupleurum D Formula (with liver qi stagnation, phlegm, and disturbed shen)
Chase Wind, Penetrate Bone Formula (with arthritis and kidney qi deficiency)
Clematis & Stephania Formula (with wind-damp, and qi and blood stagnation)
Coptis Relieve Toxicity Formula (with liver heat or fire)
Essential Yang Formula (from kidney yang deficiency)
Five Mushroom Formula (general tonic for lung, kidney, liver, spleen, and immune system)
Gastrodia & Uncaria Formula (with liver yang rising and liver wind)
He Shou Wu Tablets (with deficient blood, and kidney/liver yin deficiency)
Luo Bu Ma Formula (with liver heat or fire and dampness or phlegm)
Tang Kuei & Peony Formula (during pregnancy, with liver blood and spleen qi deficiency, and dampness)
Two Immortals Formula (menopausal, with kidney yin and yang deficiency)

**HYPERTHYROIDISM**

Gentiana Drain Fire Formula (with liver fire)
Heavenly Emperor's Formula (with heart and kidney yin deficiency fire)
Rehmannia & Scrophularia Formula (with kidney yin deficiency heat)

**HYPOCHONDRIAC PAIN**

Blood Palace Formula (with blood stasis in upper body)
Bupleurum & Tang Kuei Formula (with constrained liver qi)
Bupleurum D Formula (with liver qi stagnation, phlegm, and disturbed shen)
Corydalis Formula (analgesic)
Free & Easy Wanderer Plus (with constrained liver qi and heat)
Gentiana Drain Fire Formula (with liver/gallbladder fire, damp-heat)
Linking Formula (with yin deficiency, qi stagnation, and fire)
Minor Bupleurum Formula (with shao yang stage disorders)
Shu Gan Formula (with liver qi stagnation)

**HYPOGLYCEMIA**

Five Mushroom Formula (regulates blood glucose)
Ginseng & Astragalus Formula (with spleen and stomach qi deficiency)
He Shou Wu Tablets (with deficient blood, and kidney/liver yin deficiency)
Minor Bupleurum Formula (for liver/spleen disharmony)
Shu Gan Formula (with liver qi stagnation)

**HYPOTENSION**

Ginseng & Astragalus Formula (with spleen and stomach qi deficiency)
Essential Yang Formula (with kidney yang deficiency)
Tang Kuei & Peony Formula (liver/spleen disharmony)
Vital Treasure Formula (with kidney yang deficiency, qi and yin deficiency)

**HYPOTHYROIDISM**

Essential Yang Formula (with kidney yang deficiency)
Ginseng & Astragalus Formula (with spleen and stomach qi deficiency)
Ginseng Nourishing Formula (with qi and blood deficiency, and emotional symptoms)
Nourish Essence Formula (with kidney yin and yang deficiency, liver yin deficiency)
Vital Treasure Formula (with kidney yang deficiency, qi and yin deficiency)

**HYSTERIA** **(See EMOTIONAL INSTABILITY)**

## I

### IMMUNE SYSTEM IMPAIRED OR WEAK

Astragalus Formula (with cold and deficiency in the middle burner)
Astragalus & Ligustrum Formula (to support normal qi)
Eleuthero Tablets (with stress, kidney and spleen deficiency, and stagnation)
Five Mushroom Formula (general tonic for lung, kidney, liver, spleen, and immune system)
Ginseng Endurance Formula (with qi, blood, and yang deficiency)
Ginseng Nourishing Formula (with qi and blood deficiency, recovery from long illness)
Intestinal Fungus Formula (with intestinal heat-toxin and dampness)
Jade Screen & Xanthium Formula (with allergies, to supplement wei qi)
Jade Windscreen Formula (to supplement wei qi)
Ji Xue Formula (with qi and blood deficiency and stagnation, heat-toxin and dampness)
Minor Bupleurum Formula (to support normal qi)

### IMPOTENCE

Bupleurum D Formula (with liver qi stagnation, phlegm, and disturbed shen)
Cinnamon D Formula (with heart/kidney disharmony and exhaustion)
Eleuthero Tablets (with stress, kidney and spleen deficiency, and stagnation)
Essential Yang Formula (with kidney yang deficiency)
Ginseng Nourishing Formula (with qi and blood deficiency, calms the spirit)
Jing Qi Formula (with kidney, liver yin, and spleen qi deficiency, and constrained liver qi)
Nourish Essence Formula (with kidney yin and yang deficiency, liver yin deficiency)
Rehmannia Six Formula (with kidney and liver yin deficiency)
Rehmannia & Scrophularia Formula (with kidney yin deficiency heat)
Sea of Qi Formula (with spleen yang and kidney yang deficiency)
Vital Treasure Formula (with kidney yang deficiency, qi and yin deficiency)

### INCOHERENT SPEECH

Coptis Relieve Toxicity Formula (with fire)
Rehmannia Cool Blood Formula (with heat in the blood)

### INCONTINENCE (See URINARY INCONTINENCE)

### INDIGESTION

Bupleurum & Tang Kuei Formula (with constrained liver qi)
Earth-Harmonizing Formula (chronic, with liver/stomach disharmony, food stagnation, and heat)
Ease Digestion Formula (from wind, damp, stomach phlegm, or food stagnation)
Resolve the Middle Formula (with damp turbidity and stagnation in the middle burner)
Six Gentlemen Formula (with spleen and stomach qi deficiency, and phlegm or dampness)
Stomach-Harmonizing Formula (acute, with food stagnation and heat)
Shu Gan Formula (with liver qi stagnation)

**INFERTILITY**

Chong Release Formula (menstrual phase, with blood deficiency and stagnation)
Cinnamon & Poria Formula (with blood stasis)
Essential Yang Formula (with kidney yang deficiency and low libido)
Free & Easy Wanderer Plus (with constrained liver qi, liver blood deficiency, and heat)
Jing Qi Formula (male, low sperm count)
Mobilize Essence Formula (ovulatory phase, with blood stagnation and yin/yang deficiency)
Nourish Essence Formula (with kidney yin and yang deficiency, liver yin deficiency)
Nourish Ren & Chong Formula (follicular phase, with deficient blood and yin, and heat and stagnation in liver and heart)
Phlegm-Transforming Formula (with phlegm accumulation, deficiency, and qi or blood stagnation)
Seven Treasures Formula (with yin and jing deficiency)
Stasis-Transforming Formula (with qi and blood stagnation, and damp-heat)
Tang Kuei & Peony Formula (with liver blood and spleen qi deficiency, and dampness)
Tang Kuei & Salvia Formula (with blood deficiency and stagnation)
Two Immortals Formula (with deficiency of ren and chong channels, and deficient kidney yin and yang)
Yuan Support Formula (luteal phase, with spleen qi, kidney yang, and blood deficiency, and liver qi stagnation)
Women's Precious Formula (with qi and blood deficiency)

**INFLAMMATION, SYSTEMIC**

Curcuma Longa Formula

**INFLUENZA (FLU)**

Andrographis Formula (with heat-toxin)
Bupleurum & Cinnamon Formula (with simultaneous tai yang and shao yang patterns)
Ease Digestion Formula (from wind-damp, with stomach phlegm or food stagnation)
Gan Mao Ling Formula (from wind-heat)
Lily Preserve Metal Formula (post-illness, with lung yin deficiency)
Minor Bupleurum Formula (with shao yang stage disorders)
Mulberry & Lycium Formula (with lung heat or lung fire)
Restore the Lung Formula (post-illness, with lung qi deficiency)
Siler & Platycodon Formula (for wind-heat with heat in the interior)
Viola Clear Fire Formula (with heat-toxin)
Yin Chiao Formula (for wind-heat, initial stages)
Zhong Gan Ling Formula (from severe wind-heat)

**INSOMNIA**

Blood Palace Formula (with blood stasis in upper body)
Bupleurum D Formula (with liver qi stagnation, phlegm, and disturbed shen)
Cinnamon D Formula (with heart/kidney disharmony)
Coptis Relieve Toxicity Formula (with liver heat or fire)
Corydalis Formula (from pain)
Gastrodia & Uncaria Formula (with liver yang rising and liver wind)

Ginkgo Formula (with poor mental functioning)
Ginseng & Longan Formula (with spleen qi, heart qi, and blood deficiency)
Ginseng Nourishing Formula (with qi and blood deficiency, and emotional symptoms)
Heavenly Emperor's Formula (with heart and kidney yin deficiency fire)
He Shou Wu Tablets (with deficient blood, and kidney/liver yin deficiency)
Jing Qi Formula (with kidney, liver yin, and spleen qi deficiency, and constrained liver qi)
Linking Formula (with yin deficiency, qi stagnation, and fire)
Luo Bu Ma Formula (with liver heat or fire and dampness or phlegm)
Peaceful Spirit Formula (with spleen qi and heart qi and blood deficiency)
Rehmannia & Scrophularia Formula (with kidney yin deficiency heat)
Restful Sleep Formula (with deficient qi and heart blood, and heat)
Salvia Ten Formula (with depression and spleen qi deficiency)
True Yin Formula (with kidney and liver yin deficiency)
Two Immortals Formula (with kidney yin and yang deficiency, and fire)
Zizyphus Formula (with liver and heart blood and yin deficiency, and heat)

**INTERCOSTAL NEURALGIA**

Blood Palace Formula (with blood stasis in upper body)
Linking Formula (with yin deficiency, qi stagnation, and fire)

**INTESTINAL ABSCESS**

Intestinal Fungus Formula (with heat-toxin and dampness)
Wu Hua Formula

**INTESTINAL CRAMPING**

Corydalis Formula (for pain from)
Ease Digestion Formula (from wind, damp, stomach phlegm, or food stagnation)
Intestinal Fungus Formula (with heat-toxin and dampness)
Resolve the Middle Formula (with damp turbidity and stagnation in the middle burner)
Shu Gan Formula (with liver qi stagnation)
Wu Hua Formula (from dysentery or damp-heat)

**IRRITABILITY**

Blood Palace Formula (with blood stasis in upper body)
Bupleurum & Cinnamon Formula (with liver/spleen disharmony or shao yang stage disorders)
Bupleurum & Tang Kuei Formula (with constrained liver qi, liver blood and yin deficiency)
Bupleurum D Formula (with liver qi stagnation, phlegm, and disturbed shen)
Cinnamon D Formula (with heart/kidney disharmony)
Coptis Relieve Toxicity Formula (with internal heat or fire)
Free & Easy Wanderer Plus (with constrained liver qi, liver blood deficiency, and heat)
Gentiana Drain Fire Formula (with liver/gallbladder fire)
Heavenly Emperor's Formula (with heart and kidney yin deficiency fire)
Luo Bu Ma Formula (with liver heat or fire and dampness or phlegm)
Minor Bupleurum Formula (with shao yang stage disorders)
Peaceful Spirit Formula (with spleen qi and heart qi and blood deficiency)
Polyporus & Dianthus Formula (with heat in the interior or damp-heat)
Poria & Bamboo Formula (with stomach-gallbladder disharmony, phlegm-heat and stagnation)

Rehmannia Cool Blood Formula (with heat in the blood)
Salvia Ten Formula (with depression)
Two Immortals Formula (with kidney yin and yang deficiency, and fire)
Zizyphus Formula (with liver and heart blood and yin deficiency, and heat)

**IRRITABLE BOWEL SYNDROME**

Intestinal Fungus Formula (with heat-toxin and dampness)
Pulsatilla Intestinal Formula (with intestinal inflammation from heat-toxin
Shu Gan Formula (with liver qi stagnation)

**ITCHING**

Cinnamon Twig Formula (from wind-cold invasion or ying/wei disharmony)
Coptis Relieve Toxicity Formula (with internal heat)
Four Marvel Formula (lower body, from damp-heat)
Heavenly Emperor's Formula (painful, with heart and kidney yin deficiency fire)
Jade Screen & Xanthium Formula (from allergies)
Rehmannia Cool Blood Formula (with heat in the blood)
Siler & Platycodon Formula (for wind-heat with heat in the interior)
Tang Kuei & Tribulus Formula (with blood deficiency and dryness)
Tang Kuei & Salvia Formula (with blood deficiency and stagnation)
Wu Hua Formula (from damp-heat)
Yin Chiao Formula (due to wind-heat)

## J

**JAUNDICE**

Gentiana Drain Fire Formula (with damp-heat or liver heat)
Liver C Formula (chronic)
Lysimachia GB Formula (with damp-heat and constrained qi in the liver and gallbladder, and pain)
Minor Bupleurum Formula (with heat and phlegm in the middle burner)

**JOINT DISLOCATIONS**

Bone & Sinew Formula (second and third stage trauma)
Curcuma Longa Formula (for inflammation with qi and blood stagnation and heat)
Tieh Ta Formula (for pain, with little or no heat)
Trauma 1 Formula (first stage trauma, with swelling, heat, and pain)
Trauma 2 Formula (second stage trauma, with stasis, stiffness, and pain)

**JOINT PAIN, STIFFNESS OR SWELLING** **(See ARTHRITIS)**

## K

**KIDNEY INFECTION**

Andrographis Formula (with heat-toxin)
Polyporus & Dianthus Formula (with heat in the interior or damp-heat)
Viola Clear Fire Formula (with heat-toxin)

**KIDNEY STONES**

Amber Stone-Transforming Formula (acute or chronic)

**KNEE PAIN**

Chase Wind, Penetrate Bone Formula (from wind, cold, or dampness)
Curcuma Longa Formula (for inflammation with qi and blood stagnation and heat)
Du Huo & Loranthus Formula (with kidney and liver deficiency)
Seven Treasures Formula (with deficient jing and kidney and liver yin, and deficient blood)

**KNEES WEAK**

Chase Wind, Penetrate Bone Formula (with wind, cold, or dampness)
Du Huo & Loranthus Formula (with kidney and liver deficiency)
Essential Yang Formula (with kidney yang deficiency)
He Shou Wu Tablets (with deficient blood, and kidney/liver yin deficiency)
Nourish Essence Formula (with kidney yin and yang deficiency, liver yin deficiency)
Rehmannia Six Formula (with kidney and liver yin deficiency)
Seven Treasures Formula (with deficient jing and kidney and liver yin, and deficient blood)
True Yin Formula (with kidney and liver yin deficiency)
Vital Treasure Formula (with deficient kidney yang, qi, and yin)

**L**

**LABOR, DIFFICULT**

Ginseng & Astragalus Formula (slow to start, with middle qi deficiency)
Women's Precious Formula (with qi and blood deficiency)

**LACTATION, INSUFFICIENT**

Bupleurum & Tang Kuei Formula (with constrained liver qi, liver blood and yin deficiency)
Tang Kuei & Salvia Formula (with blood deficiency and stagnation)
Women's Precious Formula (with qi and blood deficiency)

**LARYNGITIS**

Andrographis Formula (with heat-toxin)
Eight Immortals Formula (from chronic dryness, with lung, kidney, and stomach yin deficiency)
Lily Preserve Metal Formula (chronic, with lung yin deficiency)
Pinellia & Magnolia Bark Formula (chronic, with constrained qi and phlegm)
Viola Clear Fire Formula (acute, from heat-toxin)
Yin Chiao Formula (from wind-heat)
Zhong Gan Ling Formula (acute, from wind-heat)

**LASSITUDE (See FATIGUE)**

**LEGS (See LIMBS)**

**LEUKORRHEA (See VAGINAL DISCHARGE)**

**LIGAMENTS, TORN**

Bone & Sinew Formula (second and third stage trauma)
Tieh Ta Formula (for pain, with little or no heat)
Trauma 1 Formula (first stage trauma, with swelling, heat, and pain)
Trauma 2 Formula (second stage trauma, with stasis, stiffness, and pain)

**LIGHT-HEADEDNESS (See DIZZINESS)**

**LIMBS, COLD (See COLD LIMBS)**

**LIMBS, TIRED, WEAK, AND ACHING**

Chase Wind, Penetrate Bone Formula (with wind-cold and damp painful obstruction)
Clematis & Stephania Formula (with wind-damp, and qi and blood stagnation)
Du Huo & Loranthus Formula (lower, with kidney and liver deficiency)
Essential Yang Formula (lower, with kidney yang deficiency)
Ginseng & Astragalus Formula (upper, with middle qi deficiency)
General Tonic Formula (with qi and blood deficiency, and internal cold)

He Shou Wu Tablets (with deficient blood, and kidney/liver yin deficiency)
Ji Xue Formula (with qi and blood deficiency and stagnation, heat-toxin and dampness)
Restorative Formula (with qi, blood, yin and yang deficiency, wind, and dampness)
Sea of Qi Formula (with spleen yang and kidney yang deficiency)
Tang Kuei & Peony Formula (lower, with liver blood and spleen deficiency, and dampness)
True Yin Formula (with kidney and liver yin deficiency)
Women's Precious Formula (with qi and blood deficiency)

**LIPS DRY (See DRYNESS)**

**LIVER ENZYMES ELEVATED**

Free & Easy Wanderer Plus (with liver/spleen disharmony and heat)
Liver C Formula
Minor Bupleurum Formula (with shao yang stage disorders)

**LOOSE STOOLS (See DIARRHEA)**

**LYMPH NODES, ENLARGED**

Andrographis Formula (with heat-toxin)
Curcuma Longa Formula (for inflammation with qi and blood stagnation and heat)
Gan Mao Ling Formula (from wind-heat)
Minor Bupleurum Formula (chronic, or with shao yang stage disorders)
Phlegm-Transforming Formula (chronic, with phlegm accumulation, deficiency, and qi or blood stagnation)
Viola Clear Fire Formula (from heat-toxin)
Yin Chiao Formula (from wind-heat)
Zhong Gan Ling Formula (from severe wind-heat)

## M

**MANIA**

Bupleurum D Formula (with liver qi stagnation, phlegm, and disturbed shen)
Coptis Relieve Toxicity Formula (with fire or heat)
Poria & Bamboo Formula (with stomach-gallbladder disharmony, phlegm-heat and stagnation)
Rehmannia Cool Blood Formula (with heat in the blood)

**MEASLES**

Andrographis Formula (early stage with heat-toxin)
Gan Mao Ling Formula (early stage with wind-heat)
Mulberry & Lycium Formula (with lung heat or fire)
Yin Chiao Formula (from wind-heat)
Zhong Gan Ling Formula (from wind-heat)

**MELANCHOLY, EXCESSIVE (See also DEPRESSION)**

Peaceful Spirit Formula (with spleen qi and heart qi and blood deficiency)
Salvia Ten Formula (with depression and spleen qi deficiency)
Two Immortals Formula (with kidney yin and yang deficiency, and flaring-up of fire)

**MEMORY, POOR**

Cinnamon D Formula (with heart/kidney disharmony)
Ginkgo Formula (with liver wind or fire and heart and liver blood deficiency)
Ginseng & Astragalus Formula (with middle qi deficiency)
Ginseng & Longan Formula (with spleen qi, heart qi, and blood deficiency)

Ginseng Nourishing Formula (with qi and blood deficiency, and emotional symptoms)
Heavenly Emperor's Formula (with heart and kidney yin deficiency fire)
Ji Xue Formula (with qi and blood deficiency and stagnation, heat-toxin and dampness)
Peaceful Spirit Formula (with spleen qi and heart qi and blood deficiency)
Restful Sleep Formula (with insomnia, deficient qi and heart blood, and heat)
True Yin Formula (with kidney and liver yin deficiency)

**MENARCHE, LATE**

Nourish Ren & Chong Formula (with deficient blood and yin, and heat and stagnation in liver and heart)
Women's Precious Formula (with qi and blood deficiency)

**MENOPAUSAL SYMPTOMS (See also HOT FLASHES)**

Bupleurum & Tang Kuei Formula (with constrained liver qi, liver blood and yin deficiency)
Bupleurum D Formula (with liver qi stagnation, phlegm, and disturbed shen)
Cinnamon & Poria Formula (with blood stasis)
Free & Easy Wanderer Plus (with constrained liver qi, liver blood deficiency, and heat)
Heavenly Emperor's Formula (with heart or kidney yin deficiency fire)
Mobilize Essence Formula (with blood stagnation and yin and yang deficiency)
Phlegm-Transforming Formula (with phlegm accumulation, deficiency, and qi or blood stagnation)
Rehmannia & Scrophularia Formula (with kidney yin deficiency)

Stasis-Transforming Formula (with qi and blood stagnation, and damp-heat)
Two Immortals Formula (with kidney yin and yang deficiency, and flaring-up of fire)
Women's Precious Formula (with qi and blood deficiency)
Zizyphus Formula (insomnia, with liver and heart blood and yin deficiency, and heat)

**MENOPAUSE, PREMATURE**

Nourish Ren & Chong Formula (with deficient blood and yin, and heat and stagnation in liver and heart)
Rehmannia Six Formula (with kidney and liver yin deficiency)

**MENSTRUAL BLEEDING EXCESSIVE OR ABNORMAL**

Chong Release Formula (with blood deficiency and stagnation)
Ginseng & Longan Formula (with spleen qi, heart qi, and blood deficiency)
Immortal Valley Formula (with dampness, heat, and blood stasis in lower abdomen)
San Qi Formula (controls bleeding)
San Qi Tablets (controls bleeding)

**MENSTRUAL CYCLE SHORTENED**

Gentiana Drain Fire Formula (with damp-heat or liver heat)
Yin Valley Formula (with yin deficiency dryness, heat, and blood stasis)

**MENSTRUAL PAIN**

- BUPLEURUM & TANG KUEI FORMULA (with constrained liver qi, liver blood and yin deficiency)
- CHONG RELEASE FORMULA (with blood deficiency and stagnation)
- CINNAMON & PORIA FORMULA (with blood stasis)
- CORYDALIS FORMULA (for pain from)
- FREE & EASY WANDERER PLUS (with constrained liver qi, liver blood and yin deficiency, and heat)
- MOBILIZE ESSENCE FORMULA (during ovulation, with blood stagnation and yin and yang deficiency)
- STASIS-TRANSFORMING FORMULA (with qi and blood stagnation, and damp-heat)
- TANG KUEI & PEONY FORMULA (with liver blood and spleen deficiency and dampness)
- TANG KUEI & SALVIA FORMULA (with blood deficiency and stagnation)
- WOMEN'S PRECIOUS FORMULA (with qi and blood deficiency)

**MENSTRUATION, FATIGUE AFTER**

- BUPLEURUM & TANG KUEI FORMULA (with constrained liver qi, liver blood and yin deficiency)
- NOURISH REN & CHONG FORMULA (with deficient blood and yin, and heat and stagnation in liver and heart)
- TANG KUEI & SALVIA FORMULA (with blood deficiency and stagnation)
- WOMEN'S PRECIOUS FORMULA (with qi and blood deficiency)

**MENSTRUATION, IRREGULAR**

- BUPLEURUM & TANG KUEI FORMULA (with constrained liver qi, liver blood and yin deficiency)
- CHONG RELEASE FORMULA (with blood deficiency and stagnation)
- CINNAMON & PORIA FORMULA (with blood stasis)
- FREE & EASY WANDERER PLUS (with constrained liver qi, liver blood deficiency, and heat)
- STASIS-TRANSFORMING FORMULA (with qi and blood stagnation, and damp-heat)
- TANG KUEI & PEONY FORMULA (with liver blood and spleen deficiency and dampness)
- TANG KUEI & SALVIA FORMULA (with blood deficiency and stagnation)
- WOMEN'S PRECIOUS FORMULA (with qi and blood deficiency)
- YUAN SUPPORT FORMULA (with spleen qi, kidney yang, and blood deficiency)

**MENSTRUATION, PROLONGED**

- GINSENG & ASTRAGALUS FORMULA (with spleen and stomach qi deficiency)
- GINSENG & LONGAN FORMULA (with spleen qi and blood deficiency)
- SEA OF QI FORMULA (with spleen yang and kidney yang deficiency)

**MENSTRUATION, SCANTY OR ABSENT**

- CINNAMON & PORIA FORMULA (with blood stasis)
- HE SHOU WU TABLETS (with deficient blood, and kidney/liver yin deficiency)
- MOBILIZE ESSENCE FORMULA (peri-menopausal, with blood stagnation and yin and yang deficiency)
- NOURISH REN & CHONG FORMULA (with deficient blood and yin, and heat and stagnation in liver and heart)
- STASIS-TRANSFORMING FORMULA (with qi and blood stagnation, and damp-heat)
- TANG KUEI & SALVIA FORMULA (with blood deficiency and stagnation)

Two Immortals Formula (with kidney yin and yang deficiency, and flaring-up of fire)
Yin Valley Formula (with yin deficiency dryness, heat, and blood stasis)
Women's Precious Formula (with qi and blood deficiency)

**MENTAL CONFUSION**

Cinnamon D Formula (with heart/kidney disharmony)
Ginkgo Formula (with liver wind or fire, and heart and liver blood deficiency)
Heavenly Emperor's Formula (with heart and kidney yin deficiency fire)

**MENTAL DISORDERS**

Astragalus Formula (lack of sense of self, with cold in the middle burner)
Blood Palace Formula (outbursts or extreme mood swings, with blood stagnation in upper body)
Bupleurum & Cinnamon Formula (passive-aggressive behavior, boundary issues, with liver/spleen disharmony)
Bupleurum & Tang Kuei Formula (with constrained liver qi, liver blood deficiency)
Bupleurum D Formula (with liver qi stagnation, phlegm, and disturbed shen)
Cinnamon D Formula (neurotic disorders, with heart/kidney disharmony)
Cinnamon Twig Formula (boundary issues, use low dose)
Coptis Relieve Toxicity Formula (with liver heat or fire)
Free & Easy Wanderer Plus (with constrained liver qi, liver blood deficiency, and heat)
Gastrodia & Uncaria Formula (with liver yang rising and wind)
Ginseng & Longan Formula (personality disorders, phobias, with heart blood and spleen and heart qi deficiency)
Ginseng Nourishing Formula (with qi and blood deficiency)
Heavenly Emperor's Formula (with heart and kidney yin deficiency fire)
Peaceful Spirit Formula (with spleen qi and heart qi and blood deficiency)
Pinellia & Magnolia Bark Formula (with constrained qi and phlegm)
Salvia Ten Formula (with depression)
Six Gentlemen Formula (with spleen and stomach qi deficiency and phlegm or dampness)
Restful Sleep Formula (with restlessness, deficient qi and heart blood, and heat)
Yuan Support Formula (with spleen qi, kidney yang, and blood deficiency)
Zizyphus Formula (with insomnia, liver and heart blood and yin deficiency, and heat)

**MENTAL FATIGUE OR EXHAUSTION**

Ginkgo Formula (with liver wind or fire and heart and liver blood deficiency)
Ginseng Nourishing Formula (with qi and blood deficiency)
Jing Qi Formula (with kidney, liver yin, and spleen qi deficiency, and constrained liver qi)
Peaceful Spirit Formula (with spleen and heart qi deficiency)

**MIGRAINE HEADACHE (See HEADACHE)**

**MISCARRIAGE, THREATENED OR HABITUAL**

Essential Yang Formula (with kidney yang deficiency)
Ginseng & Astragalus Formula (habitual, with middle qi deficiency)
Nourish Essence Formula (habitual, with kidney yin and yang deficiency, liver yin deficiency)
Tang Kuei & Peony Formula (threatened or habitual, with liver blood and spleen deficiency, and dampness)

Women's Precious Formula (with qi and blood deficiency)
Yuan Support Formula (with spleen qi, kidney yang, and blood deficiency)

**MONONUCLEOSIS (See EPSTEIN-BARR VIRUS)**

**MOOD SWINGS (See EMOTIONAL INSTABILITY)**

**MORNING SICKNESS**

Citrus & Pinellia Formula (with phlegm-damp)
Ease Digestion Formula
Pinellia & Magnolia Bark Formula (with constrained qi and phlegm)
Shu Gan Formula (with liver qi stagnation)

**MOTION SICKNESS**

Ease Digestion Formula
Pinellia & Magnolia Bark Formula (with constrained qi and phlegm)
Poria Five Formula (with water accumulation)

**MOUTH SORES**

Andrographis Formula (with heat-toxin)
Coptis Relieve Toxicity Formula (with liver heat or damp-heat)
Rehmannia Cool Blood Formula (with heat in the blood)

**MOVEMENT DIFFICULTY**

Clematis & Stephania Formula (with wind-damp, and qi and blood stagnation)
Curcuma Longa Formula (for inflammation with qi and blood stagnation and heat)
Du Huo & Loranthus Formula (lower body with kidney and liver deficiency)

**MUMPS**

Andrographis Formula (with heat-toxin)
Coptis Relieve Toxicity Formula (with liver heat or damp-heat)
Viola Clear Fire Formula (with heat-toxin)

**MUSCLE ACHES OR PAIN**

Clematis & Stephania Formula (with wind-damp, and qi and blood stagnation)
Corydalis Formula (for pain relief)
Juan Bi Formula (upper body, with wind-damp, cold, and blood stasis)
Restorative Formula (with qi, blood, yin and yang deficiency, wind, and dampness)

**MUSCLE SPASM**

Chase Wind, Penetrate Bone Formula (with wind-cold and damp painful obstruction)
Corydalis Formula (for pain from)
Eleuthero Tablets (with stress, kidney and spleen deficiency, and stagnation)
Gastrodia & Uncaria Formula (with liver yang rising and liver wind)
Ginseng Nourishing Formula (with qi and blood deficiency, and emotional symptoms)

**MUSCLE STRAINS**

Tieh Ta Formula

**MUSCLE TENSION**

Bupleurum & Cinnamon Formula (with liver/spleen disharmony or concurrent tai yang and shao yang patterns)
Bupleurum & Tang Kuei Formula (with constrained liver qi, liver blood and yin deficiency)
Corydalis Formula (for pain)

Head Relief Formula (in head and neck, from wind-cold, muscle tension, or trauma)
Minor Bupleurum Formula (with shao yang stage disorders)

**MUSCLE WEAKNESS (See WEAKNESS)**

**N**

**NAIL FUNGUS**

Oregano Oil Formula (topically)

**NAILS, DRY OR BRITTLE (See DRYNESS)**

**NASAL CONGESTION (See SINUS CONGESTION)**

**NASAL DISCHARGE (See SINUS DISCHARGE)**

**NAUSEA**

Bupleurum & Cinnamon Formula (with liver/spleen disharmony or concurrent tai yang and shao yang patterns)
Bupleurum & Tang Kuei Formula (with liver/spleen disharmony)
Citrus & Pinellia Formula (with stomach or spleen disharmony from phlegm-damp)
Eight Immortals Formula (with lung, kidney, and stomach yin deficiency)
Earth-Harmonizing Formula (with liver/stomach disharmony, food stagnation, and heat)
Ease Digestion Formula (from wind, damp, stomach phlegm or food stagnation)
Free & Easy Wanderer Plus (with liver/spleen disharmony and heat)
Ji Xue Formula (from chemotherapy, with qi and blood deficiency and stagnation, heat-toxin and dampness)
Minor Bupleurum Formula (with shao yang stage disorders)
Poria & Bamboo Formula (with stomach-gallbladder disharmony, phlegm-heat and stagnation)
Resolve the Middle Formula (with damp turbidity and stagnation in the middle burner)
Salvia Ten Formula (with depression)
Shu Gan Formula (with liver qi stagnation)
Six Gentlemen Formula (with spleen and stomach qi deficiency and phlegm or dampness)
Stomach-Harmonizing Formula (acute, with food stagnation and heat)

**NECK STIFF AND ACHING**

Chase Wind, Penetrate Bone Formula (with chronic wind-cold and damp painful obstruction)
Cinnamon Twig Formula (from wind-cold, when ephedra contraindicated)
Corydalis Formula (for pain)
Curcuma Longa Formula (for inflammation, with qi and blood stagnation and heat)
Gan Mao Ling Formula (from wind-heat)
Head Relief Formula (from wind-cold)
Juan Bi Formula (from wind-damp)
Minor Bupleurum Formula (with shao yang stage disorders)
Zhong Gan Ling Formula (from wind-heat)

**NEPHRITIS**

Eight Immortals Formula (chronic, with lung, kidney, and stomach yin deficiency)
Essential Yang Formula (chronic, with kidney yang deficiency)

Nourish Essence Formula (chronic, with kidney yin and yang deficiency, liver yin deficiency)
Polyporus & Dianthus Formula (acute, with heat in the interior or damp-heat)
Poria Five Formula (with impaired water metabolism)
Tang Kuei & Peony Formula (chronic, with liver blood and spleen deficiency and dampness)

**NERVOUSNESS (See ANXIETY)**

**NERVOUS EXHAUSTION**

Bupleurum & Cinnamon Formula (with liver/spleen disharmony)
Cinnamon D Formula (from sexual excess, with heart/kidney disharmony)
Eleuthero Tablets (with stress, kidney and spleen deficiency, and stagnation)
Ginseng & Longan Formula (with spleen qi, heart qi, and blood deficiency)
Ginseng Nourishing Formula (with qi and blood deficiency, and emotional symptoms)
Ji Xue Formula (with qi and blood deficiency and stagnation, heat-toxin and dampness)
Jing Qi Formula (with kidney, liver yin, and spleen qi deficiency, and constrained liver qi)
Peaceful Spirit Formula (with spleen and heart qi deficiency and blood deficiency)

**NEURASTHENIA (See NERVOUS EXHAUSTION)**

**NEUROPATHY**

Curcuma Longa Formula (for inflammation, with qi and blood stagnation and heat)
Ji Xue Formula (from chemotherapy, with qi and blood deficiency and stagnation, heat-toxin and dampness)

**NEUROTIC DISORDER (See MENTAL DISORDERS)**

**NIGHTMARES (See DREAM-DISTURBED SLEEP)**

**NIGHT SWEATS**

Astragalus Formula (with cold and deficiency in the middle burner)
Astragalus & Ligustrum Formula (to support normal qi)
Blood Palace Formula (with blood stasis in upper body)
Cinnamon D Formula (with heart/kidney disharmony)
Eight Immortals Formula (with lung, kidney, and stomach yin deficiency)
Essential Yang Formula (with kidney yang deficiency)
Ginseng & Astragalus Formula (with spleen and stomach qi deficiency)
Ginseng & Longan Formula (with spleen qi, heart qi, and blood deficiency)
Ginseng Nourishing Formula (with qi and blood deficiency and emotional symptoms)
Heavenly Emperor's Formula (with heart and kidney yin deficiency fire)
Jing Qi Formula (with kidney, liver yin, and spleen qi deficiency, and constrained liver qi)
Lily Preserve Metal Formula (with lung yin deficiency)
Nourish Essence Formula (with kidney yin and yang deficiency, liver yin deficiency)
Rehmannia & Scrophularia Formula (with kidney yin deficiency heat)
Rehmannia Six Formula (with kidney and liver yin deficiency)
True Yin Formula (with kidney and liver yin deficiency)
Two Immortals Formula (with kidney yin and yang deficiency, and flaring-up of fire)

Yin Valley Formula (with yin deficiency dryness, heat, and blood stasis)
Zizyphus Formula (with liver and heart blood and yin deficiency, and heat)

**NOCTURNAL SEMINAL EMISSIONS**

Cinnamon D Formula (with heart/kidney disharmony)
Essential Yang Formula (with kidney yang deficiency)
Heavenly Emperor's Formula (with heart and kidney yin deficiency fire)
He Shou Wu Tablets (with deficient blood, and kidney/liver yin deficiency)
Nourish Essence Formula (with kidney yin and yang deficiency, liver yin deficiency)
Rehmannia Six Formula (with kidney and liver yin deficiency)
Seven Treasures Formula (with deficient jing and kidney and liver yin, and deficient blood)
Yin Valley Formula (with yin deficiency dryness, heat, and blood stasis)

**NOCTURNAL URINATION (See URINATION, NOCTURNAL)**

**NOSE DRY (See DRYNESS)**

**NOSEBLEED**

Coptis Relieve Toxicity Formula (with heat or fire)
Mulberry & Lycium Formula (with lung heat or fire)
Rehmannia Cool Blood Formula (with heat in the blood)
San Qi Formula (controls bleeding)
San Qi Tablets (controls bleeding)

**NUMBNESS**

Clematis & Stephania Formula (lower extremities, with wind-damp and qi and blood stagnation)
Four Marvel Formula (lower body, from damp-heat)
Gastrodia & Uncaria Formula (with liver yang rising and liver wind)
Ji Xue Formula (with qi and blood deficiency and stagnation, heat-toxin and dampness)

## O

**OBESITY**

Hawthorn & Fennel Formula (with deficient qi)
Poria Fifteen Formula (with dampness, deficiency, and stagnation)
Resolve the Middle Formula (with more severe damp turbidity and stagnation in the middle burner)
Yuan Support Formula (with spleen qi, kidney yang, and blood deficiency)

**OTITIS MEDIA**

Children's Ear Formula (in infants and children)
Gentiana Drain Fire Formula (with pus)
Minor Bupleurum Formula (with shao yang stage disorders)

**OVARIAN CYSTS**

Cinnamon & Poria Formula (with blood stasis)
Mobilize Essence Formula (with blood stagnation and yin and yang deficiency)
Phlegm-Transforming Formula (with phlegm accumulation, deficiency, and qi or blood stagnation)
Stasis-Transforming Formula (with qi and blood stagnation, and damp-heat)

**OVARIAN FOLLICLE, POOR**

Nourish Ren & Chong Formula (with deficient blood and yin, and heat and stagnation in liver and heart)

**OVULATION, BLEEDING DURING**
Tang Kuei & Salvia Formula (with blood deficiency and stagnation)
Yin Valley Formula (with yin deficiency dryness, heat, and blood stasis)
**OVULATION, LATE OR PAIN WITH**
Mobilize Essence Formula (with blood stagnation and yin and yang deficiency)
Nourish Ren & Chong Formula (with deficient blood and yin, and heat and stagnation in liver and heart)

## P

**PAIN (See also BACK PAIN, HEADACHE, MENSTRUAL PAIN, etc.)**
Blood Palace Formula (fibromyalgia, with blood stasis in upper body)
Chase Wind, Penetrate Bone Formula (with wind-cold and wind-damp painful obstruction)
Cinnamon & Poria Formula (in lower abdomen, with blood stasis)
Clematis & Stephania Formula (in trunk, legs, or post-partum, with wind-damp, and qi and blood stagnation)
Corydalis Formula (analgesic)
Curcuma Longa Formula (from inflammation, with qi and blood stagnation and heat)
Du Huo & Loranthus Formula (lower body with kidney and liver deficiency)
Eleuthero Tablets (in loins, kidney and spleen deficiency, and stagnation)
Juan Bi Formula (upper body, with wind-damp, cold, and blood stasis)
Rehmannia & Scrophularia Formula (in back or at midline, with kidney yin deficiency)
Restorative Formula (chronic, in elderly or patients weakened by illness)
San Qi Tablets (from trauma or injury)
Tang Kuei & Salvia Formula (lower abdomen, with blood deficiency and stagnation)
Tieh Ta Formula (from trauma or injury)
Trauma 1 Formula (first stage trauma, with swelling, heat, and pain)
Trauma 2 Formula (second stage trauma, with stagnation, stiffness, and pain)
**PALLOR (See COMPLEXION, PALE)**
**PALMS AND/OR SOLES, HOT**
Eight Immortals Formula (with lung, kidney, and stomach yin deficiency)
Heavenly Emperor's Formula (with kidney and heart yin deficiency)
Lily Preserve Metal Formula (with lung yin deficiency)
Linking Formula (with yin deficiency, qi stagnation, and fire)
Ming Mu Formula (with concurrent weakening of vision, liver and kidney deficiency with liver heat or internal wind)
Rehmannia & Scrophularia Formula (with kidney yin deficiency)
Rehmannia Six Formula (with kidney and liver yin deficiency)
**PALPITATION**
Blood Palace Formula (with blood stasis in upper body)
Bupleurum & Tang Kuei Formula (with constrained liver qi, and liver blood and yin deficiency)
Bupleurum D Formula (with liver qi stagnation, phlegm, and disturbed shen)
Cinnamon D Formula (with heart/kidney disharmony)
Citrus & Pinellia Formula (with phlegm-damp)

Coptis Relieve Toxicity Formula (with heat or fire)
Eight Immortals Formula (with lung, kidney, and stomach yin deficiency)
Free & Easy Wanderer Plus (with constrained liver qi, liver blood deficiency, and heat)
Ginkgo Formula (with poor mental functioning, liver fire or wind, and heart and liver blood deficiency)
Ginseng & Longan Formula (with spleen qi, heart qi, and blood deficiency)
Ginseng Nourishing Formula (with qi and blood deficiency, and emotional symptoms)
Heavenly Emperor's Formula (with heart and kidney yin deficiency fire)
Peaceful Spirit Formula (with spleen qi and heart qi and blood deficiency)
Poria & Bamboo Formula (with stomach-gallbladder disharmony, phlegm-heat and stagnation)
Restful Sleep Formula (with insomnia, deficient qi and heart blood, and heat)
Salvia Ten Formula (with depression and spleen qi deficiency)
Sheng Mai Formula (with lung qi or yin deficiency, or with injury to yin from summer heat)
Tang Kuei & Salvia Formula (with blood deficiency)
Two Immortals Formula (with kidney yin and yang deficiency, and flaring-up of fire)
Women's Precious Formula (with qi and blood deficiency)
Zizyphus Formula (with liver and heart blood and yin deficiency, and heat)

**PANCREATITIS**

Corydalis Formula (pain from)
Minor Bupleurum Formula (for pathogenic qi and heat in the middle burner)

**PARASITES**

Intestinal Fungus Formula (candida)
Oregano Oil Formula (candida, worms, dysentery)
Wu Hua Formula (dysentery)

**PASSIVE-AGGRESSIVE BEHAVIOR**

Bupleurum & Cinnamon Formula (with liver/spleen disharmony)

**PELVIC INFLAMMATORY DISEASE**

Andrographis Formula (with heat-toxin)
Cinnamon & Poria Formula (chronic, with blood stasis)
Free & Easy Wanderer Plus (with constrained liver qi, liver blood deficiency, and heat)
Gentiana Drain Fire Formula (with damp-heat or liver heat)
Immortal Valley Formula (with dampness, heat, and blood stasis in lower abdomen)
Stasis-Transforming Formula (with qi and blood stagnation, and damp-heat)
Tang Kuei & Peony Formula (with liver blood and spleen deficiency and dampness)

**PELVIC CONGESTION**

Chong Release Formula (with blood deficiency and stagnation)

**PHARYNGITIS**

Andrographis Formula (with heat-toxin)
Eight Immortals Formula (chronic, with yin deficiency)
Lily Preserve Metal Formula (with lung and kidney yin deficiency)
Viola Clear Fire Formula (with heat-toxin)

Yin Chiao Formula (with wind-heat)
Zhong Gan Ling Formula (from severe wind-heat)

**PHLEBITIS**

San Qi Formula

**PHLEGM, IN DIGESTIVE SYSTEM**

Citrus & Pinellia Formula (with disharmony of stomach or spleen from phlegm-damp)
Ease Digestion Formula (acute)
Hawthorn & Fennel Formula (chronic, with obesity and deficient qi)
Intestinal Fungus Formula (with intestinal heat-toxin and dampness)
Poria Fifteen Formula (chronic, with obesity)
Resolve the Middle Formula (with damp turbidity and stagnation in the middle burner)
Six Gentlemen Formula (chronic, with spleen and stomach qi deficiency)

**PHOBIAS**

Ginseng & Longan Formula (with spleen qi, heart qi, and blood deficiency)

**PIMPLES (See ACNE)**

**PINWORMS (See WORMS)**

**PNEUMONIA**

Bupleurum & Cinnamon Formula (with concurrent tai yang and shao yang stage disorders)
Fritillaria & Pinellia Formula (with lung heat or phlegm-heat)
Ling Zhi Lung Formula (with wheezing and fluid in the lungs)
Minor Bupleurum Formula (shao yang stage disorders)
Mulberry & Lycium Formula (with lung heat or fire)
Viola Clear Fire Formula (with heat-toxin)

**PNEUMOTHORAX, SPONTANEOUS**

Lily Preserve Metal Formula (with lung and kidney yin deficiency)

**POLIOMYELITIS, SEQUELAE OF**

Du Huo & Loranthus Formula (lower body, with kidney and liver deficiency)

**POST-CONCUSSION SYNDROME**

Blood Palace Formula (with blood stasis in upper body)
Bupleurum D Formula (with liver qi stagnation, phlegm, and disturbed shen)
Ginseng & Longan Formula (with spleen qi and heart qi and blood deficiency)

**POST-NASAL DRIP**

Nourish Essence Formula (chronic, with kidney yin and yang deficiency, liver yin deficiency)
Xanthium & Magnolia Formula (acute)

**POST-OPERATIVE FATIGUE**

Astragalus & Ligustrum Formula (to support normal qi)
Astragalus Formula (with cold and deficiency in the middle burner)
General Tonic Formula (with qi and blood deficiency, and internal cold)
Ginseng & Astragalus Formula (with spleen and stomach qi deficiency)
Ginseng & Longan Formula (with spleen qi, heart qi, and blood deficiency)
Ginseng Nourishing Formula (with qi and blood deficiency)

**POST-OPERATIVE PAIN**

Astragalus Formula (with cold and deficiency in the middle burner)
Corydalis Formula (for pain)
Tieh Ta Formula (for musculo-skeletal pain)

**POST-PARTUM PAIN (See PAIN)**

**POST-PARTUM WEAKNESS, DEFICIENCY, OR FATIGUE**

Astragalus & Ligustrum Formula (to support normal qi)
General Tonic Formula (with qi and blood deficiency, and internal cold)
Ginseng & Astragalus Formula (with spleen and stomach qi deficiency)
Ginseng Nourishing Formula (with qi and blood deficiency, and emotional symptoms)
Ji Xue Formula (with qi and blood deficiency and stagnation, heat-toxin and dampness)
Tang Kuei & Peony Formula (with liver blood and spleen deficiency and dampness)
Tang Kuei & Salvia Formula (with blood deficiency)
Women's Precious Formula (with qi and blood deficiency)
Yuan Support Formula (with spleen qi, kidney yang, and blood deficiency)

**POST-TRAUMATIC STRESS DISORDER**

Bupleurum D Formula (with liver qi stagnation, phlegm, and disturbed shen)
Ginseng & Longan Formula (with spleen qi, heart qi, and blood deficiency)
Peaceful Spirit Formula (with spleen qi and heart qi and blood deficiency)
Sheng Mai Formula (for shock, with lung qi or yin deficiency)

**PRE-ECLAMPSIA (See TOXEMIA OF PREGNANCY)**

**PREGNANCY, GENERAL TONIC FOR**

Tang Kuei & Peony Formula

**PREMATURE EJACULATION**

Heavenly Emperor's Formula (with heart and kidney yin deficiency fire)
Nourish Essence Formula (with kidney yin and yang deficiency, and liver yin deficiency)
Rehmannia & Scrophularia Formula (with kidney yin deficiency heat)
Rehmannia Six Formula (with kidney and liver yin deficiency)
True Yin Formula (with kidney and liver yin deficiency)
Vital Treasure Formula (with kidney yang deficiency, qi and yin deficiency)

**PREMENSTRUAL SYNDROME**

Bupleurum & Tang Kuei Formula (with constrained liver qi, liver blood and yin deficiency)
Chong Release Formula (with blood deficiency and stagnation)
Free & Easy Wanderer Plus (same as above, but with heat)
Mobilize Essence Formula (pain from, with blood stagnation and yin and yang deficiency)
Tang Kuei & Peony Formula (with liver blood and spleen deficiency and dampness)
Women's Precious Formula (with qi and blood deficiency)

**PREMENSTRUAL WATER RETENTION**

Tang Kuei & Peony Formula (with liver blood and spleen deficiency and dampness)
Poria Five Formula (with spleen deficiency and congestion of fluids)

**PROLAPSE**

Ginseng & Astragalus Formula

**PROSTATE, SWOLLEN OR PAINFUL**

Cinnamon & Poria Formula (with blood stasis)
Prostate Formula (with spleen and kidney yang deficiency, and dampness)
Rabdosia Prostate Formula (with heat or damp-heat)

**PROSTATITIS**

Cinnamon & Poria Formula (with blood stasis)
Gentiana Drain Fire Formula (acute with heat)
Ginseng & Astragalus Formula (chronic, with spleen and stomach qi deficiency)
Prostate Formula (with spleen and kidney yang deficiency, and dampness)
Stasis-Transforming Formula (with qi and blood stagnation, and damp-heat)
Tang Kuei & Tribulus Formula (with blood deficiency and dryness)

**PSA (PROSTATE SPECIFIC ANTIGEN) ELEVATED**

Essential Yang Formula (with kidney yang deficiency)
Rabdosia Prostate Formula (with heat or damp-heat)

**PSORIASIS**

Coptis Relieve Toxicity Formula (with internal heat)
Rehmannia Cool Blood Formula (with heat in the blood)
Tang Kuei & Tribulus Formula (with blood deficiency and dryness)
Two Immortals Formula (improves in pregnancy, worse after childbirth)

**PSYCHOLOGICAL DISORDERS (See EMOTIONAL INSTABILITY or MENTAL DISORDERS)**

## R

**RASHES (See SKIN RASH)**

**RECTAL BLEEDING**

San Qi Formula (controls bleeding)
San Qi Tablets (controls bleeding)
Wu Hua Formula (with damp-heat)

**RECTAL ITCHING**

Intestinal Fungus Formula (with intestinal heat-toxin and dampness)

**RESPIRATORY INFECTION**

Andrographis Formula (with heat-toxin)
Fritillaria & Pinellia Formula (lung heat or phlegm-heat)
Gan Mao Ling Formula (early stage, from wind-heat)
Ling Zhi Lung Formula (with wheezing and fluid in the lungs)
Minor Bupleurum Formula (with shao yang stage disorders)
Mulberry & Lycium Formula (with lung heat or fire)
Viola Clear Fire Formula (with heat-toxin)
Yin Chiao Formula (initial stage upper respiratory, from wind-heat)
Zhong Gan Ling Formula (from severe wind-heat)

**RESTLESSNESS**

Bupleurum D Formula (with liver qi stagnation, phlegm, and disturbed shen)
Free & Easy Wanderer Plus (with constrained liver qi, liver blood deficiency, with heat)
Ginkgo Formula (with poor mental functioning, liver fire or wind, and heart and liver blood deficiency)
Ginseng Nourishing Formula (with qi and blood deficiency, and emotional symptoms)
Luo Bu Ma Formula (with liver heat or fire and dampness or phlegm)
Peaceful Spirit Formula (with spleen qi and heart qi and blood deficiency)
Rehmannia & Scrophularia Formula (with kidney yin deficiency heat)
Rehmannia Cool Blood Formula (with heat in the blood)

Salvia Ten Formula (with depression)
Yin Valley Formula (with yin deficiency dryness, heat, and blood stasis)
Zizyphus Formula (with liver and heart blood and yin deficiency, and heat)

**RHEUMATISM (See ARTHRITIS)**

**RHINITIS, ALLERGIC (See SINUS INFLAMMATION)**

**RINGING IN THE EAR (TINNITUS)**

Bupleurum D Formula (with liver qi stagnation, phlegm)
Children's Ear Formula (acute, with phlegm and fever)
Eight Immortals Formula (with lung, kidney, and stomach yin deficiency)
Gastrodia & Uncaria Formula (with liver yang rising and liver wind)
Nourish Essence Formula (with kidney yin and yang deficiency, and liver yin deficiency)
Poria & Bamboo Formula (with phlegm-heat and stagnation)
Rehmannia & Scrophularia Formula (with kidney yin deficiency heat)
Rehmannia Six Formula (with kidney and liver yin deficiency)

**RUNNY NOSE (See SINUS DISCHARGE)**

## S

**SCIATICA**

Chase Wind, Penetrate Bone Formula (with wind-cold or damp painful obstruction)
Clematis & Stephania Formula (with wind-damp, and qi and blood stagnation)
Corydalis Formula (for pain from)
Du Huo & Loranthus Formula (with kidney and liver deficiency)
Essential Yang Formula (with kidney yang deficiency)

**SCOLIOSIS**

Essential Yang Formula (with kidney yang deficiency)

**SCROTAL ECZEMA**

Four Marvel Formula (with dampness and heat in the lower burner)
Gentiana Drain Fire Formula (with damp-heat in the lower burner or liver heat)

**SCROTAL EDEMA**

Poria Five Formula

**SEXUAL DREAMS**

Cinnamon D Formula (with heart/kidney disharmony)

**SEXUAL DYSFUNCTION, FEMALE**

Cinnamon D Formula (with heart/kidney disharmony)
Yuan Support Formula (with spleen qi, kidney yang, and blood deficiency)

**SEXUAL DYSFUNCTION, MALE**

Essential Yang Formula (with kidney yang deficiency)
Prostate Formula (with prostate symptoms)
Stasis-Transforming Formula (with qi and blood stagnation, and damp-heat)
Vital Treasure Formula (with kidney yang deficiency, qi and yin deficiency)

**SEXUAL EXHAUSTION, MALE**

Cinnamon D Formula (with heart/kidney disharmony)
Ginseng Nourishing Formula (with qi and blood deficiency, and emotional symptoms)
Jing Qi Formula (with kidney, liver yin, and spleen qi deficiency, and constrained liver qi)

Nourish Essence Formula (with kidney yin and yang deficiency, and liver yin deficiency)
True Yin Formula (with kidney and liver yin deficiency)

**SEXUAL INTERCOURSE, PAIN WITH**
Cinnamon D Formula (with heart/kidney disharmony)
Yin Valley Formula (with yin deficiency dryness, heat, and blood stasis)

**SHEN UNSTABLE (See also PSYCHOLOGICAL DISORDERS)**
Cinnamon D Formula (with heart/kidney disharmony)

**SHINGLES (See HERPES ZOSTER)**

**SHOCK**
Sheng Mai Formula (with lung qi or yin deficiency, or with injury to yin from summer heat)

**SHORTNESS OF BREATH**
Astragalus Formula (with cold and deficiency in the middle burner)
Essential Yang Formula (with kidney yang deficiency)
General Tonic Formula (with qi and blood deficiency, and internal cold)
Ginseng & Astragalus Formula (with spleen and stomach qi deficiency)
Ginseng Endurance Formula (with qi, blood, and yang deficiency)
Ginseng Nourishing Formula (with qi and blood deficiency, and emotional symptoms)
Mulberry & Lycium Formula (with lung heat or lung fire)
Poria Five Formula (with congestion of fluids)
Restore the Lung Formula (with lung qi deficiency)
Sheng Mai Formula (with lung qi or yin deficiency, or with injury to yin from summer heat)
Six Gentlemen Formula (with spleen and stomach qi deficiency and phlegm or dampness)

**SHOULDERS SORE OR STIFF**
Bupleurum D Formula (with liver qi stagnation, phlegm, and disturbed shen)
Gan Mao Ling Formula (from wind-heat)
Juan Bi Formula (with wind-damp, cold, and blood stasis)
Minor Bupleurum Formula (with shao yang stage disorders)
Zhong Gan Ling Formula (from wind-heat)

**SINUS CONGESTION**
Children's Ear Formula (with congested ears)
Cinnamon Twig Formula (from wind-cold)
Gan Mao Ling Formula (from wind-heat)
Jade Screen & Xanthium Formula (from allergies, and wind-damp)
Xanthium & Magnolia Formula (acute, from wind-cold)
Xanthium Nasal Formula (acute, with heat, dampness, or phlegm
Yin Chiao Formula (from wind-heat)

**SINUS DISCHARGE**
Gan Mao Ling Formula (from wind-heat)
Jade Screen & Xanthium Formula (from allergies, and wind-damp)
Jade Windscreen Formula (chronic, from allergies)
Nourish Essence Formula (with kidney yin and yang deficiency, liver yin deficiency)
Viola Clear Fire Formula (yellow or green, with heat-toxin)
Xanthium & Magnolia Formula (acute, from wind-cold)
Xanthium Nasal Formula (acute, with heat, dampness, or phlegm

**SINUS INFECTION**

Andrographis Formula (with heat-toxin)
Gan Mao Ling Formula (early stage, from wind-heat)
Siler & Platycodon Formula (for wind-heat with heat in the interior)
Viola Clear Fire Formula (with heat-toxin)
Xanthium Nasal Formula (acute, with heat, dampness, or phlegm
Zhong Gan Ling Formula (from severe wind-heat)

**SINUS INFLAMMATION AND PAIN**

Andrographis Formula (with heat-toxin)
Curcuma Longa Formula (chronic, with qi and blood stagnation and heat)
Head Relief Formula (from wind-cold)
Jade Screen & Xanthium Formula (from allergies and wind-damp)
Xanthium Nasal Formula (acute, with heat, dampness, or phlegm)

**SKIN DRY (See DRYNESS)**

**SKIN RASH**

Andrographis Formula (with heat-toxin)
Cinnamon Twig Formula (with disharmony of ying and wei)
Coptis Relieve Toxicity Formula (with internal heat)
Four Marvel Formula (with dampness and heat in the lower burner)
Free & Easy Wanderer Plus (liver blood deficiency and blood heat)
Gentiana Drain Fire Formula (with damp-heat)
He Shou Wu Tablets (with deficient blood, and kidney/liver yin deficiency)
Intestinal Fungus Formula (with intestinal heat-toxin and dampness)
Jade Screen & Xanthium Formula (from allergic reaction)
Margarita Complexion Formula (red or itchy, with heat in the blood or stomach heat)
Mulberry & Lycium Formula (with lung heat or fire)
Oregano Oil Formula (topically, for skin infection)
Pulsatilla Intestinal Formula (with intestinal inflammation from heat-toxin)
Rehmannia Cool Blood Formula (red, with intense itching from heat in the blood)
Siler & Platycodon Formula (for wind-heat with heat in the interior)
Tang Kuei & Salvia Formula (with blood deficiency)
Tang Kuei & Tribulus Formula (with blood deficiency and dryness)
Women's Precious Formula (with qi and blood deficiency)
Wu Hua Formula (with damp-heat)
Yin Chiao Formula (with wind-heat)

**SLEEP, DISTURBED OR RESTLESS (See INSOMNIA)**

**SMOKING WITHDRAWAL**

Bupleurum D Formula (with liver qi stagnation, phlegm, and disturbed shen)
Lily Preserve Metal Formula (with lung yin deficiency)

**SNORING**

Fritillaria & Pinellia Formula (lung heat or phlegm-heat)
Minor Bupleurum Formula (with shao yang stage disorders)
Pinellia & Magnolia Bark Formula (with constrained qi and phlegm)

**SORES**

Coptis Relieve Toxicity Formula (with internal heat)
Four Marvel Formula (oozing in legs, with dampness and heat in the lower burner)
General Tonic Formula (chronic, with qi and blood deficiency, and internal cold)

Ginseng & Astragalus Formula (slow to heal, with spleen and stomach qi deficiency)
Ginseng Nourishing Formula (chronic, with qi and blood deficiency)
He Shou Wu Tablets (with deficient blood, and kidney/liver yin deficiency)
Rehmannia Cool Blood Formula (painful, with heat in the blood)
Siler & Platycodon Formula (for wind-heat with heat in the interior)
Wu Hua Formula (with damp-heat)

**SORE THROAT (See THROAT, SORE)**

**SPONTANEOUS EMISSIONS**

Jing Qi Formula (with kidney, liver yin, and spleen qi deficiency, and constrained liver qi)
Nourish Essence Formula (with kidney yin and yang deficiency, liver yin deficiency)
Rehmannia & Scrophularia Formula (with kidney yin deficiency heat)
True Yin Formula (with kidney and liver yin deficiency)

**SPOTS IN VISION (See VISION, SPOTS IN)**

**SPRAINS OR STRAINS**

Bone & Sinew Formula (second and third stage trauma)
Tieh Ta Formula (for pain, with little or no heat)
Trauma 1 Formula (first stage trauma, with swelling, heat, and pain)
Trauma 2 Formula (second stage trauma, with stagnation, stiffness, and pain)

**STIES**

Coptis Relieve Toxicity Formula (with heat or fire)
Gentiana Drain Fire Formula (with damp-heat)
Siler & Platycodon Formula (for wind-heat with heat in the interior)

**STOMACH ACHE OR PAIN**

Bupleurum & Cinnamon Formula (with liver/spleen disharmony or concurrent tai yang and shao yang patterns)
Bupleurum D Formula (acute, burning with liver invading stomach)
Bupleurum & Tang Kuei Formula (with liver/spleen disharmony)
Corydalis Formula (for pain from)
Ease Digestion Formula (from wind, damp, stomach phlegm or food stagnation)
Free & Easy Wanderer Plus (with liver/spleen disharmony and heat)
Linking Formula (with yin deficiency, qi stagnation, and fire)
Minor Bupleurum Formula (with shao yang stage disorders)
Poria & Bamboo Formula (with stomach-gallbladder disharmony, phlegm-heat and stagnation)
Shu Gan Formula (with liver qi stagnation)
Stomach-Harmonizing Formula (acute, with food stagnation and heat)

**STOMACH FLU (See GASTROENTERITIS)**

**STOOLS, DRY, HARD, OR DIFFICULT TO PASS (See also CONSTIPATION)**

He Shou Wu Tablets (with deficient blood, and kidney/liver yin deficiency)
Luo Bu Ma Formula (with liver heat or fire and dampness or phlegm)
Persica & Cistanches Formula (moistens and unblocks the intestines)
Rehmannia Cool Blood Formula (with heat in the blood)
Tang Kuei & Salvia (with blood deficiency and stagnation)

**STOOLS, ERRATIC**

Bupleurum & Tang Kuei Formula (with liver/spleen disharmony)
Ease Digestion Formula (from wind, damp, stomach phlegm or food stagnation)

Eight Immortals Formula (with lung, kidney, and stomach yin deficiency)
Ginseng & Astragalus Formula (for warm drinks, with spleen and stomach qi deficiency)
Jade Source Formula (extreme, with yin deficiency fire and deficient fluids)
Linking Formula (with yin deficiency, qi stagnation, and fire)
Rehmannia & Scrophularia Formula (with kidney yin deficiency heat)
Rehmannia Cool Blood Formula (with heat in the blood and no desire to swallow)
Seven Treasures Formula (lower, with deficient yin, jing and blood)
Sheng Mai Formula (with lung qi or yin deficiency or with injury to yin from summer heat)
True Yin Formula (with kidney and liver yin deficiency)
Yin Chiao Formula (with wind-heat)

**THROAT, SENSATION OF SOMETHING CAUGHT IN**

Pinellia & Magnolia Bark Formula (with constrained qi and phlegm)

**THROAT, SORE**

Andrographis Formula (with heat-toxin)
Coptis Relieve Toxicity Formula (with heat or fire)
Eight Immortals Formula (dry, with lung, kidney, and stomach yin deficiency)
Fritillaria & Pinellia Formula (with lung heat or phlegm-heat)
Gan Mao Ling Formula (from wind-heat)
Heavenly Emperor's Formula (with heart and kidney yin deficiency fire)
Jade Screen & Xanthium Formula (from allergies)
Lily Preserve Metal Formula (and dry, with lung yin deficiency)
Minor Bupleurum Formula (with shao yang stage disorders)
Oregano Oil Formula (anti-microbial)
Rehmannia & Scrophularia Formula (or dry, with kidney yin deficiency heat)
Rehmannia Cool Blood Formula (and dry, with heat in the blood)
True Yin Formula (and dry, with kidney and liver yin deficiency)
Viola Clear Fire Formula (with heat-toxin)
Yin Chiao Formula (from wind-heat)
Zhong Gan Ling Formula (from wind-heat)

**THYROID TUMORS, BENIGN**

Phlegm-Transforming Formula (with phlegm accumulation, deficiency, and qi or blood stagnation)

**TIDAL FEVER (See FEVER)**

**TINNITUS (See RINGING IN THE EAR)**

**TIREDNESS (See FATIGUE)**

**TONSILLITIS**

Andrographis Formula (with heat-toxin)
Coptis Relieve Toxicity Formula (with heat or fire)
Gan Mao Ling Formula (with wind-heat)
Gentiana Drain Fire Formula (from liver fire)
Minor Bupleurum Formula (shao yang stage)
Viola Clear Fire Formula (with heat-toxin)
Yin Chiao Formula (with wind-heat)
Zhong Gan Ling Formula (with severe wind-heat)

**TOOTHACHE**

Coptis Relieve Toxicity Formula (with heat or fire)
Corydalis Formula (for pain)
Head Relief Formula (from wind-cold, muscle tension, or trauma)
Rehmannia Six Formula (with kidney and liver yin deficiency fire)

**TOXEMIA OF PREGNANCY (PRE-ECLAMPSIA)**

Poria Five Formula (with retention of fluids)
Tang Kuei & Peony Formula (with liver blood and spleen deficiency and dampness)

**TOXICITY, FEELING OF**

Coptis Relieve Toxicity Formula (with heat or fire, damp-heat or heat in blood)
Free & Easy Wanderer Plus (with constrained liver qi and heat)
Hawthorn & Fennel Formula (with obesity, phlegm, and food stagnation)
Ji Xue Formula (with qi and blood deficiency and stagnation, heat-toxin, and dampness)
Poria Fifteen Formula (with obesity, phlegm, and food stagnation)
Resolve the Middle Formula (with damp turbidity and stagnation in the middle burner)
Siler & Platycodon Formula (for wind-heat with heat in the interior)

**TRAUMATIC INJURY**

Bone & Sinew Formula (second and third stage trauma)
Chase Wind, Penetrate Bone Formula (chronic stage, with wind-cold and wind-damp, with qi and blood stagnation)
Curcuma Longa Formula (inflammation, with qi and blood stagnation and heat)
San Qi Formula (controls bleeding)
San Qi Tablets (controls bleeding)
Tieh Ta Formula (acute stage)
Trauma 1 Formula (first stage trauma, with swelling, heat, and pain)
Trauma 2 Formula (second stage trauma, with stagnation, stiffness, and pain)

**TUBERCULOSIS, PULMONARY**

Bupleurum & Cinnamon Formula (with concurrent tai yang and shao yang patterns)
Eight Immortals Formula (with lung, kidney, and stomach yin deficiency)
Mulberry & Lycium Formula (with lung heat or fire)

**U**

**ULCER**

Astragalus Formula (gastric, peptic or duodenal, with cold and deficiency in the middle burner)
Bupleurum & Cinnamon Formula (gastric or duodenal, from liver/spleen disharmony with mixed signs of heat and cold)
Bupleurum & Tang Kuei Formula (peptic, with liver/spleen disharmony)
Bupleurum D Formula (pre-ulcer, with liver qi stagnation, and liver invading stomach)
Coptis Relieve Toxicity Formula (with heat or fire)
Ease Digestion Formula (acute symptoms)
Linking Formula (with yin deficiency, qi stagnation, and fire)
Minor Bupleurum Formula (with shao yang stage patterns)

Oregano Oil Formula (for helicobacter pylori)
Poria & Bamboo Formula (with stomach-gallbladder disharmony, phlegm-heat and stagnation)
San Qi Formula (controls bleeding)
Tang Kuei & Peony Formula (with blood and spleen deficiency and liver/spleen disharmony)

**UPPER RESPIRATORY INFECTION (See RESPIRATORY INFECTION)**

**URINARY BLADDER PAIN**

Corydalis Formula (analgesic)

**URINARY INCONTINENCE**

Essential Yang Formula (with kidney yang deficiency)
Nourish Essence Formula (with kidney yin and yang deficiency, liver yin deficiency)
Sea of Qi Formula (with spleen yang and kidney yang deficiency)

**URINARY RETENTION**

Essential Yang Formula (with kidney yang deficiency)
Hawthorn & Fennel Formula (with obesity)
Polyporus & Dianthus Formula (with heat in the interior, or damp-heat)
Poria Fifteen Formula (with obesity)
Poria Five Formula (with retention of fluids)
Rehmannia & Scrophularia Formula (with kidney yin deficiency heat)
Rehmannia Six Formula (with kidney and liver yin deficiency fire)

**URINARY TRACT INFECTION**

Amber Stone-Transforming Formula (from bladder or kidney stones)
Andrographis Formula (with heat-toxin)
Coptis Relieve Toxicity Formula (with heat or fire)
Essential Yang Formula (chronic, with kidney yang deficiency)
Four Marvel Formula (with dampness and heat in the lower burner)
Gentiana Drain Fire Formula (acute, damp-heat)
Polyporus & Dianthus Formula (with heat in the interior, or damp-heat)
Rehmannia & Scrophularia Formula (with kidney yin deficiency heat)
Rehmannia Six Formula (with kidney and liver yin deficiency fire)
Two Immortals Formula (chronic, with kidney yin and yang deficiency, and flaring-up of fire)
Viola Clear Fire Formula (with heat-toxin)

**URINATION, DIFFICULT**

Bupleurum D Formula (with liver qi stagnation and cold in the lower burner)
Eleuthero Tablets (with stress, kidney and spleen deficiency, and stagnation)
Essential Yang Formula (with kidney yang deficiency)
Free & Easy Wanderer Plus (with liver qi stagnation and heat)
Hawthorn & Fennel Formula (with obesity)
Luo Bu Ma Formula (with liver heat or fire and dampness or phlegm)
Polyporus & Dianthus Formula (dark, hot, with heat in the interior or damp-heat)
Poria Fifteen Formula (with obesity)
Poria Five Formula (with retention of fluids)
Prostate Formula (with prostate symptoms)
Rehmannia & Scrophularia Formula (with kidney yin deficiency heat)
Rehmannia Cool Blood Formula (scanty, yellow, with heat in the blood)

Siler & Platycodon Formula (for wind-heat with heat in the interior)
Tang Kuei & Peony Formula (with liver blood and spleen deficiency and dampness)

**URINATION, EXCESSIVE OR FREQUENT**

Essential Yang Formula (with kidney yang deficiency)
Jade Source Formula (with yin deficiency fire and deficient fluids)
Nourish Essence Formula (with kidney yin and yang deficiency, liver yin deficiency)
Prostate Formula (with prostate symptoms)
Sea of Qi Formula (with spleen yang and kidney yang deficiency)
Two Immortals Formula (with kidney yin and yang deficiency, and flaring-up of fire)

**URINATION, NOCTURNAL**

Essential Yang Formula (with kidney yang deficiency)
Nourish Essence Formula (with kidney yin and yang deficiency, liver yin deficiency)
Prostate Formula (with prostate symptoms)
Sea of Qi Formula (with spleen yang and kidney yang deficiency)

**URINATION, PAIN WITH (See also URINARY TRACT INFECTION)**

Amber Stone-Transforming Formula (from bladder or kidney stones)
Corydalis Formula (for pain and spasms)

**URTICARIA (See HIVES)**

**UTERINE BLEEDING, DYSFUNCTIONAL**

Bupleurum & Tang Kuei Formula (with constrained liver qi, liver blood and yin deficiency)
Chong Release Formula (with blood deficiency and stagnation)
Cinnamon & Poria Formula (with blood stasis)
General Tonic Formula (with qi and blood deficiency, and internal cold)
Ginseng & Astragalus Formula (with spleen and stomach qi deficiency)
Ginseng & Longan Formula (with spleen qi, heart qi, and blood deficiency)
Immortal Valley Formula (with dampness, heat, and blood stasis in lower abdomen)
Phlegm-Transforming Formula (with phlegm accumulation, deficiency, and qi or blood stagnation)
Polyporus & Dianthus Formula (with heat in the interior or damp-heat)
San Qi Formula (stops bleeding)
San Qi Tablets (stops bleeding)
Stasis-Transforming Formula (with qi and blood stagnation, and damp-heat)
Tang Kuei & Salvia Formula (with blood deficiency and stagnation)
Women's Precious Formula (with qi and blood deficiency)

**UTERINE FIBROIDS**

Cinnamon & Poria Formula (with blood stasis)
Phlegm-Transforming Formula (with phlegm accumulation, deficiency, and qi or blood stagnation)

**V**

**VAGINAL DISCHARGE**

Astragalus Formula (clear or white, with cold and deficiency of middle burner)
Bupleurum & Tang Kuei Formula (white, with liver qi stagnation)

Coptis Relieve Toxicity Formula (with heat or fire)
Four Marvel Formula (with dampness and heat in the lower burner)
Free & Easy Wanderer Plus (yellowish, with liver qi stagnation and heat)
Ginseng & Astragalus Formula (with spleen and stomach qi deficiency)
Ginseng & Longan Formula (with spleen qi, heart qi, and blood deficiency)
Gentiana Drain Fire Formula (yellowish and/or foul-smelling, with damp-heat)
Immortal Valley Formula (with dampness, heat, and blood stasis in lower abdomen)
Sea of Qi Formula (clear or white, with spleen yang and kidney yang deficiency)
Seven Treasures Formula (profuse, white, or clear, with deficient jing and kidney and liver yin, and deficient blood)
Tang Kuei & Peony Formula (with liver blood and spleen deficiency, and dampness)
Women's Precious Formula (with qi and blood deficiency)
Yin Valley Formula (with yin deficiency dryness, heat, and blood stasis)

**VAGINAL YEAST INFECTIONS (See YEAST INFECTION)**

**VAGINITIS, NON-SPECIFIC**

Four Marvel Formula (with dampness and heat in the lower burner)
Gentiana Drain Fire Formula (with damp-heat in liver)
Immortal Valley Formula (with dampness, heat, and blood stasis in lower abdomen)
Yin Valley Formula (with yin deficiency dryness, heat, and blood stasis)

**VARICOSE VEINS**

San Qi Tablets

**VERTEBRAL SUBLUXATION**

Bupleurum & Cinnamon Formula (with shao yang pattern)

**VERTIGO (See DIZZINESS)**

**VISION, BLURRED**

Gastrodia & Uncaria Formula (with liver yang rising and liver wind)
He Shou Wu Tablets (with deficient blood, and kidney/liver yin deficiency)
Jing Qi Formula (with kidney, liver yin, and spleen qi deficiency, and constrained liver qi)
Ming Mu Formula (liver and kidney deficiency with liver heat or internal wind)
Minor Bupleurum Formula (with shao yang patterns)
Rehmannia Six Formula (with kidney and liver yin deficiency)
Tang Kuei & Salvia Formula (with blood deficiency)
True Yin Formula (with kidney and liver yin deficiency)
Zizyphus Formula (with liver and heart blood and yin deficiency)

**VISION, SPOTS IN**

Blood Palace Formula (with blood stasis in upper body)
He Shou Wu Tablets (with deficient blood, and kidney/liver yin deficiency)
Ming Mu Formula (liver and kidney deficiency, with liver heat or internal wind)
Tang Kuei & Salvia Formula (with blood deficiency)
True Yin Formula (with kidney and liver yin deficiency)
Women's Precious Formula (with qi and blood deficiency)

**VISUAL ACUITY, DECREASED**

Jing Qi Formula (with kidney, liver yin and spleen qi deficiency, and constrained liver qi)

Ming Mu Formula (liver and kidney deficiency, with liver heat or internal wind)

**VOMITING**

Bupleurum & Cinnamon Formula (with liver/spleen disharmony or concurrent tai yang and shao yang patterns)

Citrus & Pinellia Formula (with phlegm-damp)

Coptis Relieve Toxicity Formula (with heat or fire)

Ease Digestion Formula (from wind, damp, stomach phlegm, or food stagnation)

Free & Easy Wanderer Plus (with liver/spleen disharmony, and heat)

Ji Xue Formula (from chemotherapy, with qi and blood deficiency and stagnation, heat-toxin, and dampness)

Linking Formula (of sour fluid, with yin deficiency, qi stagnation, and fire)

Lysimachia GB Formula (with damp-heat and constrained qi in the liver and gallbladder)

Minor Bupleurum Formula (with shao yang stage patterns)

Pinellia & Magnolia Bark Formula (with qi stagnation in stomach)

Poria Five Formula (immediately after drinking or with retention of fluids)

Poria & Bamboo Formula (with stomach-gallbladder disharmony, phlegm-heat and stagnation)

Resolve the Middle Formula (with damp turbidity and stagnation in the middle burner)

Shu Gan Formula (acute, with liver qi stagnation and phlegm)

Six Gentlemen Formula (with spleen and stomach qi deficiency, and phlegm or dampness)

Stomach-Harmonizing Formula (with food stagnation and heat)

**VOMITING BLOOD**

Coptis Relieve Toxicity Formula (with heat or fire)

Rehmannia Cool Blood Formula (with heat in the blood)

San Qi Formula (controls bleeding)

San Qi Tablets (controls bleeding)

**VULVAR ITCHING (See GENITAL ITCHING)**

## W

**WALKING, DIFFICULTY**

Clematis & Stephania Formula

Du Huo & Loranthus Formula (with kidney and liver deficiency)

Ji Xue Formula (from neuropathy, with qi and blood deficiency and stagnation, heat-toxin, and dampness)

**WARTS**

Siler & Platycodon Formula (for wind-heat with heat in the interior)

**WATER RETENTION (See EDEMA)**

**WEAKNESS, GENERALIZED OR AFTER SURGERY OR ILLNESS**

Astragalus & Ligustrum Formula (to support normal qi)

Astragalus Formula (with cold and deficiency in the middle burner)

Eleuthero Tablets (with stress, kidney and spleen deficiency, and stagnation)

Essential Yang Formula (with kidney yang deficiency)

Five Mushroom Formula (general tonic for lung, kidney, liver, spleen, and immune system)
General Tonic Formula (with qi and blood deficiency, and internal cold)
Ginseng & Astragalus Formula (with spleen and stomach qi deficiency
Ginseng & Longan Formula (with spleen qi, heart qi, and blood deficiency)
Ginseng Endurance Formula (with qi, blood, and yang deficiency)
Ginseng Nourishing Formula (chronic, with qi and blood deficiency, and emotional symptoms)
He Shou Wu Tablets (with deficient blood, and kidney/liver yin deficiency)
Ji Xue Formula (with qi and blood deficiency and stagnation, heat-toxin, and dampness)
Jing Qi Formula (with kidney, liver yin, and spleen qi deficiency, and constrained liver qi)
Nourish Essence Formula (with kidney yin and yang deficiency, liver yin deficiency)
Sea of Qi Formula (with spleen yang and kidney yang deficiency)
Sheng Mai Formula (with lung qi or yin deficiency or with injury to yin from summer heat)
Tang Kuei & Peony Formula (during pregnancy, with blood and spleen deficiency and dampness)
Tang Kuei & Salvia Formula (with blood deficiency and stagnation)
Women's Precious Formula (with qi and blood deficiency)

**WEIGHT GAIN (See OBESITY)**

**WEIGHT, LOSS OF**

Ginseng & Astragalus Formula (with spleen and stomach qi deficiency
Ginseng Nourishing Formula (with qi and blood deficiency and emotional symptoms)
Jade Source Formula (with yin deficiency fire and deficient fluids)
Salvia Ten Formula (with depression)

**WHEEZING (See also ASTHMA)**

Five Mushroom Formula (general tonic for lung, kidney, liver, spleen, and immune system)
Lily Preserve Metal Formula (with lung yin deficiency)
Ling Zhi Lung Formula (for kidneys not grasping lung qi, with phlegm)
Mulberry & Lycium Formula (with lung heat or fire)
Pinellia & Magnolia Bark Formula (with constrained qi and phlegm)
Restore the Lung Formula (with lung qi deficiency)

**WORMS**

Oregano Oil Formula

## Y

**YEAST INFECTION**

Gentiana Drain Fire Formula (vaginal)
Intestinal Fungus Formula (intestinal)
Oregano Oil Formula (vaginal or intestinal)
Immortal Valley Formula (with dampness, heat, and blood stasis in lower abdomen)

## GLOSSARY OF CHINESE MEDICAL TERMS USED

**BLOOD DEFICIENCY**–Clinical manifestations include pale or sallow complexion, pale lips, dizziness, poor memory, blurring of vision, palpitations, insomnia, numbness of hands and feet, a pale tongue and thready pulse.

**BLOOD STAGNATION OR STASIS**–Manifests in symptoms such as fixed, boring or stabbing pain, mass tumors which do not move, hemorrhage with dark blood and clots, purple lips and nails, purple blotches or bruises on skin, purple tongue and wiry, choppy or knotted pulse.

**CHONG CHANNEL**–Also called the Penetrating Vessel. Has a regulating effect on all twelve regular channels and regulates menstruation. Symptoms of this channel include menstrual irregularities, miscarriage, uterine bleeding, insufficient lactation, lower abdominal pain, and in men, seminal emission, impotence, prostatitis.

**COLD**–Caused by cold pathogenic factor or diminished vital function; marked by intolerance of cold, fondness for warmth, loose bowels, pale tongue with white coating, slow pulse, etc.

**COLD IN THE MIDDLE BURNER**–Usually refers to cold in the spleen and stomach. Marked by cold and pain over the stomach, anorexia, abdominal fullness, belching, vomiting thin fluid, diarrhea, lassitude and cold limbs.

**CONSTRAINED HEAT**–Refers to heat generated by a heat pathogen that is lodged in a specific tissue. Clearing/draining actions are usually not enough. Constrained heat requires substances that disperse heat.

**CONSTRAINED LIVER–(QI STAGNATION)**

**DAMPNESS**–Caused externally by damp pathogenic factor or internally by a dysfunction of the spleen and kidney in promoting water circulation and distribution. Symptoms include heaviness in the limbs, headache as if the head were tightly bound, fullness in the chest, joint pains and swelling, diarrhea, abdominal fullness, sallow face, edema of the lower limbs, turbid discharges, etc.

**DAMP-HEAT**–A combination of dampness and heat, which produces varying symptoms depending on the part of the body affected. Symptoms include loss of appetite, nausea, vomiting, bitter taste and stickiness in the mouth, heaviness of the body and limbs, fullness of the chest, lassitude, jaundice, loose stools or diarrhea with blood or mucus, offensive odor of stools, burning in anus, scanty yellow urine, abdominal pain and distension, eczema, swelling and burning pain in the testes, yellow foul-smelling leukorrhea, frequency and/or urgency of urination, burning pain in the urethra, dribbling urination, turbid, deep yellow urine. Pulse is rapid and slippery; tongue is red with a sticky, yellow coating.

**DEFICIENCY**–Deficiency of vital energy and lowered body resistance. Some deficiency symptoms include: emaciation, listlessness, lassitude, shortness of breath, pallor, insomnia, poor memory, spontaneous and night sweating, nocturnal enuresis, pain alleviated by pressure. Tongue is dry with little or no coating; pulse is weak and thready.

**DEFICIENCY HEAT OR FIRE**–Caused by a deficiency of yin; symptoms include afternoon or low grade fever, malar flush, dry mouth, insomnia with mental restlessness, anxiety, feverish sensations in the palms and soles, night sweats, constipation, concentrated urine, etc. Tongue is red with little coating; pulse is rapid, thready, and empty.

**DISPERSION**–The action of scattering a concentration of a pathogen or dislodging the pathogen so it can be cleared out.

**DRYNESS**–One of the six pathogenic factors which prevails in autumn or in dry climates; causes consumption of body fluids with symptoms such as red eyes, dry nose and throat, dry cough, dry skin, constipation, reduced urination, etc. Also an internal condition caused by impairment of yin.

**ENCUMBRANCE**–Refers to an accumulation, usually of dampness, damp-heat, or phlegm, which restricts the normal functioning of an organ.

**EXTERIOR (See also INTERIOR)**–Refers to the depth of disease. Exterior syndromes are caused by invasion of the six pathogenic factors, which first attack the superficial portions of the body. In general, these syndromes are of sudden onset and short duration. Chief symptoms include intolerance to cold or wind, fever, headache, nasal obstruction and superficial pulse.

**ESSENCE**–(also known as "Jing"), refers to the combination of the energy which makes up a person's inherited constitution and the energy derived from food. It resides mostly in the kidneys and is the basis of growth, reproduction, and development. It is also the source of kidney qi and of constitutional strength. Deficiency of essence results in variety of symptoms such as stunted growth, poor bone development or bone deterioration, infertility, habitual miscarriage, loose teeth, hair falling out or prematurely gray, poor sexual function, impotence, weakness of knees, ringing in the ears, poor memory, poor concentration, dizziness, lowered body resistance, and chronic allergies.

**FIRE**–A severe form of internal heat. Fire is always associated with a specific organ (e.g., heart/pericardium, liver/gallbladder, lung, stomach, or spleen) and always flares upward. Manifestations include: high fever, restlessness, insomnia, mania, delirium, thirst, sweating, mouth and tongue ulcers, swollen and painful gums, headache, congestion of the eyes.

**FOOD STAGNATION**–Symptom pattern includes: stomach pain and distension, loss of appetite, foul belching, acid regurgitation, vomiting. Tongue may have a thick, sticky coating.

**HEART BLOOD DEFICIENCY**–Symptom pattern includes: giddiness, pallor, palpitation, insomnia, forgetfulness, and a fine and weak pulse.

**HEART QI DEFICIENCY**–Symptom pattern includes: palpitation, shortness of breath on exertion, spontaneous sweating, and a fine, weak or irregular pulse.

**HEART YIN DEFICIENCY**– Symptom pattern includes: mental irritability, palpitation, insomnia, low fever, night sweats, flushed cheeks, thirst, and a fine, rapid pulse.

**HEAT**–Caused by pathogenic heat or by excessive vital function. Marked by feverishness, flushed face, thirst, craving for cold drinks, constipation, red tongue with yellow coating, rapid pulse.

**HEAT IN THE BLOOD**–Marked by restlessness or mania, feeling of heat, skin diseases with red eruptions, mouth ulcers, itching, excessive menstrual bleeding, hemorrhage, dry mouth, red tongue, rapid pulse.

**HEAT-TOXIN**–Refers to toxic heat that is generated by bacterial or viral infection.

**INTERIOR (See also EXTERIOR)**–Refers to the depth of the disease. Interior syndromes are mostly severe or chronic and deep. In interior diseases the pathogenic factors are on the interior of the body and attack the organs.

**JING (See ESSENCE)**

**KIDNEY YANG DEFICIENCY**–Symptom pattern includes: pallor, cold limbs, soreness and weakness of the lumbar region and knee joints, nocturnal urination, impotence, infertility, dizziness, ringing in the ears, a pale tongue with white coating, and a deep, weak pulse.

**KIDNEY YIN DEFICIENCY**–Symptom pattern includes: low back pain, weak knees, lassitude, general weakness, vertigo, ringing in the ears, thirst, flushed cheeks, mental irritability, afternoon fever, night sweats, nocturnal emissions, yellow urine, constipation, red tongue with little coating, and a thready, rapid pulse.

**LIVER BLOOD DEFICIENCY**–Symptom pattern includes: sallow face, blurring of vision, dry eyes, spasms of muscles and tendons, dizziness, mental irritability, insomnia, absent or scanty menstruation, prolonged menstrual cycle, pale tongue or lips.

**LIVER FIRE**–Symptom pattern includes: dizziness, headache, flushed face, red eyes, bitter taste in the mouth, mental irritability, anger outbursts. In severe cases symptoms include: mania, nosebleed, blood in the urine, or coughing blood. Tongue is scarlet red on tip and sides, with yellow coating. Pulse is wiry and rapid.

**LIVER HEAT**–Marked by mental irritability, bitter taste in mouth, thirst, etc. Similar to Fire but not as severe.

**LIVER QI STAGNATION**–Manifests in irritability, tendency to anger, dizziness, abdominal and hypochondriac pain and distension, fullness in chest, excessive sighing, breast distension, belching, loss of appetite, nausea, sensation of a foreign body in throat, menstrual disorders.

**LIVER/SPLEEN DISHARMONY**–Symptom pattern includes: abdominal pain and distension, diarrhea or loose stools, belching, vomiting, acid regurgitation.

**LIVER WIND**–Usually resulting from liver fire or deficient blood, symptoms include: dizziness and vertigo, convulsions, tremors, spasms and numbness.

**LIVER YANG RISING**–Manifests in headache with distending sensation in the head, dizziness and vertigo, ringing in the ears, flushed face, red eyes, irritability, insomnia with dream-disturbed sleep, palpitations, poor memory, red tongue, and a tight and rapid pulse.

**LIVER YIN DEFICIENCY**–Symptom pattern includes: dizziness, headache, ringing in the ears, blurred vision, dry eyes, insomnia, night sweats, feverishness in palms and soles, thirst, dry throat. Pulse is thready and taut. Tongue is reddened with little coating.

**LUNG HEAT**–Marked by cough with thick or yellow phlegm, pain in the chest, and shortness of breath.

**LUNG YIN DEFICIENCY**–Manifests in symptoms such as dry or blood tinged cough, or cough with a small amount of sticky sputum, dryness of the mouth and throat, afternoon fever, malar flush, night sweats, feverishness in palms and soles. Tongue is red with little coating. Pulse is thready and rapid.

**MIDDLE QI DEFICIENCY**–(Also called deficiency of the middle burner.) Refers to deficiency of qi of the spleen and stomach, resulting in hypofunction of those organs, digestive disorders, weakness etc. **(See SPLEEN AND STOMACH QI DEFICIENCY)**

**NORMAL QI**–Body energy made up of qi inherited from parents, qi from food, and qi from air. Responsible for the movement, functioning and warmth of the body and for protection from disease.

**PAINFUL OBSTRUCTION**–Obstruction of vital energy and blood flow, usually bringing on pains, specifically arthritis; due to wind, cold and dampness blocking the channels of the limbs.

**PATHOGENIC FACTORS**–The causes of disease. Pathogenic factors include wind, cold, dampness, heat, dryness, and fire. These can be of exterior origin (related to extreme or sudden climatic changes such as invasion by wind-cold) or they can be internally generated, such as liver-wind.

**PHLEGM**–Results from an accumulation of bodily fluids due to a dysfunction of the lung, spleen, and kidney and impairment of water metabolism. Clinical manifestations are many and vary depending on the area of the body affected. Symptoms can include cough with profuse sputum, asthmatic breathing, fullness in the chest, palpitations, coma, manic-depressive disorders, lymph node swelling, nodules under the skin, dizziness, blurred vision, sensation of a foreign body in the throat, edema, general body aching and heaviness, nausea, vomiting of sticky fluid, borborygmus, stomach and abdominal discomfort.

**PHLEGM-HEAT**–Often seen in lung or stomach patterns, clinical manifestations include: yellow-sticky phlegm, barking cough with profuse yellow or green sputum, fullness in the chest, asthma, dry mouth and lips, restlessness. Tongue is red with a sticky, yellow coating. Pulse is rapid and slippery.

**PROTECTIVE QI (See WEI QI)**

**QI DEFICIENCY**–Symptoms include: general weakness, lethargy, shortness of breath, weak voice, spontaneous sweating, loss of appetite, abdominal distension, loose stools, frequent urination, palpitations and an empty pulse.

**REN CHANNEL**–Also known as the Conception Vessel, this channel has a regulating effect on all yin channels of the body. It regulates menstruation and nurtures the fetus. Symptoms of the ren channel include menstrual irregularities, white vaginal discharge, miscarriage, infertility, abdominal masses, enuresis.

**SHAO YANG STAGE DISORDER**–Refers to an intermediate stage of an illness where the pathogenic factors remain between the exterior and the interior. Pathological manifestations include: alternating chills and fever, fullness in the costal and hypochondriac regions, lack of appetite, mental restlessness, vomiting, bitter taste in mouth, dry throat, blurring of vision. Pulse is tight.

**SHEN (See UNSTABLE OR DISTURBED SHEN)**

**SPLEEN DAMPNESS**–Symptoms include: lack of appetite, sticky taste in the mouth or loss of sense of taste, nausea, fullness in the chest and abdomen, feeling of heaviness, loose stools, headache as if head were bound. Tongue has sticky coating. Pulse is slippery.

**SPLEEN QI DEFICIENCY**–Clinical manifestations include: sallow complexion, emaciation, tiredness, dislike of speaking, reduced appetite, abdominal distension, loose stools, prolapse. Tongue is pale with a thin white coating. Pulse is empty, weak, or thready.

**SPLEEN YANG DEFICIENCY**–Symptom pattern includes: pallor, cold limbs, poor appetite, abdominal distension which is worse after eating, dull abdominal pain which improves with warmth and pressure, loose stools. Tongue is pale with a white coating. Pulse is deep and slow.

**STOMACH PHLEGM**–Symptoms include: nausea, vomiting of sticky fluid, stomach and abdominal fullness and discomfort, borborygmus. Tongue coating is sticky and pulse is slippery.

**STOMACH QI DEFICIENCY**–Clinical manifestations include: uncomfortable feeling in the stomach, no appetite, lack of taste sensation, loose stools, tiredness (especially in the morning), weak limbs. Tongue is pale. Pulse is weak and empty especially in the middle position of the right hand.

**SUMMER HEAT**–One of the six pathogenic factors. Pathogenic summer heat is caused by prolonged exposure to blazing sun on hot days or to a hot room with poor ventilation. Summer heat consumes qi and yin and may disturb the mind. Symptoms include: excessive sweating, thirst, shortness of breath, lassitude, and concentrated urine; and in extreme cases, fever, restlessness, red, dry skin, and delirium or coma. May combine with damp to produce dizziness, heaviness in the head, stifling sensation in the chest, nausea, poor appetite, diarrhea, and general sluggishness.

**TURBIDITY**–Murky fluids due to weak transformation/transportation function of the spleen or to ingestion of spoiled food, too much alcohol, etc. Often associated with dampness.

**UNSTABLE OR DISTURBED SHEN**–Shen is translated as "spirit." It refers to the mind, consciousness, the force of the personality, and the connection to the spiritual aspects of humanness. When shen is disturbed or unstable, symptoms arise such as insomnia, unclear or muddled thinking, poor memory, restlessness, hysteria, incoherent speech, delirium, mania.

**WEI QI**–Refers to defensive energy, which protects the body from invasion by external pathogenic factors.

**WIND**–One of the six pathogenic factors. External wind is usually combined with one of the other pathogenic factors (cold, heat, dampness, and dryness), which depend on wind to invade the body. Symptoms of external wind include: headache, stiff neck, nasal obstruction, sneezing, itching or pain in the throat, facial puffiness, aversion to wind, joint pains, and a superficial pulse. Internal or endogenous wind causes symptoms such as headaches, stiff neck, irritability, dizziness, fainting, high fever, delirium, coma, convulsions, tremors, tics, blurred vision, numbness, facial paralysis, wandering pains.

**WIND-COLD**–Symptoms include: aversion to cold, shivering, sneezing, cough, runny nose with watery or white discharge, slight fever or no fever, neck pain and stiffness. Pulse is tight and superficial. Tongue looks normal (normal color, thin, white coating).

**WIND-HEAT**–Symptoms are similar to those above except with symptoms of heat such as fever, yellow mucus, sore throat, swollen tonsils, thirst, sweating. Pulse is floating and rapid. Tongue is red on the tip or sides, with a thin, white, or yellowish coating.

**WIND-DAMP**–Symptoms include: itchy skin, rashes, hives, fever, aversion to cold, sweating, neck pain and stiffness, body aches and heaviness, swollen joints. Pulse is superficial and slippery.

## *GLOSSARY SOURCES*

*Chinese Acupuncture and Moxibustion.* Foreign Languages Press, 1987.

*Dictionary of Traditional Chinese Medicine.* Beijing Medical College, 1985.

Wiseman, N. and Ye, F. *A Practical Dictionary of Chinese Medicine.* Paradigm Publications, 1998.

# *REFERENCES*

Scheid, V., Bensky, D., Ellis, A., and Barolet, R. *Chinese Herbal Medicine: Formulas and Strategies, 2nd Edition.* Seattle: Eastland Press, 2009.

Bensky, D., Clavey, S., Stoger, E., and Gamble, A. *Chinese Herbal Medicine: Materia Medica, 3rd Edition.* Seattle: Eastland Press, 2004.

Hsu, H.Y. *Oriental Materia Medica: A Concise Guide.* Long Beach, Calif.: Oriental Healing Arts Institute, 1986.

Zhu, C.H. *Clinical Handbook of Chinese Prepared Medicines.* Brookline, Mass.: Paradigm Publications, 1989.